Global Compensation

Compensation is a systematic approach to providing monetary value and other benefits to employees in exchange for their work and service. But pay and conditions becomes a more complicated issue for multinational companies which operate across different locations and cultures, and who employ an increasingly diverse range of personnel.

This unique new text gives an in-depth and detailed analysis of the key themes and emerging topics faced by global enterprises when dealing with compensation issues today. The first section, "Foundational concepts", looks at the design of compensation packages for a number of different employee groups; from supply chain management to research and development, as well as ethical considerations when dealing with a global context, and the concept of performance-related pay. The second section, "Global applications", looks at current debates in the field, including the influence of national cultures on compensation schemes, discrepancies in CEO pay, and contrasts in wages between industry types.

Part of Routledge's *Global Human Resource Management* series, and written by the most eminent researchers in the field, *Global Compensation: Foundations and perspectives* is an invaluable text for any student of Human Resource Management, Business and Management, or any practitioner working in this area.

Luis R. Gomez-Mejia holds the Horace Steele Chair in the Management Department at Arizona State University, USA. His publications have appeared in most major management journals, including *Academy of Management Journal*, *Academy of Management Review*, *Administrative Science Quarterly*, *Personnel Psychology*, *Journal of Management* and *Strategic Management Journal*.

Steve Werner is an Associate Professor of Management at the University of Houston, USA. He has published over three dozen academic and practitioner papers on HRM and international business. Professor Werner serves on the editorial board of the *Human Resource Management Journal* and *Human Resource Management Review*.

Routledge Global Human Resource Management Series

Edited by Randall S. Schuler, Susan E. Jackson, Paul Sparrow and Michael Poole

Routledge Global Human Resource Management is an important new series that examines human resources in its global context. The series is organized into three strands: Content and issues in global human resource management (HRM); Specific HR functions in a global context; and Comparative HRM. Authored by some of the world's leading authorities on HRM, each book in the series aims to give readers comprehensive, in-depth and accessible texts that combine essential theory and best practice. Topics covered include cross-border alliances, global leadership, global legal systems, HRM in Asia, Africa and the Americas, industrial relations, and global staffing.

Managing Human Resources in Cross-Border Alliances
Randall S. Schuler, Susan E. Jackson and Yadong Luo

Managing Human Resources in Africa
Edited by Ken N. Kamoche, Yaw A. Debrah, Frank M. Horwitz and Gerry Nkombo Muuka

Globalizing Human Resource Management
Paul Sparrow, Chris Brewster and Hilary Harris

Managing Human Resources in Asia-Pacific
Edited by Pawan S. Budhwar

International Human Resource Management (second edition)
Policy and practice for the global enterprise
Dennis R. Briscoe and Randall S. Schuler

Managing Human Resources in Latin America
An agenda for international leaders
Edited by Marta M. Elvira and Anabella Davila

Global Staffing
Edited by Hugh Scullion and David G. Collings

Managing Human Resources in Europe
A thematic approach
Edited by Henrik Holt Larsen and Wolfgang Mayrhofer

Managing Human Resources in the Middle East
Edited by Pawan S. Budhwar and Kamel Mellahi

Managing Global Legal Systems
International employment regulation and competitive advantage
Gary W. Florkowski

Global Industrial Relations
Edited by Michael J. Morley, Patrick Gunnigle and David G. Collings

Managing Human Resources in North America
Current issues and perspectives
Edited by Steve Werner

Global Leadership
Research, practice, development
Edited by Mark Mendenhall, Gary Oddou, Allan Bird and Martha Maznevski

Global Compensation
Foundations and perspectives
Edited by Luis R. Gomez-Mejia and Steve Werner

Global Performance Management
Edited by Arup Varma, Pawan S. Budhwar and Angelo DeNisi

Forthcoming:

Managing Human Resources in Central and Eastern Europe
Edited by Michael J. Morley, Noreen Heraty and Snejina Michailova

Global Careers
Michael Dickmann and Yehuda Baruch

Global Compensation

Foundations and perspectives

Edited by
Luis R. Gomez-Mejia
and Steve Werner

Routledge
Taylor & Francis Group

LONDON AND NEW YORK

First published 2008
by Routledge
2 Park Square, Milton Park, Abingdon, Oxon OX14 4RN

Simultaneously published in the USA and Canada
by Routledge
270 Madison Ave, New York, NY 10016

Routledge is an imprint of the Taylor & Francis Group, an informa business

Typeset in Times New Roman and Franklin Gothic by
Book Now Ltd, London
Printed and bound in Great Britain by
TJ International Ltd, Padstow, Cornwall

British Library Cataloguing in Publication Data
A catalogue record for this book is available from the British Library

Library of Congress Cataloging in Publication Data
Global compensation / edited by Luis R. Gomez-Mejia & Steve Werner.
    p. cm.
1. Compensation management–Cross-cultural studies. 2. International business
enterprises–Personnel management–Cross-cultural studies. 3. International
business enterprises–Cross-cultural studies. 4. Globalization–Economic aspects.
I. Gomez-Mejia, Luis R. II. Werner, Steve, 1964-

HF5549.5.C67G55 2008
658.3'2–dc22   2008000878

ISBN10: 0–415–77502–7 (hbk)
ISBN10: 0–415–77503–5 (pbk)

ISBN13: 978–0–415–77502–1 (hbk)
ISBN13: 978–0–415–77503–8 (pbk)

To my dear Ani, Alex, Dulce and Vince.
Luis R. Gomez-Mejia

To Naomi and Luke with all my love.
Steve Werner

Contents

Illustrations

Figures

Tables

Notes on contributors

David B. Balkin is a Professor of Management in the Leeds School of Business at the University of Colorado, Boulder. He has published dozens of articles and numerous books on strategic compensation, and other various aspects of compensation and human resource management.

Pascual Berrone is an Assistant Professor of General Management in the IESE Business School at the University of Navarra, Spain. His current research interests focus on various aspects of the interface between corporate governance mechanisms and corporate social responsibility.

Carmelo Cennamo is a PhD candidate in strategic management at the Instituto de Empresa Business School in Madrid, Spain. His research interests include stakeholder management theory, corporate governance, corporate strategy, and institutional factors affecting firms' strategic options.

Björn Claes is a PhD candidate at the Instituto de Empresa Business School in Madrid, Spain. His research interests are in the field of the human side of operations and supply chain management, including supply chain behavior, performance measurement, and supply chain cooperation.

Charles H. Fay is a Professor of Human Resources and Chair of the HRM Department in the School of Management and Labor Relations at Rutgers, the State University of New Jersey. A pioneer in compensation research, he has authored numerous articles and books on various aspects of compensation.

Richard Floersch is Executive Vice President and Chief HR Officer at McDonald's Corporation, Oak Brook, Illinois. He leads the HR team at McDonald's in developing and implementing HR strategies intended to create value for the more than 32,000 McDonald's stores across the world.

Monica Franco-Santos is a research fellow at the Centre for Business Performance in Cranfield School of Management, UK. Her research interests include the design, implementation, management, and impact of performance measurement systems.

Barry Gerhart is the Bruce R. Ellig Distinguished Chair in Pay and Organizational Effectiveness in the School of Business at the University of Wisconsin-Madison.

His research interests include compensation, human resource strategy, employee attitudes/behaviors, and research methods.

Katalin Takacs Haynes is an Assistant Professor at Texas A&M University. She received her PhD in strategic management from Arizona State University. Her research interests include the relationship between the institutional environment and corporate governance, and social issues in management.

Robert L. Heneman is Director of Graduate Programs in Labor and Human Resources and Professor of Management and Human Resources in the Max M. Fisher College of Business, the Ohio State University. His primary areas of research, teaching, and consulting are compensation, performance management, staffing, and work design.

Marianna Makri is an Assistant Professor of Strategic Management at the University of Miami. Her research interests include CEO pay, corporate governance, and management of technology and innovation.

Gregorio Sánchez Marín is an Associate Professor of Human Resource Management in the Department of Management and Finance at the University of Murcia, Spain. His current research interests focus on executive pay, compensation strategy, and family firms' management.

Joseph J. Martocchio is a Professor in the Institute of Labor and Industrial Relations at the University of Illinois at Champaign. He is the author of numerous articles and two books on such human resource management issues as compensation, benefits, employee training, and absenteeism.

Edilberto (Ed) Montemayor is an Associate Professor in the School of Labor and Industrial Relations at Michigan State University. His current research focuses on employment ethics, with a particular emphasis on the ethical quality of strategies, policies, and practices affecting employee pay and benefits.

Jerry Newman is SUNY Distinguished Teaching Professor at the State University of New York, Buffalo, School of Management. He is author of the classic textbook *Compensation* (with George Milkovich) and *My Secret Life on the McJob: Lessons from Behind the Counter Guaranteed to Supersize Any Management Style*, both published by McGraw-Hill.

Jordan Otten is an Assistant Professor in the Business-Society Management Department at the Rotterdam School of Management at the Erasmus University, The Netherlands. His research interests include executive pay and corporate governance.

Niti Pandey is a doctoral student at the Institute of Labor and Industrial Relations at the University of Illinois. Her research interests include employee benefits, intergenerational issues in the workplace, and team effectiveness in the healthcare setting.

Aino Salimäki is Researcher and PhD candidate at the Department of Industrial Engineering and Management, Helsinki University of Technology. Her main research interests include the prevalence, effectiveness, and consequences of pay for performance practices in the global context. Her chapter was written while she was on sabbatical at the Ohio State University.

Editors

> **Luis R. Gomez-Mejia** is a Council of 100 Distinguished Scholar and Professor of Management in the W.P. Carey School of Business at Arizona State University. He has published over 100 articles and written or edited a dozen management books in such areas as CEO pay, compensation strategy, and HRM in small firms.
>
> **Steve Werner** is an Associate Professor of Management in the C.T. Bauer College of Business at the University of Houston. He has published dozens of articles in such areas as compensation, human resource management, and international management.

Foreword

Global Human Resource Management is a series of books edited and authored by some of the best and most well-known researchers in the field of human resource management. This series is aimed at offering students and practitioners accessible, coordinated, and comprehensive books in global HRM. To be used individually or together, these books cover the main bases of comparative and international HRM. Taking an expert look at an increasingly important and complex area of global business, this is a groundbreaking new series that answers a real need for serious textbooks on global HRM.

Several books in this series, *Global Human Resource Management*, are devoted to human resource management policies and practices in multinational enterprises. For example, some books focus on specific activities of global HRM policies and practices, such as global compensation, global staffing, and global labour relations. Other books address special topics that arise in multinational enterprises across the globe, such as managing HR in cross-border alliances, developing strategies and structures, and developing the HR function in multinational enterprises. In addition to books on various HRM activities and topics in multinational enterprises, several other books in the series adopt a comparative, and within region, approach to understanding global human resource management. These books on comparative human resource management can adopt two major approaches. One approach is to describe the HRM policies and practices found at the local level in selected countries in several regions of the world. The second approach is to describe the HRM issues and topics that are most relevant to the companies in the countries of the region.

This book, *Global Compensation: Foundations and perspectives*, utilizes both the multinational enterprise perspective and the comparative human resource management perspective. That is, it addresses multinational enterprise issues in global compensation *and* it provides an understanding of compensation issues and topics in several countries around the globe. The authors have done this in part by organizing the book into two major sections, with one focusing on comparative issues and topics and the other focusing on the multinational enterprise perspective.

In order to provide the most expertise possible in undertaking this book, the authors have taken a co-editorship approach. Together, Luis Gomez-Mejia and Steve Werner have gathered many of the most knowledgeable researchers to produce an outstanding book that provides the reader with an excellent understanding of global compensation in MNEs and in several countries around the globe. In addition to writing some of the chapters themselves, the co-editors have done a superb job in organizing the contributions of their many contributors. All 16 chapters fit together very effectively. This book is extremely well conceptualized and well written. No doubt it is a highly valuable book for any global human resource student and scholar or any global human resource professional.

This Routledge series, *Global Human Resource Management*, is intended to serve the growing market of global scholars and professionals who are seeking a deeper and broader understanding of the role and importance of human resource management in companies as they operate throughout the world. With this in mind, all books in the series provide a thorough review of existing research and numerous examples of companies around the world.

Because a significant number of scholars and professionals throughout the world are involved in researching and practicing the topics examined in this series of books, the authorship of the books and the experiences of companies cited in the books reflect a vast global representation. The authors in the series bring with them exceptional knowledge of the human resource management topics they address, and in many cases the authors have been the pioneers for their topics. So we feel fortunate to have the involvement of such a distinguished group of academics in this series.

The publisher and editor also have played a major role in making this series possible. Routledge has provided its global production, marketing and reputation to make this series feasible and affordable to academics and practitioners throughout the world. In addition, Routledge has provided its own highly qualified professionals to make this series a reality. In particular we want to indicate our deep appreciation for the work of our series editor, Francesca Heslop. She has been very supportive of the series from the very beginning and has been invaluable in providing the needed support and encouragement to us and to the many authors in the series. She, along with other staff including Simon Whitmore, Russell George, Victoria Lincoln, Jacqueline Curthoys, Lindsie Court, Simon Alexander, and Elisabet Sinkie, has helped make the process of completing this series an enjoyable one. For everything they have done, we thank them all.

Randall S. Schuler, Rutgers University and GSBA Zurich
Paul Sparrow, Lancaster University
Susan E. Jackson, Rutgers University and GSBA Zurich
Michael Poole, Cardiff University

Preface

This book is part of Routledge's Global HRM series edited by Randall Schuler, Susan Jackson, Paul Sparrow and Michael Poole. As the title suggests, the book focuses on global compensation. It is intended for a global audience. It provides an overview of the issues MNEs face when determining pay and benefits for a global workforce. It also provides an overview of national differences in the pay and benefits of workers and executives.

The purpose of the book

Although it is of critical importance to organizations, there is relatively little written about international aspects of compensation. This book is a response to the need for a coherent source of information on compensation in the global context. We believe that it will be useful to students, academics, and HR professionals working in the area of compensation. This book can serve several purposes. First, it can serve as a text book. Because it covers international aspects of compensation in great depth, it can serve as a useful supplement to an introductory compensation text or an international HRM text. The book can also stand alone as a text for a course in international compensation. Second, it can be useful to HR practitioners for coverage of and solutions to current HR issues in global compensation. Finally, the book can be a useful source for academics studying compensation to help frame further theoretical and empirical research in the largely under-researched international area.

The organization of the book

The book has two major sections. The first section, titled Foundational concepts, provides an overview of different aspects of compensation in a global context, which includes an analysis of current hot topics in global compensation. The chapters are written by a strong international mix of up and coming scholars. Chapter 1, by Gregorio Sánchez Marín, covers the basis for compensation differences around the world, while Chapter 2, by the same author, shows the national differences in compensation among European, American and Asian countries. Chapter 3, by Edilberto (Ed) Montemayor, introduces the important point of ethical consideration in the design of global compensation systems. Chapter 4, by Monica Franco-Santos, provides a foundation of the important issues involved in the design of a pay for performance system in global contexts. Chapters 5 and 6, look at the use of incentives on special groups, to foster behaviors that further a firm's competitive advantage in a global context. Chapter 5, by Björn Claes, looks at the design of compensation for supply chain managers, while Chapter 6, by Marianna Makri, looks at the design of compensation for research and development managers and executives. Chapters 7, 8 and 9 look at the compensation system design of executives. Chapter 7, by Katalin Takacs Haynes, looks at factors that affect national differences in the compensation of executives. Chapter 8, by Carmelo Cennamo, looks at how the compensation package of global executives can affect how firms address the concerns of all stakeholders. Finally, Chapter 9, by Pascual Berrone and Jordan Otten, looks at internal and external determinants of executive pay world wide.

The second section, titled Global applications, is an analysis of various aspects of global compensation from the perspectives of leading scholars in the field of compensation. Much of what we know about compensation has been written by these scholars. This section presents their perspectives on the current state of compensation in a global context. Chapter 10, by Charles H. Fay, addresses the issue of global convergence in the design and outcomes of compensation systems. Chapter 11, by Barry Gerhart, questions the true impact of national culture on compensation. Chapter 12, by Aino Salimäki and Robert L. Heneman, looks at national differences in pay for performance plans as well as pay for performance plans for global employees. Chapter 13, by Jerry Newman and Richard Floersch, looks at global wages in industries with low barriers to entry and how they differ from other industries. Chapter 14, by Joseph J. Martocchio and Niti Pandey, looks at the national differences in benefits among countries around the world. Chapters 15 and 16 focus on CEO pay. Chapter 15, by David B. Balkin, explores why CEO pay in the US is so much higher than in other countries, while Chapter 16, by Pascual Berrone and Luis R. Gomez-Mejia, explores how the incentive packages of global CEOs can be designed to be more beneficial for society. Overall, the chapters cover a wide range of topics and perspectives that, we believe, will help further the dialogue about the important issues in compensation practices around the world.

Acknowledgments

We are very grateful to the chapter authors for their valuable contributions and their professionalism throughout the process. We would also like to thank the series editors, Susan Jackson, Michael Poole, Randall Schuler, and Paul Sparrow, for their help and guidance in the process of publishing this book.

Luis R. Gomez-Mejia and Steve Werner

SECTION 1

Foundational concepts

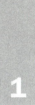

The influence of institutional and cultural factors on compensation practices around the world

Gregorio Sánchez Marín

The globalization of economies, a process which is clearly leaving its mark on today's world, has led to many changes such as the disappearance of trade barriers, the interdependence of economies, greater mobility of people and the progressive homogenization of culture. These factors, together with the increase in international competition, have modified the way in which organizations are managed. The main consequence has been the rise of the international company. Transnational businesses came onto the scene in the 1950s, when there was an intensification of international exchange and a subsequent increase in the number of firms selling their products on new markets and setting up filial companies abroad.

One may, therefore, state that the internationalization processes of companies have influenced globalization and have been encouraged by it. What challenges arise from globalization and the increase of competition in terms of managing organizations? In the first place, there are those emerging from having to trade in different countries with different levels of economic development, different legal and political systems, varied national and organizational cultures, with workers of different skills, expectations, values and motivations. Such internationalized organizations need, on the one hand, to attempt to adapt to the cultural and institutional contexts of the countries in which they are operating and, on the other, to set up a more global and homogenized organization which aligns and harmonizes its management structures throughout its offices, be they at home or abroad.

One of the basic pillars of success of international organizations is a correct adaptation of human resource management (HRM). If an organization is able to apply international management of human resources which can be adapted to the cultural demands and the expectations of all the employees, while at the same time configuring a global strategy, then it is more likely to achieve a competitive advantage (Scullion and Starkey, 2000). Thus, HRM practices should adopt a global view so that the organization is able to select, promote, reward and train its employees fittingly so that they, in turn, may contribute to overcoming the challenges presented by internationalization. (See Chapters 10 and 11 for more on this issue.)

In such a scenario compensation assumes a highly relevant role. Management of compensation practices in the sphere of global business is subject to the same adaptation conditions and requirements as other areas of HRM and maybe even more so since decisions on compensation have special impacts on employees and arouse greater social and even political sensitivity (Gomez-Mejia and Welbourne, 1991).

According to Bloom and colleagues (2003), compensation systems in the international arena require a more global approach which must move between two main objectives: (1) strategic alignment-compensation systems must be adapted to the organizational context to support and improve the corporate aims; and (2) adaptation to the institutional and cultural context – compensation systems must be adjusted to the local contexts within which the international firm is working. The balance struck between these two objectives can lead to compensation becoming a key element in the international success of the company. (See Chapter 11 for a different perspective on this.) This chapter seeks to analyze the role of compensation from an international perspective and to examine the main factors affecting it while studying how organizations can adapt their design to improve performance and increase motivation among employees, and hence, their competitive level.

Compensation in a global context

In order to understand compensation within an international context it is necessary, first of all, to recognize the existing differences and similarities between the various contexts in which the company operates, and then be in a position to handle such differences appropriately. Milkovich and Newman (2008) believe that employee compensation design hinges on the variations presented by four key factors – institutional, economic, organizational and individual. The changes – be they greater or smaller – that these factors impose in the different countries will be reflected in the changes that the organization may have to undertake when designing different compensation systems in the different territories in which it works.

Each factor is made up of a set of subfactors. The institutional factors are determined in the main by political structures and cultural traditions along with social contracts and trade union power. Business organizations are also of influence. The economic factors are integrated in the existing level of competitiveness and the degree of market development, the differences in ownership structures of the organizations and the characteristics of the tax systems. The organizational factors which may influence compensation design are related to the degree of autonomy enjoyed by the employees, the level of technology and innovation, and strategic aims. Finally, the individual factors refer to aspects connected with employees of international firms: demographic characteristics, level of knowledge and skills, attitudes, motivations and preferences.

Studies on compensation carried out at a local level (a single country) have analyzed almost all the factors. However, when the analysis is extended to the international sphere some factors assume much greater importance and their analysis requires special attention. Milkovich and Newman (2008) consider that a compensation analysis from a global perspective needs to focus primarily on five of the factors/subfactors: (1) social contracts; (2) trade unions; (3) capital markets and ownership structure; (4) management autonomy; and (5) institutional and cultural framework. These factors have been shown to be particularly important when explaining the variations which are produced in international compensation practices.

In terms of its being part of a social contract, Milkovich and Newman (2008) state that labor relations go beyond employee–employer interchange. This interchange also includes the state, all the owners of the other companies (acting at an individual or, through business associations, at a collective level) and all the employees (likewise acting at an individual or, through their unions, at a collective level). The relations and expectations of these three parties constitute the social contract. In this sense, it is clear that different people in different countries have different expectations and beliefs about the roles of government, unions, employees, employers and business organizations with respect to compensation. Thus, any understanding of the compensation phenomenon must include an understanding of the social contract established in each country. Efforts to modify employee compensation systems involve changes in the expectations of all parties to the social contract.

Perhaps the most extreme example of the effects of the social contract in compensation systems is that which relates to the degree of centralization within the compensation frameworks of different countries. According to Freeman and Katz (1994), the USA, United Kingdom and Canada use highly decentralized compensation systems with minimum government intervention. Countries such as Japan, Germany and Spain usually establish compensation systems of average centralization since they are controlled by the sector to which the company belongs. Elsewhere, Sweden, Denmark and Belgium have highly centralized frameworks with heavy government intervention, which form national wage systems.

Another example of a determining factor in international compensation design, and one which is related to the social contract, is the differing presence of trade unions in the different countries. Several papers (Katz and Darbishire, 2000; Boyer, 2001) have highlighted the high union membership in European countries such as Sweden and Denmark and the low membership in countries such as the United Kingdom. At the other end of the spectrum is the low union membership in Asian countries such as South Korea or Japan, and also in the case of the USA. Although some data seem to point to a downward trend in trade union power in countries where they have traditionally been very strong, the influence of collective agreements should not be overlooked. For example, in France or Spain, between 81 percent and 90 percent of workers are covered by collective agreements, although only 9 to 15 percent are members of a trade union (Boyer, 2001).

How does this affect international compensation systems? Union presence may, depending on the country in question, give rise to greater or lesser freedom for the organization when establishing its compensation system, and it may determine the level of resistance or involvement of the employees in the system. Thus, for example, in some countries, such as Germany or Belgium, employee compensation is established through a collective agreement with employees (even if they are not members of a union). Elsewhere in the European Union there is an attempt to set up employee boards which will be involved in any change in the companies' compensation systems where they work (Milkovich and Newman, 2008).

Another aspect, related to the above, which may influence the design of the compensation system is social legislation. For example, within the European Union, the United Kingdom is the country with the fewest legal requirements. There is no minimum salary, no maximum number of hours and no formal methods of participation. The system is similar in the USA and Japan. In contrast, France and Germany have the most heavily regulated social welfare systems – Spain too, but to a lesser extent. In this sense, the element that can most influence compensation systems is labor costs and, especially, social costs (which are included in the compensation), costs which the organization must meet in all these countries (Brewster and Harris, 1999). Although high labor costs usually go hand in hand with higher levels of productivity (Schwab *et al.*, 2000), which compensates for the higher salaries, it does often lead to negative decisions such as relocating the company in countries where labor costs are cheaper.

From an economic standpoint, the financial and ownership structures differ in organizations around the world and these differences may be important in understanding international compensation systems. For example, in the USA the ownership structure of organizations and access to capital is much less concentrated than in the majority of countries (National Center for Employee Ownership, 2005). At the other end of the spectrum there is South Korea, whose economic structure depends to a large extent on six huge corporations which are closely linked to six families (Ungson *et al.*, 1997). In countries such as Germany and Spain, while the situation is not as extreme as in Asia, there are also high ownership concentrations by a small number of large banks which are majority shareholders in the largest, most important companies in their respective countries (Turner, 1998; Crespi and Garcia-Cestona, 2001). The different ownership models have consequences for certain compensation systems. Hence, Milkovich and Newman (2008), among others, hold that the establishment of incentives linked to an increase in the value of shares or share purchase options for employees makes little sense in large corporations in countries with high concentrations of ownership. Nevertheless, ownership in small, recently created businesses normally operates outside traditional channels, and so offering ownership linked incentives may be more effective when seeking to attract new employees.

The clearest illustration of the importance of ownership structure has been seen in China and in the Eastern European countries. As a result of the social and political upheavals in these places, a huge variety of forms of ownership have come about. For example, while state owned companies are still the majority employers in China, the private companies with foreign shareholders and wholly foreign companies now account for 50 percent of total profits in that country. In the new Chinese private businesses employees have different values and expectations from those in the public sector. The same can be said of the expectations of employers (i.e. the social contract), which are substantially different. Zhou and Martocchio (2001) illustrate how ownership structure has led to a change in salary preferences and in the expectations of Chinese workers. Those authors report that private sector employees prefer more performance linked compensation than their public sector counterparts.

Management autonomy refers to the degree of discretion which managers enjoy when dealing strategically with a compensation system. This level of autonomy is inversely related to the degree of centralization of the compensation system. The majority of companies in the USA or the United Kingdom, for example, enjoy greater freedom of action and decision when designing or modifying their employees' compensation system than their counterparts in other European countries. In EU countries, there is generally more government and legislative intervention and strong trade union pressure, all of which reduces autonomy from directors of organizations when it comes to aligning compensation with business strategy or market conditions (Fajertag, 2000). It is not only governments and trade unions which can limit managerial discretion. Corporative policies are also influential. Compensation decisions taken at the mother company of a multinational and then exported to the filial firms in the other countries, could align themselves to the corporate strategy, although not in the economic or sociocultural context of such countries (Roth and O'Donnell, 1996; Brewster and Harris, 1999). For example, North American multinationals which emphasize performance based compensation could expand such a policy to their filial companies in Asian countries, for example Japan, where egalitarian compensation systems are preferred, which supposes a limit to the autonomy of local managers when adapting compensation systems to local cultural conditions.

The above example leads us to ask how the institutional and cultural factors of a certain country or territory might exercise any influence of significance in the design of compensation systems. The institutional and cultural environment has been and still is without doubt the factor considered as most responsible for changes and adaptations in international compensation systems and, hence, that which has generated most research in recent times.

Institutional factors and compensation design

Institutional theory and, in particular, the contemporary neo institutionalist current (Meyer and Scott, 1983; Scott, 1987; Zucker, 1987) has become one of the most interesting technical frameworks to explain the behavior of organizations which have to face up to turbulent, changing environments where uncertainty reigns and seems to be ever more important. This approach considers organizations as systems which incorporate symbols and regulating processes that condition and determine social behavior (Scott, 1995).

According to the institutional perspective, organizations are conditioned by their social context and so they seek to adopt structures and processes which best adapt to the standards, values and beliefs held within the "institutional environment." Thus, the behavior of an organization usually responds to the search for legitimacy and social acceptance (Suchman, 1995) within its own context with the final aim of increasing, through these, its likelihood of survival.

The vision of organizations that this theory proposes stems from the conception of these as institutions made up of normative, cognitive or regulative structures which provide stability and meaning to the social behavior and which are upheld by various interests (cultures, structures and routines) which act at different levels (Scott, 1995). Likewise, each of these structures or pillars on which organizations rest involves various bases of acceptance, mechanisms, logics, indicators and sources of legitimacy.

The regulative pillar highlights the role of institutions in limiting and regulating behavior. It affects the establishing of rules, their control, the stipulation of sanctions and rewards as strategies which govern future behaviors. The normative pillar underlines the importance of the values and norms which arise formally or informally. Values are usually defined as desirable while norms determine how things should be done and what means should be employed. The cognitive pillar gathers the rules which make up the nature of the reality and create the frameworks in which meanings can be developed. The behavior of the individual is thus assumed to be a consequence of the internal representation the individual has of their environment.

DiMaggio and Powell (1983) see institutional effects as being dissipated through three social mechanisms, coercion, the normative and mimicry, each of which rests on one of the pillars. The coercive forces are associated with the regulative pillar and they reflect how structures such as the state can put pressure on organizations to accept institutional rules. Normative pressures derive from the role of the players – professional organizations, academic institutions or consultants – who issue the norms. Last, the mimetic mechanisms are associated with the cognitive pillar and act through processes of cloning or imitating benchmark organizations which are successful or which have better results and which belong to the same environment.

Thus, DiMaggio and Powell (1983) refer to "institutional isomorphism" as the phenomenon which, as a consequence of the action of the three forces or institutional mechanisms, leads to organizations being ever more homogeneous in form in each organizational field or group of organizations, which on aggregate makes up a recognized area of institutional life.

According to the above arguments, institutional theory can, on the one hand, predict practices and behaviors of an organization from different perspectives, which may proceed from legitimated cultural perceptions, traditions of the sector or management methods (Eisenhardt, 1988), and, on the other, the institutional framework can be used to explain the homogeneity between organizations in certain management and administration practices (Suchman, 1995). Of course, both aspects of the theory have been and can be applied to the sphere of HRM, as Wright and McMahan (1992) show. For these authors, many HRM practices may be the result of social construction processes through which external entities influence the creation and implementation of practices which slowly acquire some legitimation.

Institutional and compensation theory

Institutional theory can, within HRM processes, clearly help to explain factors which are of influence in the design of compensation systems. As regards the first aspect, the perceptions of society on compensation practices of an organization can affect its status within the environment or context in which it obtains its financial and human resources. Gomez-Mejia and Wiseman (1997) have suggested that if a firm is overgenerous towards its directors, its reputation may suffer, with a subsequent loss of social support. Employing experts and professionals who are supposedly independently designing compensation systems may serve to avoid such a negative effect. This may be a mechanism which bestows social legitimacy on the organization.

Regarding the homogeneity of compensation practices among organizations, Finkelstein and Hambrick (1989) point out that firms belonging to different sectors of activity present different wage models and compensation structures which can be explained by the influence of the consultant agencies. Shaw *et al.* (2002) explain the power of compensation systems and the degree of wage dispersion as elements which favor implantation of the organization strategy by combining classical economic perspective with institutional and equity theories. Eisenhardt (1988) found that the age of the businesses is one variable that most strongly explains whether to pay a fixed amount or to use commissions. This is due to the types of practices that were considered most opportune for the institutional environment in question when the business was set up. St-Onge *et al.* (2001) empirically confirmed that incentives systems for directors which are based on stock options not only serve to align the interests of principal and agent, but are also used in a symbolic sense as a sign that the company is imitating the practices carried out by other firms within the sector (independently of whether these provide greater or lesser efficiency for the organization). Thus, performance based compensation systems are not only used to minimize agency problems (Lazear, 1999), but also as mechanisms which the organization uses to offer a specific image in its environment and to attract a certain type of employee.

Thus, from an institutionalist viewpoint, compensation systems become more of a signal or announcement that the organization considers itself as belonging to a certain social context. This interpretation has given rise to the development of a good number of studies which focus on analyzing the role of the so-called symbolic compensation policies (Westphal and Zajac, 1994, 1998; Zajac and Westphal, 1995; Fernandez-Alles *et al.*, 2006).

Symbolic compensation and legitimacy

Westphal and Zajac (1994) espouse the need to adopt new foci in the study of compensation which go beyond the more economical aspects (mainly agency theory), because of the difficulty of demonstrating consistent empirical relations between compensation and organizational efficiency (Jensen and Murphy, 1990). From an institutional viewpoint, real compensation practices differ a priori from the formal designs because of the influences of political and cultural forces and that of certain customs of the sector which make it easier to talk about symbolic rather than rational compensation.

Zajac and Westphal (1995) coined the term "symbolic compensation" to refer to that type of compensation which does not maximize organizational efficiency, but which results from the pressures of the institutional environment. Adoption by part of the organization of a certain compensation system is what indicates that the organization belongs to and is conditioned by its social context. In the same vein, St-Onge *et al.* (2001) express the idea that institutional theory may be useful in predicting how, over time, institutional and mimetic pressures induce companies to adopt similar compensation practices in their quest to achieve the necessary legitimacy within their environments and ensure their survival.

This supposes that although organizations might be capable of designing their compensation systems to improve the overall performance of the firm, the process may be influenced by the trends or social conventions of the institutional environment in which they operate (Meyer and Rowan, 1977) and which, in the long run, may have greater effects on the final outcome of the design of the compensation practices.

Various studies have confirmed how the institutional environment exercises a significant influence on several aspects and components of compensation. Eisenhardt (1988) was one of the pioneers in this sense when she sought an additional explanation (beyond economic reasoning) of how sellers' payments were established. She took 54 small shops located in the same business area and found that the compensation policies designed for the sales staff were governed by both economic variables (agency) and institutional factors. Specifically, she found that the age of the business was one of the most influential factors in compensation, meaning that the compensation design chosen reflected the institutional environment prevailing at the time the business was set up. Over time, the compensation scheme gained legitimacy and was rarely called into question or examined.

Westphal and Zajac, through several later studies, developed and confirmed the influence of institutional factors in the formation of the symbolic compensation in senior management spheres. In particular, Westphal and Zajac (1994) took a sample of 570 large American firms and started from the idea that the adoption of long term incentive plans (based, for example, on organization performance or share distribution) can be explained from a political and institutional perspective. They found a separation between real compensation and symbolic compensation: a large number of firms adopt, but do not use long term incentive schemes for their senior directors, which implies that rather than trying to bring together the interests of the managers and the shareholders, these firms are seeking legitimacy within their environment by symbolically controlling agency costs.

Using a sub-sample of the same database reduced to 352 firms, Zajac and Westphal (1995) continued the analysis of institutional, demographic, economic and political determinants in long term incentive systems used in senior management. Confirming the results of the previous study, they found that although agency theory is the dominant perspective in explaining the raison d'être of these incentive systems, because of the need to align interests and supervision, it is institutional theory which offers the explanation as to why this type of incentive acquires a symbolic value over time. Thus, institutional logic tends to win over time, even when the use of these systems in reducing agency problems remains unclear.

In their third paper in this area, Westphal and Zajac (1998) again confirm the influence of the institutional environment on senior management compensation. They check in particular how the announcement to adopt incentive plans which align the highest director's pay with shareholder interests has important consequences for the organization, both internally, since it reduces the amount of control by the board of directors, and externally, since the stock market reacts positively, regardless of whether these plans are later put into practice or not. The findings confirm the importance of the institutional environment of the organization.

In a wider sense, Staw and Epstein (2000) also analyze the role of management compensation from the perspective of management trends and tendencies. They find that while implanting popular management techniques does not have any economic effects for the 100 biggest American industrial corporations, it does positively affect how the company is perceived within its environments both in terms of reputation and of innovative capacity and quality. They also show that the use of these techniques clearly influences the design of senior management compensation systems. Specifically, both the basic salary and the short term incentives of the CEO are positively related to these management trends: compensation (salary plus bonuses) gets higher as the implantation of techniques such as total quality or management by aims is announced. These results show how legitimacy can be achieved through various management practices and how these influence the design of compensation systems.

St-Onge *et al.* (2001) focus on a specific system of long term incentives – stock options – and analyze their efficiency and the role of the institutional environment. They conducted interviews on 18 directors from different Canadian firms. From the opinions they were given, they reported that stock option programs set up by firms do not align the interests of directors and shareholders over the long term. Rather, there is a need to imitate incentive practices observed in other firms in the same sector, so that they act at a symbolic level which legitimizes and justifies their use.

Finally, Fernandez-Alles and colleagues (2006), provide a more general analysis of whether variable compensation systems are conditioned only by efficiency or whether they reflect a search for improved legitimacy. They show how the design of variable compensation among employees (management and non management) does not always achieve financial objectives or interest alignment, as agency theory upholds, but also has social aims, like achieving legitimacy, consistent with institutional theory.

In short, the studies carried out to date have underlined the clear influence of the institutional environment in the design of compensation systems, which is why institutional factors are being incorporated more and more into the analysis of compensation as a way of obtaining an explanatory framework which is closer to reality (Zajac and Westphal, 1995). It has been confirmed that the management of compensation practices, both of basic salary and of short and long term incentives, does not only take into account the fundamentals of economic reasoning but also elements of a symbolic character, which are used as a means of gaining legitimacy within the social context the organization belongs to. Furthermore, the implantation of popular management practices such as total quality is an influencing factor in the organization's design of its compensation practices.

Cultural factors and compensation design

Culture can be defined as the mental programming shared by a group of people which is based on a set of common values, beliefs and assumptions (Hofstede, 1991). This shared mental diagram directly influences the way information is processed and interpreted and hence actions and behaviors. Because of its characteristics, culture differs from one group of people to another and it has been shown to be a relatively stable component of countries (Hofstede, 1993). Culture can be considered as the "software of the mind," which is deeply rooted in day to day living and is therefore highly resistant to change (Newman and Nollen, 1996).

Sources and consequences of culture

The explanatory framework provided by Tosi and Greckhamer (2004) can help understanding of the sources or origins of a culture and, more importantly, its consequences in the structure and functioning of organizations. Differences in national culture emerge as a set of forces which are the result of history, geography, resources, climate and other factors of the country. A set of cultural values comes out of these which are elements of people's cognitive maps and are reflected in the social system and the institutions of a culture (Shaw, 1990). Cultural values in turn influence the structure and functioning of the economic organizations of the country, aspects of an organization's design (including the compensation systems), management philosophies, styles of leadership and motivation techniques (Tosi and Greckhamer, 2004).

Although numerous studies have sought to identify the cultural differences between countries, it is perhaps Hofstede (1980) who has provided the most comprehensible framework for the different cultural diagrams and values of nations. This writer carried out an ambitious project for IBM which involved surveying 116,000 of the company's employees in 50 countries. It was found that cultural differences can be built up on various dimensions:

(1) Power distance. This indicates the degree to which individuals are willing to accept a greater or lesser hierarchical structure which underlines to a greater or lesser extent the differences in status between subordinates and superiors. The greater the power distance, the more noticeable the difference between superiors and subordinates (e.g. Mexico, Arab nations, Malaysia). In contrast, individuals in societies of short power distance (e.g. Netherlands, Sweden, Australia) will probably be less tolerant of inequalities between levels and job categories than in countries where greater power distance is considered as normal.

(2) Uncertainty avoidance. This is related to how members of a society face up to risk with greater or lesser caution. A low level of uncertainty avoidance supposes a higher tolerance to risk and to the unknown. A consequence is lower levels of stress in the individuals of this culture (e.g. Greece, Portugal, Italy). A high level of uncertainty avoidance is related to countries where the citizens constantly seek to minimize risks and to control uncertainty. As a result of striving to maintain security individuals in such societies suffer more tension and stress (e.g. Sweden, Denmark, Singapore).

(3) Individualism vs collectivism. This reflects the degree to which individuals of a certain society value independence over belonging to a group. Countries with high individualism positively value and give weight to goals, autonomy and personal privacy (e.g. USA, United Kingdom, Canada). In contrast, a high level of collectivism (or low individualism) is found in countries where central values are established on the basis of group loyalty, commitment to the rules of the group, participation in group activities, social cohesion and intense participation (e.g. Japan, South Korea, Indonesia).

(4) Masculinity vs femininity. This characterizes the degree to which a society values more positively and promotes characteristics of masculine and feminine behavior. It also reflects how rigid the stereotypes are in the roles played by men and women. A country that scores high in masculinity accepts the philosophy that men or male values are dominant in the society's business dealings. It also values highly aspects such as material possessions and aggression in the search for greater wealth (e.g. Germany, Austria, USA). A feminine society on the other hand puts emphasis on behaviors directed towards care and health. The individuals of these countries give more positive value to the quality of their lives than to material possessions. Moreover, the role of the woman is less predetermined, less of a stereotype and has a wider range of opportunities (e.g. Norway, Finland, the Netherlands).

It seems that the role played by culture in different countries in explaining and understanding possible variations and differences in the design of compensation systems is a key one. On the one hand, money can have very different connotations in a society, depending on the amount obtained, where it is obtained, how it is obtained and how it is used to pay the employees (Zelizer, 1989). On the other, to the extent that the values of the national culture are seen to be reinforced, it becomes more likely that individuals will behave in ways aimed at improving performance. This is because the compensation practices are consistent with existing expectations, behaviors and routines which transcend the workplace and do not divert employees' attention (Newman and Nollen, 1996).

Adjusting compensation practices to culture

The design of compensation systems that are adapted to employees' cultural expectations could, therefore, contribute to giving these firms a competitive advantage. Starting from Hofstede's classification, some studies have sought to establish relations between the design of the compensation system and the dimensions of the national culture in order to check such aspects. Specifically, Gomez-Mejia and Welbourne (1991) at a theoretical level, and Pennings (1993), Schuler and Rogovsky (1998) and Tosi and Greckhamer (2004), at the empirical level, have established relations between each of the dimensions of national culture and the compensation system or practice that may be the most appropriate and that which contributes most to improving the efficiency of the international business.

Gomez-Mejia and Welbourne (1991) in relation to the first dimension, indicate that countries with a high power distance require hierarchical compensation systems with large differences in earnings which reflect differences in status and position between superiors and subordinates. Countries with a low power distance require more egalitarian systems which reflect small differences in earnings and with shared incentives (profit sharing). As regards the second dimension, countries with uncertainty avoidance usually give a lot of weight to fixed pay and systems are characterized by being centralized and very oriented towards internal equity. For countries with low uncertainty avoidance, variable pay is a key element in the compensation mix, the systems are very decentralized and flexible and there is a lot more emphasis on the quest for external equity. As for the third dimension, Gomez-Mejia and Welbourne (1991) state that compensation based on individual performance and personal achievements, the use of exclusively extrinsic rewards and the quest for external equity are the most appropriate practices for countries with an individualist culture. On the other hand, compensation based on group performance, the use of intrinsic rewards (as well as extrinsic ones) and an emphasis on internal equity is best for the collectivist culture. Finally, the more masculine societies are characterized by compensation policies which favor inequalities according to gender and usually reward masculine characteristics and stereotypes both financially and when it comes to promotion. Feminine societies foster more egalitarian compensation systems which do not make sexual discriminations and in which access to reward and promotion are not dependent on one's meeting a certain stereotype.

Schuler and Rogovsky (1998) use data from 24 countries to analyze the links between culture and compensation practices. These authors find, first, that international firms operating in countries with high levels of uncertainty avoidance should use stable compensation systems, based on length of service and skills. Second, for such firms to be able to increase their productivity through performance based compensation, they need to take into account the culture in question. Individual incentives work better for countries with high levels of individualism. Third, firms need to consider the culture of the destination country when using social benefit programs. The results suggest that in countries with high levels of masculinity there is less use of maternity programs, childcare services, flexitime, career flexibility and so on. However, there is no need to take into consideration uncertainty avoidance levels when offering social benefits. Fourth, international companies need to take into account the culture of the destination country before making use of ownership based incentives. Share plans or share options could be more appropriate for very individualist cultures and with low levels of uncertainty avoidance. In short, national culture provides an important explanation of the variance in use of different compensation practices in different countries by international companies.

In the sphere of senior management, Pennings (1993) examines compensation in the United Status, France and Holland through a qualitative study based on interviews of 67 directors of 29 organizations in these three countries. The results are consistent with the cultural differences of the countries (according to Hofstede's dimensions), thus confirming that the pay of a director is designed according to the cultural values of each nation. In short, American compensation systems are more formally instituted; they have larger variable components at both short and long term, which means that directors' salaries are very high. (See Chapter 15 for more on this topic.) In France and Holland, formalization is lower (specific compensation plans are even non existent in some cases) and incentives systems have little effect on the director's final pay. This is especially significant in France, where pay in the majority of companies is fixed.

Finally, Tosi and Greckhamer (2004) relate Hofstede's cultural dimensions with three compensation dimensions of the CEO – total compensation, proportion of variable compensation and the compensation ratio of the CEO with respect to that of the lowest employee level. To do this, they used the Towers Perrin database for 1997 to 2001, which contains information on the earnings of directors in 23 countries. The main findings of the study were: (1) the three compensation dimensions analyzed are related to power distance, and so the compensation of the CEO in a certain culture is fundamentally the reflection of the structure's strength and influence in the society; (2) total compensation and the proportion of variable compensation are more directly related to the culture's degree of individualism; and (3) uncertainty avoidance as a symbol of risk clearly influences the proportion of the variable compensation of the CEO.

In short, the empirical findings clearly show the importance of national culture in the management of compensation systems. The studies confirm that culture contributes to understanding the compensation designs applied in different countries. As Bloch and Parry (1989) indicate, there exist different ways in which compensation practices are adapted to the cognitive schemes of different cultures and these will similarly vary from society to society and affect the "cultural matrix" in which money is incorporated.

Conclusions

One of the basic pillars of success of organizations operating within an international context is the correct adaptation of their staff management processes. If the organization is able to apply HRM which adapts to the institutional and cultural conditioners and to the expectations of all the employees, it is more likely that it will achieve some competitive advantage. Human resource practices must, therefore, adopt a global perspective which allows the organization to select, conserve, promote, compensate and train employees so that they can contribute to overcoming the challenge of internationalization.

How do international businesses carry out the development and deployment of compensation systems in the different countries in which they operate? Different factors influence the design of the compensation systems and configure the different orientations or strategic alternatives. The compensation strategy will generally reflect the stance of the company in respect to two contrasting pressure categories (Bloom *et al.*, 2003): one which causes the organization to design a global compensation strategy which supports the worldwide corporative strategy of the firm, and another which demands that the organization adapts to the different local contexts in which it operates.

Institutional theory (DiMaggio and Powell, 1983; Scott, 1987), is useful to explain the practices and behavior of an organization which derive from legitimated cultural perceptions of sector traditions or management methods. Likewise, the institutional framework explains the homogeneity between organizations in some of their management and administration practices. Of course, both aspects have been applied to the study of compensation systems, whose design may be the result of social construction processes in which certain external entities influence the creation and implantation of compensation practices which slowly achieve legitimacy.

Several studies have confirmed that the management of compensation practices, both in its fixed components (basic salary) and its variable ones (short or long term incentives) not only take into account fundamentals of economic reasoning but also elements of a symbolic nature which are used to acquire legitimacy in the social context to which the organization belongs. Furthermore, the fact that an organization implants popular management practices (such as total quality or management by aims) influences the orientation and design of its own compensation practices, which will be more likely to be moderated by achieving legitimacy than by the search for efficiency.

As for the role of the cultures of the different countries in explaining and understanding the possible variations in the designs of compensation systems at an international level, the studies have found clear, significant relations between compensation practices and national culture. Pennings (1993), Schuler and Rogovsky (1998) and Tosi and Greckhamer (2004) have found that, in general, countries with a high power distance require hierarchical compensation systems with large differences in salaries. Countries with high uncertainty avoidance usually put a lot of weight on fixed wages. Pay based on individual performance and personal achievements, the use of exclusively extrinsic compensations and the search for equity are practices which are better suited to countries of individualist culture. Finally, more masculine societies are characterized by compensation policies which favor inequality according to sex and which generally favor masculine stereotype characteristics, both financially and when promoting.

In short, it can be affirmed that the research to date has served to highlight the enormous influence of the institutional context on the design of compensation systems. Institutional factors are being incorporated more and more into the analysis of compensation, as a way of developing an explicative framework which is closer to reality (Zajac and Westphal, 1995).

Nevertheless, further studies serving to enrich this area are required. As Chow (2004) states in one of the most recent analyses of institutional and cultural factors and their impact on HRM, future works must go beyond the theoretical limits (creating richer theoretical frameworks which combine economic and socio-psychological theories) and also the empirical limits (improving the quality of the data and of the construct's measurement scales) to contribute to improving knowledge on the influence of institutional and cultural context in the design of organizations' compensation systems.

References

Bloch, M. and Parry, J.P. 1989. Introduction: Money and the morality of exchange. In J.P. Parry (ed.), *Money and the morality of exchange*: 1–32. Cambridge: Cambridge University Press.

Bloom, M., Milkovich, G.T. and Mitra, A. 2003. International compensation: Learning from how managers respond to variations in local host contexts. *International Journal of Human Resource Management*, 14: 1350–67.

Boyer, G. 2001. Review symposium: Converging divergences: Worldwide changes in employment systems. *Industrial and Labor Relations Review*, 54(3): 681–2.

Brewster, C. and Harris, H. (eds). 1999. *International human resource management: Contemporary issues in Europe*. London: Routledge.

Chow, I.H. 2004. The impact of institutional context on human resource management in three Chinese societies. *Employee Relations*, 26: 626–42.

Crespi, R. and Garcia-Cestona, M.A. 2001. Ownership and control of Spanish listed firms. In F. Barca and M. Becht (eds), *The control of corporate Europe*: 207–27. Oxford: Oxford University Press.

DiMaggio, P.J. and Powell, W.W. 1983. The iron cage revisited: Institutional isomorphism and collective rationality in organizational fields. *American Sociological Review*, 48: 147–60.

Eisenhardt, K.M. 1988. Agency and institutional theory explanations: The case of retail sales compensation. *Academy of Management Journal*, 31: 488–511.

Fajertag, G. (ed.). 2000. *Collective bargaining in Europe 1998–1999*. Brussels: European Trade Union Institute.

Fernandez-Alles, M., Cuevas-Rodriguez, G. and Valle-Cabrera, R. 2006. How symbolic remuneration contributes to the legitimacy of the company: An institutional explanation. *Human Relations*, 59: 961–92.

Finkelstein, S. and Hambrick, D. 1989. Chief executive compensation: A synthesis and reconciliation. *Strategic Management Journal*, 9: 543–58.

Freeman, R. and Katz, L.F. 1994. *Differences and changes in wage structures*. Chicago, IL: University of Chicago Press.

Gomez-Mejia, L.R. and Welbourne, T.M. 1991. Compensation strategy in a global context. *Human Resource Planning*, 14(1): 29–42.

Gomez-Mejia, L.R.and Wiseman, R.M. 1997. Reframing executive compensation: An assessment and outlook. *Journal of Management*, 23: 291–374.

Hofstede, G. 1980. *Culture's consequences: International differences in work-related values*. Newbury Park, CA: Sage.

——— 1991. *Cultures and organizations*. London: McGraw-Hill.

——— 1993. Cultural constraints in management theories. *Academy of Management Executive*, 7: 81–93.

Jensen, M.C. and Murphy, K.J. 1990. Performance and top management incentives. *Journal of Political Economy*, 98: 225–64.

Katz, H. and Darbishire, O. 2000. *Converging divergences: Worldwide changes in employment systems*. Ithaca, NY: Cornell University Press.

Lazear, E.P. 1999. Personnel economics: Past lessons and future directions. *Journal of Labor Economics*, 17: 199–236.

Meyer, J.W. and Rowan, B. 1977. Institutionalized organization: Formal structure as myth and ceremony. *American Journal of Sociology*, 83: 340–63.

Meyer, J.W. and Scott, W.R. 1983. *Organizational environments: Ritual and rationality*. Beverly Hills, CA: Sage.

Milkovich, G.T. and Newman, J.M. 2008. *Compensation* (9th edition). New York: Irwin/McGraw-Hill.

National Center for Employee Ownership 2005. New data show employee ownership to be widespread. www.nceo.org/library/widespread.html.

Newman, K.L. and Nollen, S.D. 1996. Culture and congruence: The fit between management practices and national culture. *Journal of International Business Studies*, 27: 753–78.

Pennings, J.M. 1993. Executive reward systems: A cross-national comparison. *Journal of Management Studies*, 30: 261–80.

Roth, K. and O'Donnell, S. 1996. Foreign subsidiary compensation strategy: An agency theory perspective. *Academy of Management Journal*, 39: 678–703.

Schuler, R.S. and Rogovsky, N. 1998. Understanding compensation practice variations across firms: The impact of national culture. *Journal of International Business Studies*, 29: 159–77.

Schwab, K., Porter, M., Sachs, J., Warner, A. and Levison, M. 2000. *The global competitiveness report 2000. World Economic Forum*. Cambridge, MA: Harvard University Press.

Scott, W.R. 1987. The adolescence of institutional theory. *Administrative Science Quarterly*, 32: 493–511.

—— 1995. *Institutions and organizations*. London: Sage.

Scullion, H. and Starkey, K. 2000. In search of the changing role of the corporate human resource function in the international firm. *International Journal of Human Resource Management*, 11: 1061–81.

Shaw, J. 1990. A cognitive categorization model for the study of inter-cultural management. *Academy of Management Review*, 15: 626–45.

Shaw, J.D., Gupta, N. and Delery, J.E. 2002. Pay dispersion and workforce performance: Moderating effects of incentives and interdependence. *Strategic Management Journal*, 23: 491–512.

Staw, B.M. and Epstein, L.D. 2000. What bandwagons bring: Effects of popular management techniques on corporate performance, reputation, and CEO pay. *Administrative Science Quarterly*, 45: 523–56.

St-Onge, S., Magnan, M., Thorne, L. and Raymond, S. 2001. The effectiveness of stock option plans. A field investigation of senior executives. *Journal of Management Inquiry*, 10: 250–66.

Suchman, M. 1995. Managing legitimacy: Strategic and institutional approaches. *Academy of Management Review*, 20: 571–610.

Tosi, H.L. and Greckhamer, T. 2004. Culture and CEO compensation. *Organization Science*, 15: 657–70.

Turner, L. (ed.). 1998. *Negotiating the new Germany: Can social partnership survive?* Ithaca, NY: Cornell University Press.

Ungson, G.R., Steers, R.M. and Park, S.H. 1997. *Korean enterprises: The quest for globalization*. Boston, MA: Harvard Business School.

Westphal, J.D. and Zajac, E.J. 1994. Substance and symbolism in CEO's long-term incentive plans. *Administrative Science Quarterly*, 39: 367–90.

—— 1998. The symbolic management of stockholders: Corporate governance reforms and shareholder reactions. *Administrative Science Quarterly*, 43: 127–53.

Wright, P.M. and McMahan, G.C. 1992. Theoretical perspectives for strategic human resource management. *Journal of Management*, 18: 295–320.

Zajac, E.J. and Westphal, J.D. 1995. Accounting for the explanations of CEO compensation: Substance and symbolism. *Administrative Science Quarterly*, 40: 283–308.

Zelizer, V.A. 1989. The social meaning of money: "Special monies." *American Journal of Sociology*, 95: 342–77.

Zhou, J. and Martocchio, J.J. 2001. Chinese and American managers' compensation awards decision. *Personnel Psychology*, 54: 115–45.

Zucker, L. 1987. Institutional theories of organizations. *Annual Review of Sociology*, 13: 443–64.

National differences in compensation

The influence of the institutional and cultural context

Gregorio Sánchez Marín

This chapter presents the main characteristics of the compensation systems designed by organizations in different countries in the three economically most important geographical areas of the world: Europe (Spain and Germany), America (USA and Mexico) and Asia (Japan and China). The aim is to provide a view of the similarities and differences in compensation in an international sphere and to see how it is influenced by institutional and cultural factors as described in Chapter 1. The data are based in the main from the paper by Gomez-Mejia and Sanchez (2006). See Chapter 14 for a detailed discussion of national differences in benefits.

Compensation in Europe: Spain and Germany

In this section we describe the compensation systems in Europe, specifically in Spain and in Germany. The discussion includes an analysis of national context and its effects on basic salary, level of hierarchy, external equity, use of variable pay, use of performance measures and benefits.

Spain

Due to the restrictive laws and existing regulations in Spain, management of compensation is one of the most difficult processes for strategic management. This high level of intervention has direct implications when analyzing the procedure used to establish compensation. The procedure will vary according to professional categories. Thus, in the case of directors, 74 percent of firms adopt an individualized approach and use personal contracts. When it comes to technical staff, the number of personal contracts falls to 47 percent, while for the remaining categories (administration, operators) the traditional method is the collective agreement at a national or sector level (Cranfield-Esade, 2000).

Furthermore, regulations are clearly reflected in how the social benefits are set up. National health, unemployment and incapacity for work are obligatory and are financed by payments made by the workers and management alike. Moreover, on a voluntary basis, organizations offer other benefits, foremost among which figure pension schemes and health and life insurance. To a lesser extent Spanish firms also offer social benefits such as tax services, canteen subsidies, loans and company vehicles.

According to a study by Romero and Valle (2001) on a group of large firms, the most important features of the compensation systems are:

- When fixing the basic salary, the compensation system tends to be based more on the job or professional category the person holds than on his or her skills and capabilities. Changes to the basic salary are the effect of experience and length of service.
- Although the compensation system is characterized by several levels, most companies do not consider themselves as having a very hierarchical system, meaning that large differences do not exist between the top and bottom salaries in the organization.
- In most firms, competitiveness outside the compensation system is achieved by offering similar amounts to the average for the industry sector in question, with the exception of the large businesses in each sector, which are normally the leaders in this field. Rather than compete in terms of compensation components, comparisons are made at the total compensation level.
- The wage system is heavily conditioned by the important weight of the basic or fixed salary, which usually ranges from a minimum of 70–75 percent for managerial jobs to a maximum of 90–95 percent for non managerial jobs.
- The variable part of the salary, in contrast, has little effect on total pay, and is primarily connected with the level of individual performance and, to a lesser extent, with the skills and capabilities of the person.
- As for performance based earnings or incentive schemes, those most used are bonuses for meeting short term targets (sales, profits, etc). Links between payment and long term objectives are only found in 22 percent of firms.
- From the view of administration, there are opposing ideas on the transparency of the compensation system although the policy most favored seems to be that oriented more towards salary secrecy. Moreover, wage systems are usually quite centralized and have regulated, formal procedures.

Further, Romero and Valle (2001) suggested that a trend towards the variable part assuming a greater weight was emerging, though there was debate on the criteria to be used and on the methods and procedures to bring it into practice.

Other studies have confirmed this trend. For example, Cranfield-Esade (2000) points out that the use of variable pay does seem to be increasing. In 1992 it was used by 49 percent of businesses, but in 2002 the figure had climbed to 82 percent (in the case of general directors). Performance based compensation has become the most widespread form of variable compensation, although its usage depends on the hierarchical level. For managers the mean is 61 percent, while for employees it stands at merely 25 percent. The Cranfield-Esade Study also points out the low use of other incentive systems like team or group based bonuses which are only used in 18 percent of firms in the case of management and in 8 percent for unskilled workers.

In general, compensation for Spanish firms does not differ much from that of many other nearby countries, but there is a still a long way to go to achieve truly strategic orientation in compensation management, which is considered a determining factor of the sustained competitiveness of firms.

Germany

The Germans are famed for paying special attention to rules and norms, and also to symbols of power and social prestige, and this leads to a highly formal and regulated style of HRM. Another characteristic of Germany's labor relations is the direct participation of employees through union representation in the running of the business, which is known as codetermination (Dolan *et al.*, 2007).

Given the above, the compensation system traditionally favored in Germany is highly conditioned and deeply set in the social relations maintained by firms, workers and government. As a result of these social relations there is, on the one hand, very generous compensation for employees and, on the other, a highly regulated compensation system as a result of control exerted by government and collective negotiation at the sectorial level (Gresch and Stadelmann, 2001). These characteristics are summarized below:

- The compensation system is usually based more on the job held by the worker than on his or her skills and capacities. In particular the basic salary is established according to work assessment, although the age of the employee does have some influence.
- The compensation structure has many levels with small differences between each and the compensation systems are, therefore, predominantly egalitarian.
- Regarding external equity policies, the predominant pay level is that fixed at the level of the competition. Comparison of salaries between organizations is made on the basis of "tariffs" agreed between unions and employers at an industry level which establish the basic salary for the job.
- With respect to compensation components, the basic salary has a very important specific weight in the total pay – between 70 percent and 80 percent, depending on the professional category. The basic salary is fixed according to the value of the job as stipulated in the tariffs agreed on by the social agents.
- Variable compensation has traditionally had quite a low standing in the wage package, accounting for less than 15 percent in most organizations. For non managerial jobs, the variable amount is usually established in the tariff agreements.
- In terms of incentives, annual bonuses or extras are most used, and these are a reward for better efficiency in performing tasks. Efficiency measures are usually negotiated specifically for each sector and for each job, and are then included in the tariffs agreed on by unions and employers. Manager employees are not included in these agreements and they normally enjoy incentives based on objectives and company results, while a few also receive stock options.
- The German social system guarantees substantial social benefits for employees which can account for up to a third of the total compensation. These include social security, unemployment benefits, health and maternity programs and so on, which are financed by specific taxes paid by employees and employers. Other voluntary benefits are also included, such as pension plans, insurance, savings plans and so on.
- The administration of the compensation system in German forms is characterized by its large centralization aimed at achieving correct cost control. It can be classified as bureaucratic and of somewhat inflexible policies.

Apart from the above, it is necessary to also consider some recent factors which are beginning to modify some of the typical characteristics. An aging population with a low birth rate, high pensions and unemployment benefits, a large number of early retirements and high unemployment have led to a serious increase in the costs borne by the national health system in Germany. Additionally, the inflexibility of the job market has meant slow creation of jobs and a high level of dislocations. The outcome is that German firms are now demanding greater autonomy to negotiate their own tariff agreements and to attempt to improve the economic conditions for each company. There is also an increasing interest in developing new compensation systems based on individual and overall performance. Finally, new ways are being sought to ensure job security by linking it to business results (Boyer, 2001).

Compensation in the USA and Mexico

In this section we describe the compensation systems in the USA and in Mexico. The discussion includes an analysis of national context and its effects on basic salary, level of hierarchy, external equity, use of variable pay, use of performance measures and benefits.

United States

One basic distinguishing feature of the United States is its labor relations system. This is reflected by its scarce trade union presence (only 14 percent of employees are covered by collective agreements) and minimum government intervention. The system has relatively little regulation and the different parties, employer and employees, are allowed a lot of freedom to negotiate work conditions. The only norms which have to be fulfilled in work relations in general are the state laws which have rulings on minimum levels in aspects such as discrimination, equal opportunities, social benefits, safety, health and dismissals (Gomez-Mejia and Sanchez, 2006). With these general norms as the basis, companies are free to negotiate job conditions and salaries for each employee at the individual or collective level, which is local, and at a national or sector level (Stone, 1998).

Apart from the high decentralization of regulations on job relations, there is also the generally voluntary nature of social security. This, along with pensions, is controlled by Congress (trade union and company organizations are not involved) which legislates on minimum social protection, with the focus on organization aspects of collective negotiation. It is then the social interlocutors who define the job relations and social cover programs.

Given the above, Milkovich and Newman (2008) indicate that the typical US compensation system is characterized more by exchange than by commitment between the firm and the employee, which implies a shorter term vision of compensation with less guarantee of job security. Another basic pillar is strict control of salary costs, not through state intervention but by linking these to individual or group performance. Related to this is the third defining feature, the difference in earnings among employees, normally accounted for by the performance of the latter. This creates very unegalitarian salaries which depend heavily on outcomes and effort. Finally, because of strong competitiveness, employee pay (both basic salary and incentives) is heavily conditioned by external market trends.

The specific features of compensation systems can be summarized along the lines of the comments of Gomez-Mejia and Sanchez (2006) and Milkovich and Newman (2008):

- The compensation system is based on the job when fixing the basic salary. The basic salary is calculated according to the internal valuation of the jobs and their "market price." In recent years, skills and competence of employees have begun to be considered as defining elements of internal compensation structures.
- The compensation structure is characterized by few salary levels, although the differences between these are usually sizeable. There is, therefore, a strong hierarchy, especially when managerial and non managerial jobs are compared.
- Regarding external equity policy, American firms clearly tend to follow what is determined by the market and go for the average salary of the competition. When comparing with competitors special attention is paid to levels of variable pay and incentives rather than to the fixed salary.
- Among compensation components, the basic salary has a moderate specific weight. This value ranges between a maximum of 60 percent for non management employees to a minimum of 35 percent for management employees.
- Variable pay, in contrast, tops the bill for American employees. It has a relative weight ranging from 30 percent for non management employees to 55 percent for managers.
- Performance based compensation systems are the main variable pay system. Stand outs among these are the bonus plan for the individual and profit sharing or gainsharing systems based on group performance at the department or corporate level.
- Special mention needs to be made of long term incentives, which have a very high specific weight (on average 35 percent of the total pay) and are usually based on variations in the firm's share values. They are widely used in share purchase options and shares awarded for performance.
- Social benefits assume special importance in the employees' pay package since, unlike in the majority of other countries, it is the employer who provides most of these on a voluntary basis. The most important voluntary benefits, in monetary terms, are payments for time off work – holidays, leave, free days – followed by insurance and medical benefits, then pension schemes and savings plans. These benefits become an efficient tool in attracting, keeping and motivating employees.
- Compensation administration is usually flexible and based on very informal policies and procedures. Decision making is relatively decentralized to favor rapid adjustment to individual and organizational conditions.

Although compensation design has been shown to be a tool which helps to foster performance and productivity, it does bring some drawbacks and weaknesses with it, especially those stemming from the high risk assumed by employees and from the impact of that risk on decision making at management level. Employees also have little trust in the organization and they suffer from a lack of commitment and identification resulting from the short term approach of the system, from the continuous changes and modifications, and from the lack of job security (Milkovich and Newman, 2008).

Mexico

Mexico has undergone important change in recent years in terms of HRM. This has been motivated by globalization and by the country's becoming a member of NAFTA (North American Free Trade Agreement) in 1994. The climax was a world congress on human resources in 2002, at which Mexican businesses devoted unprecedented attention to this issue.

There is cultural diversity in Mexico. Three geographical areas need to be mentioned as the view of HRM varies from one to another (Dolan *et al.*, 2007): (1) the south, with its serious difficulties for political, social and economic development, which is characterized by extremely pro-employee HRM that is heavily State regulated; (2) the center of the country; and (3) the north and, in particular the northwest (around Monterrey), which is one of the most industrialized areas of Latin America and which has the highest indexes of development in the country. It is here that there is the greatest concern for HRM because of the productivity and competitive needs of businesses.

In seeking to improve its industrialization, Mexico has, over the last 40 years, fostered implantation of foreign businesses in its lands by offering high rates of productivity and very low labor costs (one special and extreme case is that of the assembly plant firms, which manufacture products of high technological content, in the area bordering with the USA). This set up has been officially maintained by the State using the argument that low salaries make the country more competitive in attracting direct investment and thus, make Mexico a "center of low cost manufacturing."

Within this context of improving industry and driving productivity, HRM takes on an increasingly important role. In theory, management sees HRM as responsible for promoting norms for labor competence with a structure that responds to the current and future conditions of the labor world and responsible for fostering a new culture of collaboration and consensual proposals that will generate opportunities for development and improved compensation for employees.

The majority of HR managers do not sit on the management committee (Arias-Galicia, 2005). In fact, many of them sit on the second or third levels of the firm's hierarchy. Consequently, HRM does not usually play any strategic role, making it difficult for human capital to adapt to changes in the environment and to become a key competitive factor.

Since the majority of Mexican firms are fundamentally cost strategy based (as occurs, for example, in the assembly plants), HR policies tend to be quite traditional and aimed more at administration than management. As Arias-Galicia (2005) points out, the human factor in the Mexican firm today does not receive the attention it deserves.

This traditional view also holds for the design of compensation systems. The first thing to note is that pay in Mexico is fixed. The salaries also represent, in general, a tenth or even a twentieth of what workers are paid in the most developed countries.

One positive aspect can be found in the fact that with the new work systems, Mexican employees now figure among the most productive in the industrialized world. This has occurred with the development of variable compensation systems, especially in the manufacturing sector, which are linked to performance assessments of the individual and the organization as a whole. Nevertheless, in spite of increased productivity, salaries have fallen 24 percent in real terms over the last 20 years (Gallagher, 2005). Former social advances such as benefits arising from long term association with a company are being constantly devalued in favor of individualization and competition, meaning that a series of social salary associated benefits are decreasing and are now limited merely to those required by law.

On top of that, there remains the abysmal disparity in salaries which exists within firms. Senior managers at large Mexican firms earn similar salaries to their US counterparts. At the other end of the scale, however, employees are among the lowest paid workers in the world. This is a clear consequence of the importance of the hierarchical structure in the Mexican business culture and the paternalistic approach to labor relations.

Compensation in Asia: Japan and China

In this section we describe the compensation systems in Asia, specifically in Japan and in China. The discussion includes an analysis of national context and its effects on basic salary, level of hierarchy, external equity, use of variable pay, use of performance measures and benefits.

Japan

Labor relations in Japan traditionally rest on three basic pillars: (1) job security in a particular company; (2) compensation and promotion systems based on the length of service; and (3) the firm's trade unions – decentralized institutions which represent the employees of a single company. These three basic aspects substantially influence and shape the characteristics of the compensation systems, which can be summarized as follows (Shibata, 2000; Yashiro, 1996):

- The compensation system tends to place more emphasis on the person than on the job when establishing the basic salary: length of service with the firm and the skills the workers possess will be more decisive in establishing their basic salary than will the value of their job or their performance. Any modifications are governed mostly by length of service.
- Promotions, which come with a change in salary, are made according to assessment by supervisors of the training and skills of employees, and not just of performance. In most firms, employees rise according to the classification of their jobs, and according to length of service and merit.
- The compensation is made up of many levels with small differences between them since increases based on merit or length of service are very small. The structure can, therefore, be considered egalitarian.
- Japanese firms tend to set pay levels at the same level as the competition. The information they use to fix the level comes from comparing a series of tables which relate the basic salary to the employee's age.
- The wage package is characterized by a high weight for fixed salary, ranging from 60 to 80 percent of the total pay and determined by the rank of the individual within the organization.

- The variable part is relatively low – between 20 percent and 40 percent of the total pay – depending on the position held in the organization. The higher the position the higher the proportion. Performance has little weight in determining the variable part.
- Variable pay is largely based on a short term bonus received twice a year and calculated by multiplication of the basic salary by a collectively negotiated index. It is not, therefore, of a clearly incentive behavior related nature. Bonuses varying according to performance are only used at the top management levels.
- A small part of variable pay is based on assessment by superiors, who also decide on promotions. The assessment considers cooperation skills as the overriding factor, ahead of other factors such as performance.
- The compensation system is usually open and transparent to encourage mutual and lasting trust between the organization and its employees. Compensation decisions are centralized, in line with Japanese paternalism, and compensation administration is highly formalized and based on specific procedures.

The lack of economic growth in Japan in the last 10 years together with the huge importance that length of time at the firm has when calculating pay has meant that Japanese firms have had to face up to a significant increase in labor costs, higher even than that of their international competitors. In response, many Japanese firms have tried to maintain long term approaches to labor relations instead of the traditional lifelong ones (Kato, 2002). Some compensation models have also undergone change, in particular those for younger, more flexible employees. Under the traditional model, these employees had lower earnings (based on time with the firm) and little chance of improvement, but they are now finding more attractive compensation in other international firms operating in Japan based on higher salaries and incentives for performance (Morishima, 2002). As a consequence, many large Japanese businesses, for example Toyota, Toshiba or Mitsubishi, are abandoning tradition and increasing their variable payment in line with employee performance.

China

The philosophical ideas of Confucius, which still prevail today in the People's Republic of China, underlie the importance of education, obedience to authority and interpersonal harmony as aspects which must direct the actions and attitudes of the individual. This philosophy, linked to traditional Chinese values of harmony, collectivity, perseverance, reciprocity and family duty, has a strong influence on the development of labor relations in Chinese businesses and, hence, in the design of the management of human resource practices, including those of compensation (Chou, 2004).

Moreover, in China there are several socioeconomic aspects which help to understand the reasons for certain compensation practices (Chou, 2004): (1) there has been a high growth of economic and business activity in recent years; (2) despite the huge growth in private initiatives, the state companies continue to dominate economic activity, and traditional Chinese values and early communist principles are still clearly predominant in these companies; (3) trade union activity is very strong in businesses and almost all workers are affiliated to them – the unions are controlled by the Communist Party and they are usually seeking collaboration rather than confrontation; (4) the job market is characterized by an excess of unqualified labor, while there is a shortage of staff for managerial and professional jobs; (5) there is scarce general development of the functions of human resources within organizations. These are merely administrative and of bureaucratic content.

Taking into account the cultural and institutional environment in which they are developed, compensation practices are characterized by the following aspects (Chou, 2004; Lowe *et al.*, 2002):

- The compensation system is characterized by the length of time the person has been in the firm as the main element for establishing and modifying the basic wage of the employee, and so it rewards loyalty to the firm.
- Promotions, which come with a rise in the employee's basic salary, are established principally on the basis of the length of time the employee has held his or her position, rather than on performance. Job security is usually guaranteed by the firm.
- Performance assessments are, therefore, not carried out by any formal, rigorous or individualized method which measures effort. It is rather a professional classification based on the technical qualification of the employee and the importance of that job within the organization.
- The compensation structure can be considered as egalitarian since differences in salary between jobs and levels are low and "politically" not desirable.
- The wage packet is heavily weighted towards fixed salaries, which are determined by the technical category of the job and, above all, by the length of time the worker has been with the company. The variable part is low because performance is barely relevant in determining total employee salary.
- Variable pay is established through group incentives. Employee incentives are established annually through gainsharing systems. Profit sharing, on the other hand, is not frequently used. Individual incentives and bonuses are practically non existent.
- Social benefit schemes are widespread and an important element (much more than variable payment) in the salary package. Given the paternalistic and state role of the employer, benefits are aimed at covering a broad spectrum of needs such as health, unemployment and sick leave.
- Compensation administration is, like the rest of HRM, centralized, not very formalized and based on vague unspecified procedures. It is not common for information on compensation mechanisms to be shared or available.

Nevertheless, it should be pointed out that the shift towards capitalism in China in recent years has led to the arrival of multinationals with more Westernized management practices. In the area of compensation this is creating a change from the egalitarian system with its importance on the length of time employees are with the company, to an alternative, more individualized system with importance placed on performance. It is yet to be seen if this system, based more on efficiency and individualism than collectivity, loyalty and commitment, will be able to take on and transform traditional Chinese values (Chou, 2004).

Conclusions

This chapter has provided examples of how the compensation systems of different countries, belonging to different geographical areas (Europe, America and Asia) clearly vary according to the cultural and institutional environment in which they are developed. Countries of Anglo Saxon culture, for example the USA, adopt exchange compensation systems, implying a shorter term vision with fewer guarantees of job security and conditioned by market trends. The basis is a strong control of wage costs by linking compensation to individual performance, and this supposes a wide disparity of earnings. Countries of oriental culture, such as China or Japan, design traditional compensation systems characterized by commitment and long term loyalty on both sides. Length of service, to the detriment of performance, is the main element for establishing wage increases. The pay package is characterized by the important weight of fixed earnings, which supposes very egalitarian salaries which are governed by rigid internal policies of the organization rather than by the market. Elsewhere, in countries of European culture such as Germany or Spain, the compensation systems are closely regulated and controlled as a result of collective negotiation and state intervention. As a result, compensation is generous and protects employees – high salaries, high fixed earnings, low performance linked incentives and wide benefit systems and social benefits. Finally, countries such as Mexico, with their Hispano-American culture, are characterized by compensation systems which are not highly formalized and an overwhelming inequality between the high and low levels of the organization. Salary levels are extremely low in general terms compared to other more developed countries. Moreover, the wage package is predominantly a fixed salary with very few social benefits.

On reflection, this chapter has shown how organizations are absorbed in their institutional environments, which in turn influence the compensation policies and practices adopted. The economic, political, legal, social and, above all, cultural structures all generate configurations that give rise to different employee compensation systems. From an institutional angle, therefore, management of compensation systems is closely linked to and influenced by institutional context factors. Organizations which act in various institutional and cultural contexts logically make use of different compensation practices. Thus, it seems clear that the relation between compensation practices and the efficiency these will have depends on how far they fit in with the institutional and cultural environment (Chou, 2004).

References

Arias-Galicia, L.F. 2005. Human resource management in Mexico. In M.M. Elvira and A. Davila (eds), *Managing human resources in Latin America: An agenda for international leaders*: 179–90. London: Routledge.

Boyer, G. 2001. Review symposium: Converging divergences: Worldwide changes in employment systems. *Industrial and Labor Relations Review*, 54(3): 681–2.

Chou, I.H. 2004. The impact of institutional context on human resource management in three Chinese societies. *Employee Relations*, 26: 626–42.

Cranfield-Esade 2000. *Gestión Estratégica de Recursos Humanos. Una década de investigación. Informe de conclusiones España 2000*. Esade, Barcelona: Departamento de Dirección de Recursos Humanos.

Dolan, S., Valle Cabrera, R., Jackson, S.E. and Schuler, R.S. 2007. *La gestión de los recursos humanos* (2nd edition). Madrid: McGraw-Hill.

Gallagher, K.P. 2005. *FDI as a sustainable development strategy: Evidence from Mexican manufacturing*. Working Paper, Center for Latin American Studies, University of Berkeley, California.

Gomez-Mejia, L.R. and Sanchez, G. 2006. *La retribución y los resultados de la organización: Investigación y práctica empresarial*. Madrid: Prentice Hall-Financial Times.

Gresch, T. and Stadelmann, E. 2001. *Traditional pay system in Germany*. Russelsheim: Adam Opel AG.

Kato, T. 2002. The end of lifetime employment in Japan? Evidence from national surveys and field research. *Journal of Japanese and International Economies*, 15: 489–514.

Lowe, K.B., Milliman, J., De Cieri, H. and Dowling, P.J. 2002. International compensation practices: A ten-country comparative analysis. *Human Resource Management*, 41(1): 45–66.

Milkovich, G.T. and Newman, J.M. 2008. *Compensation* (9th edition). New York: Irwin/McGraw-Hill.

Morishima, M. 2002. Pay practices in Japanese organizations: Changes and non-changes. *Japan Labor Bulletin*, 1: 8–13.

Romero, M.G. and Valle, R. 2001. Strategy and manager's compensation: The Spanish case. *International Journal of Human Resource Management*, 12: 218–42.

Shibata, H. 2000. The transformation of the wage and performance appraisal system in a Japanese firm. *International Journal of Human Resources Management*, 11: 294–313.

Stone, R.J. 1998. *Human resource management* (3rd edition). Milton, Australia: Jacaranda Wiley Ltd.

Yashiro, M. 1996. *Human resource management in Japanese companies in the future*. New York: Organization Resource Counselors.

Universal and national norms for Organizational Compensation Ethics

3

Using severance pay as an illustration

Edilberto (Ed) Montemayor

Many compensation strategies, policies and decisions have a significant impact on employees' lives. For example, the decision to terminate long-term employees without any compensation for their service to the firm reduces the employees' medium-term income because employees who are involuntarily terminated seldom obtain employment at their previous compensation level. Consequently, compensation strategies, policies and decisions have an ethical dimension because ethical considerations are relevant whenever someone's decisions result in harm to others who are not involved in making such decisions (Morris, 2004).

However, the literature has rarely examined Organizational Compensation Ethics, which deals with the moral dimension of compensation practices. The adjective "Organizational" is used to indicate the ideas presented here focus on the organizational level of analysis, a notion seldom addressed explicitly in extant literature that is explained in the next section. One can define Organizational Compensation Ethics as *the set of norms, principles and standards that provide guidance to judge and/or improve the moral quality of strategies, policies and decisions affecting employee pay and benefits* (a similar definition is provided by McAfee and Anderson, 1995).

The purpose of this chapter is to motivate a conversation regarding this important topic. I will argue compensation scholarship and practice are ethically deficient because they take a transactional view of employment, which ignores significant financial investments employees make in the firm they work for. The next section explains the difference between three levels of analysis in Business Ethics (institutional, organizational and personal), setting the stage for the middle section of the manuscript. The third section adopts ideas from Integrative Social Contracts Theory, a well-known Business Ethics theory, to propose the moral obligations a business firm has towards its employees, can be understood in terms of a hierarchy of universal, national and firm-specific norms. The fourth section uses well-established theory and research in Classical Economics to argue employees make significant financial investments in the firm they work for by agreeing to work under a deferred compensation scheme and/or investing in firm-specific human capital. Based on the view of employees as financial investors, the fifth section proposes five universal norms for Organizational Compensation Ethics, which are derived from globally accepted corporate governance principles. The sixth section uses severance pay to exemplify the ideas presented previously in the chapter, which ends with a conclusions section that explores the implications these ideas have for compensation scholarship and practice.

Levels of analysis in Business Ethics

Some Business Ethics scholars (e.g. Goodpaster, 2001; Heugens *et al.*, 2006) have noted that ethics and its related theories are applied at multiple levels of analysis: institutional, organizational and personal. *Institutional Business Ethics* concerns the morality of the business firm as a specific institution in society. *Organizational Business Ethics* concerns the moral quality of a specific business firm and its conduct. *Personal Business Ethics* concerns the moral quality of individuals and their conduct within a business setting.

Regrettably, much of the conceptual Business Ethics literature is not clear or precise enough about the level(s) it addresses. This is problematic because a clear and precise specification of the level of analysis addressed is a critical first step in theory development whose neglect seriously undermines the value and validity of any theoretical statement (Klein *et al.*, 1994; Rousseau, 1985).

It is important to be clear about the level of analysis addressed because the objects and phenomena that are relevant for ethical inquiry differ across the three levels of analysis (Goodpaster, 2001). Business Ethics at the institutional level of analysis includes the ethical analysis and evaluation of issues such as "affirmative action" or "outsourcing" across society in general. In contrast, Business Ethics at the organizational level of analysis includes the ethical analysis and evaluation of the strategies, policies and decisions by a specific business firm and the results it obtains when it pursues "affirmative action" or "outsourcing" objectives. Finally, Business Ethics at the personal level of analysis includes the ethical analysis and evaluation of the actual implementation (or execution) of its affirmative action (or outsourcing) policies by individual managers in the firm.

Additionally, it is important to be precise about the level of analysis addressed because the three levels of analysis listed above require different theoretical foundations. At the most aggregate level, Institutional Business Ethics requires a theoretical foundation that specifies (1) the nature of the common (social) good; (2) the contribution various institutions should make to the common good; and (3) the appropriate ways for institutions to make such contributions (Welch, 1998). That is, the theoretical foundation for Institutional Business Ethics should draw from Political Philosophy, Social Ethics and the so-called "theory of the firm" (which has focused mostly on the debate/contrast between the "shareholder" and the "stakeholder" views of the firm). At the least aggregate level, Personal Business Ethics concerns the moral quality of human beings and their conduct. Therefore classic Moral Philosophy (General Ethics) theory provides a suitable foundation for Personal Business Ethics. However, Organizational Business Ethics concerns the moral quality of a distinct entity – the business firm – and its conduct. The organizational level of analysis in Business Ethics is distinct in that organizational systems, processes and behavior generally "defy attempts to apply traditional [Ethics] theory and detached philosophical wisdom" (Barker, 2002: 1099) because traditional Ethics theory focuses on the individual level of analysis.

Consequently, the theoretical foundation for any sort of Business Ethics at the organizational level, including Organizational Compensation Ethics, should rest on its own logic independent of individual-level Moral Philosophy theories (Phillips and Margolis, 1999). Two ideas can provide a theoretical foundation in the particular case of Organizational Compensation Ethics: (1) the premise that norms in Organizational Compensation Ethics have universal roots but vary depending on each organization's context; and (2) the investment nature of employment relationships.

A hierarchy of norms for Organizational Compensation Ethics

This chapter is based on the premise that Organizational Compensation Ethics norms have common universal roots, but vary depending on each organization's context. This premise was derived from a well-known Business Ethics theory called Integrative Social Contracts Theory developed by Donaldson and Dunfee (1999). They have argued convincingly that the moral obligations a business firm has can be understood as the result of a multi-level hierarchy of norms where norms at each level must be compatible with norms at higher levels.

According to Integrative Social Contracts Theory, the top level is comprised of a few vague *universal norms* (called hyper-norms by the theory's authors), which represent foundational moral principles. In practice, the notion of universal norms has been problematic because Donaldson and Dunfee established somewhat unrealistic standards for their identification. Donaldson and Dunfee argued that universal norms manifest in substantial agreement among widely shared religious, philosophical and cultural beliefs. Accordingly, they proposed identification of universal norms can be based on their explicit endorsement by: (1) prominent world-wide organizations such as the United Nations; (2) regional government organizations such as the Organization of America States (OAS) and the Organization for Economic Cooperation and Development (OECD); (3) international business organizations such as the International Chamber of Commerce; and (4) international communities of relevant professionals (Hartman *et al.*, 2003).

I would argue it is more realistic to think universal norms manifest when a vast majority of countries in the world accept (or endorse) them, either explicitly through legislation and/or policy, or implicitly through their conduct. For the sake of illustrating the concept, let's assume we agree that there is a universal norm stipulating that *persons who work have the right to just and favorable remuneration that supports adequately the health and well-being of workers and their families*, which is based on Articles 23 and 25 of the United Nations Declaration of Human Rights.

Integrative Social Contracts Theory also proposes a middle level comprised of somewhat less vague *national norms*, called macro-social norms by the theory's authors. National norms represent broad understandings that establish basic standards for social and economic interaction among people in a particular society. National norms related to the same universal norm(s) are likely to differ across countries for a host of historical, developmental and cultural reasons. National norms applicable to employment relationships are manifest in labor and employment legislation, in the judicial interpretation of such legislation, and in typical practices among firms in the country (Boatright, 2002; Macneil, 1980). For example, countries may differ in their interpretation of the universal "just and favorable remuneration" norm mentioned above. This would manifest in country differences in terms of: (1) minimum wage and other legislation that establishes pay rates (or changes to pay rates); (2) the manner by which such legislation is revised over time; and (3) the typical practices firms have for setting and changing pay rates.

Consistent with this idea, a recent study which was part of the International Wage Flexibility Project (see Dickens *et al.*, 2006) estimated there is considerable variation in "real wage rigidity" among European Union countries, where "real wage rigidity" was defined as the percentage of workers who should not have received a pay increase above the expected rate of inflation, but did due to wage-setting institutions and systems in each country. Finland and Sweden seem to have the most real wage rigidity with levels larger than twice the average across all countries in the study. In contrast, Denmark, France, Greece, Netherlands and Switzerland seem to have the least real wage rigidity with levels below one-third of the average across all countries in the study.

The bottom level is comprised of *firm-specific norms* (called community-specific norms by the theory's authors) which are "shared understandings about the moral norms relevant to specific economic interactions" (Donaldson and Dunfee, 1999: 262). Firm-specific norms manifest in the firm's tacit endorsement (and/or adoption) of the principles implicit in practices that are typical among their labor market competitors and in the firm's past practices. For example, firms that assert their strategy is to provide "competitive" pay rates acquire a moral obligation to sustain a certain pay level relative to the relevant labor market(s). This expectation (and the corresponding moral obligation) is reinforced whenever firms adjust pay rates after analyzing compensation survey data as it is the prevailing practice among medium and large firms in many countries.

In sum, in order to understand the moral obligations a business firm has towards its employees one should consider: (1) a set of universal norms, which depend on one's view of the employment relationship; (2) national norms, which may vary across countries for a host of historical, developmental and cultural reasons; and (3) firm-specific norms, which derive from the typical practice among the firm's labor market competitors and the firm's past behavior.

The approach proposed here for the definition of universal norms for Organizational Compensation Ethics relates to the notion that a business firm is a hub of economic exchange relationships with multiple groups of *resource contributors* (shareholders, customers, employees, etc.). However, the firm has qualitatively different relationships with each group of resource contributors. Consequently, ethical thinking can become more precise and applicable if it focuses on the relationship between the firm and a specific resource contributing group, say the firm's employees (Orlando, 1999).

Accordingly, the particular set of moral obligations that one believes business firms have towards their employees will depend on one's view of the employment relationship. Unfortunately, compensation scholarship and practice are ethically deficient because they are based on a transactional view of employment relationships that makes qualitative, unrealistic and unfair distinctions between the relationship the firm has with its employees and the relationship the firm has with its capital investors.

The investment nature of employment relationships

In general, one may distinguish between two kinds of economic exchange relationships – (spot market) trade relationships and investment relationships – a distinction that has ethical relevance. Trade relationships do not create ongoing rights and obligations for the parties involved. Trade exchanges in competitive spot markets are regarded as self-contained in the sense that the parties meet their respective obligations while completing their transactions. Theoretically, spot-market trade does not create any rights or obligations for the parties involved because sellers receive a price that reflects the full economic value of their contribution. For example, the trade transaction between a customer buying a gallon of milk and the convenience store owner involved does not create any subsequent obligations for either party. Theoretically, spot-market trade occurring within competitive markets in equilibrium produces fair outcomes because the parties trade voluntarily, are well informed and have equal (or at least comparable) bargaining power, and because the price set by the market equals the economic value of what is traded. This condition has been called "marginal productivity justice" (see McClelland, 1990) when applied in the context of employment relationships (Budd, 2004).

In contrast, investment relationships create ongoing rights and obligations for the parties involved. Investment relationships are considered to be long term and to entail substantial risks because the resources invested are "locked in" to the relationship and cannot be withdrawn easily, because there is considerable uncertainty due to an unpredictable future, and because the ultimate value of such investments will depend on future developments (Boatright, 2002). For example, people who purchase stock shares in a particular business firm are said to acquire ownership rights due to their investment relationship with that firm. Thus, investment relationships are open-ended in the sense that risk, assumed to be intrinsic to investment relationships, creates ongoing ownership rights for investors and the correlative ongoing fiduciary obligations for those managing such investment.

Neo-classic Economics asserts price in competitive spot markets in equilibrium equals the economic value of what is traded. Consequently, sellers who accept a lower price than their contribution is economically worth are making a financial investment in the relationship and should expect future benefits. This means employees who accept compensation that is lower than the economic value of their work (their so-called marginal revenue product) are making a financial investment in their relationship with the firm. This is exactly what happens according to Neo-classic Economics explanations for the relationship between pay and seniority that is very common across all sorts of firms and jobs: many employees work under a delayed compensation agreement with the firm and/or invest in firm-specific human capital (Ehrenberg and Smith, 2003).

A substantial body of research (see for example Barth, 1997; Hutchens, 1989; James and Johnson, 2000) supports the existence – across occupations and nations – of a delayed compensation scheme proposed by Lazear (1998). He proposed that many employees work under a delayed compensation agreement in which employees are paid less than they are economically worth early in their career with the firm expecting that they will be paid more than they contribute later in their career or after retirement.

Additionally, many employees invest in firm-specific human capital. The theory of human capital (which also has received extensive empirical support) asserts that the economic value of a person's contributions depends on the individual's work-relevant knowledge, skills and abilities. Human Capital Theory distinguishes between general human capital (such as knowledge and skills acquired through formal education) and firm-specific human capital (such as in-depth knowledge of the firm's products, markets and customers). Building firm-specific human capital benefits both the firm and its employees because the firm will have a more productive workforce over time while employees' economic worth (and their deserved compensation) will also increase over time. However, expenditures on firm-specific human capital would be wasted if employees left the firm, therefore employees must share in the cost of their firm-specific human capital by working some time for less than the economic value of their contributions to the firm (Reynolds *et al.*, 1998).

Thus, many employees have made significant financial investments in the firm by agreeing to work under a delayed compensation scheme and/or by investing in firm-specific human capital. Unfortunately for employees, their contributions to the firm's financial capital are not recorded in the firm's accounting system and are ignored in prevailing compensation theory and practice, which treat employment as a (spot market) transaction through which employees sell their labor services in exchange for compensation. Such a transactional view of employment relationships is ethically deficient because it leads to the expropriation of the deferred compensation many employees are owed and/or the destruction of significant financial investments in firm-specific human capital that many employees made.

An ethically oriented firm ought to keep in mind employees make significant financial investments when deciding on its strategies, policies and practices related to employee pay and benefits. It should be noted the so-called shareholder view of the firm, which provides the background for the transactional view of employment behind current compensation scholarship and practice, asserts that those who make financial investments in the firm acquire ownership rights and those who manage the firm have the obligation to act in a manner that recognizes and respects such rights. However, investors with ownership rights face the so-called "agency problem" when they entrust financial assets to the firm's managers because managers' interests may conflict with the investors' (Jensen and Meckling, 1994). This calls for the appropriate "corporate governance" regime, which allocates power and decision-making authority among owners and managers and promotes transparent and efficient allocation and utilization of the firm's financial resources (Roe, 1998; Shleifer and Vishny, 1997).

Corporate Governance and universal norms for Organizational Compensation Ethics

The Organization for Economic Cooperation and Development (OECD) – which comprises developed countries that accept representative democracy and a free market economy – proposed in 1999 a set of principles of corporate governance including guidelines concerning rights for financial investors (called "shareholders" in OECD statements expressing these principles) and the correlative obligations for the firm's senior managers. These principles were revised in 2004 and have gained recognition and acceptance world wide (Jesover and Kirkpatrick, 2005).

An analytical review of OECD's guidelines regarding financial investors suggests the firm and its top management have at least five basic moral obligations towards financial investors: (1) the obligation to make decisions that are consistent with long-term investor interests; (2) the obligation to disclose significant information in a timely and accurate manner; (3) the obligation to prevent abusive self-dealing by senior managers; (4) the obligation to share the firm's financial success with its investors; and (5) the obligation to ensure financial investors recover (at least part of) their investment when the investor–firm relationship ends.

Consequently, to the extent one accepts the fact that employees make significant financial investments in the firm and agree with OECD's Corporate Governance principles, one should also accept that Organizational Compensation Ethics should include the following basic moral obligations that firms have toward employees: (1) the obligation to make decisions that are consistent with long-term employee interests; (2) the obligation to inform employees in a timely and accurate fashion about conditions and situations likely to affect their investment in the firm; (3) the obligation to avoid policies and decisions affecting managers' compensation that contradict the corresponding policies and decisions affecting other employees' compensation; (4) the obligation to share the firm's financial success with its employees; and (5) the obligation to ensure employees recover (at least part of) their deferred compensation and/or firm-specific human capital investments when the employment relationship ends.

A full review of all the basic moral obligations business firms have towards employees (when viewed as financial investors) is beyond the scope of this chapter. However, seeking to motivate a conversation regarding this important topic, the next section explores one implication of the fifth obligation listed above: *the firm has the moral obligation to ensure employees recover (at least part of) their deferred compensation and/or firm-specific human capital investments when the employment relationship ends.* In the case of shareholders, publicly traded firms fulfill the corresponding obligation with the help of secondary markets in stock exchanges (which exist in many countries) and/or through the firms' stock repurchase programs. Likewise, firms can fulfill this obligation towards their employees by providing fair severance compensation in recognition of the financial investment employees make through deferred compensation and/or investments in firm-specific human capital.

Universal and national norms regarding severance pay

As stated above, a pragmatic application of Integrative Social Contracts Theory would imply universal norms of an Organizational Compensation Ethics manifest when a vast majority of countries in the world accept (or endorse) them either explicitly through legislation and/or policy statements, or implicitly through their conduct. Such seems to be the case for severance pay, understood as lump-sum payments for employees who have been dismissed ("unjustly," "unfairly," or "without cause") for reasons other than inappropriate behavior (Vodopivec, 2004).

Severance pay is a widespread element in employment legislation and in compensation practices across the world. Holzmann *et al.* (2003) reported the most thorough review of severance pay legislation across the world that is currently available. A select portion of their findings is presented in Table 3.1 overleaf. Holzmann and colleagues found only

Table 3.1 National severance pay mandate by region

Region	No mandated severance		Mandated severance	
High income OECD	Belgium Germany Japan Netherlands New Zealand	Norway Sweden Switzerland United States	Canada (1.3) Denmark (1.5) Australia (2.0) Finland (2.0) Great Britain (2.4) Ireland (2.5)	France (2.7) Greece (5.8) Austria (9.0) Spain (12.0) Italy (18.0) Portugal (20.0)
Sub-Saharan Africa	Benin Burkina Faso Ghana Madagascar Mali	Nigeria Uganda Zambia Zimbabwe	Senegal (1.0) Botswana (3.0) South Africa (5.0) Cameroon (6.7) Cote D'ivoire (6.7) Niger (6.7)	Ethiopia (9.3) Kenya (10.0) Tanzania (12.0) Malawi (20.0) Mozambique (28.5)
Europe and Central Asia	Romania		Bosnia-Herzegovina (1.0) Kazakhstan (1.0) Kyrgyz Republic (1.0) Russia (1.0) Ukraine (1.0) Armenia (2.0) Bulgaria (2.0) Czech Republic (2.0) Moldova (2.0) Slovak Republic (2.0) Uzbekistan (2.0) Azerbaijan (3.0)	Belarus (3.0) Georgia (3.0) Latvia (3.0) Poland (3.0) Estonia (4.0) Yugoslavia (4.0) Hungary (5.0) Lithuania (6.0) Albania (10.0) Croatia (10.0) Macedonia (10.0) Slovenia (10.0) Turkey (20.0)
Rest of Asia	Singapore		Mongolia (1.0) Hong Kong (2.0) India (6.0) Taiwan (7.0) Indonesia (9.0) Bangladesh (9.3) Thailand (10.0) Vietnam (10.0)	China (12.0) Malaysia (13.3) Nepal (20.0) North Korea (20.0) Pakistan (20.0) Philippines (20.0) South Korea (20.0) Sri Lanka (57.0)
Latin America and Caribbean	Jamaica		Brazil (2.0) Nicaragua (5.0) Panama (5.0) Venezuela (5.0) Uruguay (6.0) Costa Rica (8.0) Honduras (8.0) Barbados (10.0) Chile (11.0)	Peru (12.0) Dominican Rep. (15.3) Mexico (16.3) Argentina (20.0) Bolivia (20.0) Colombia (20.0) Ecuador (20.0) Guatemala (20.0)
Middle East and North Africa	Yemen		Tunisia (3.0) Egypt (6.0) Morocco (6.0) Lebanon (10.0) Algeria (12.0)	Saudi Arabia (17.5) Syria (17.5) Iran (20.0) Israel (20.0) Jordan (20.0)

Source: Holzmann *et al.* (2003).

10 in 113 countries studied (or 9 percent) failed to mandate severance pay. The other 103 countries (or 91 percent) have legislation that mandates a defined severance pay benefit specifying the requirements for and the magnitude of severance payments, and/or legislation that mandates severance benefits should be defined through collective bargaining. That is, Holzmann *et al.*'s data show more or less general agreement across the world with the principle that firms owe severance compensation to workers dismissed for reasons other than inappropriate behavior.

Further analysis of the data Holzmann and colleagues reported for the countries that mandate a specifically defined severance pay benefit yields some interesting conclusions. For the sake of argument clarity, the following observations focus on the case of dismissed workers with 20 years of seniority representing middle-aged workers who usually fare poorly after losing their job. Holzmann *et al.*'s data suggest the typical (median) mandate is a severance bonus around 7.5 months of earnings for workers with 20 years of service. Additionally, their data suggest one-third of the countries with defined benefit severance legislation require employers to pay dismissed workers with 20 years of seniority more than 10 months of earnings as severance compensation.

Finally, and perhaps most interestingly, Holzmann *et al.*'s data suggest drastic regional differences, which are presented in Table 3.2 below. Table 3.2 indicates that the richest group of countries (high-income OECD countries) and the poorest group (Sub-Saharan Africa) are more or less evenly split regarding whether to mandate severance pay or not. In contrast, there is an almost absolute consensus about mandating severance pay in each of the other four groups: only one country in each group does not mandate either a specifically defined or a collectively bargained severance pay benefit. Further, when it is mandated, the typical (median) severance pay for workers with 20 years of service is: (1) quite modest in high-income OECD countries (which may be somewhat surprising) and in the group of Eastern Europe and Asian countries in transition to a market economy (which is understandable given their twentieth-century history); (2) "moderate," within the context of Holzmann *et al.*'s data, in Sub-Saharan countries; and (3) most generous among the three other country groups: Asia, Latin America and the Caribbean and Middle East and North Africa.

In sum, except for the poorest and richest countries in the world, one could argue there is a (somewhat) universal norm that firms owe severance compensation to workers dismissed for reasons other than inappropriate behavior. In contrast, there are wide

Table 3.2 Summary statistics – mandated severance by region

Region	Countries mandate	Payout for 20 years of service		
		Minimum	*Median*	*Maximum*
High-income OECD	12 of 21 countries	1.3 months	2.6 months	20.0 months
Sub-Saharan Africa	11 of 20 countries	1.0 months	6.7 months	28.5 months
Europe and Central Asia	25 of 26 countries	1.0 months	3.0 months	20.0 months
Rest of Asia	16 of 17 countries	1.0 months	11.0 months	57.0 months
Latin America and Caribbean	17 of 18 countries	2.0 months	12.0 months	20.0 months
Middle East and North Africa	10 of 11 countries	3.0 months	14.5 months	20.0 months

Source: Holzmann *et al.* (2003).

differences across regions and between countries in each region when it comes to the magnitude of this benefit.

Conclusions

This chapter proposes that the moral obligations one believes business firms have towards their employees will depend on one's view of the employment relationship, and criticizes prevailing compensation scholarship and practice as ethically deficient because they are based on a transactional view of employment relationships, which makes qualitative, unrealistic and unfair distinctions between the relationship the firm has with its employees and the relationship the firm has with its capital investors.

I argue well-established Economics theory and research supports the fact that employees make significant financial investments in the firm by agreeing to work under a deferred compensation scheme and/or investing in firm-specific human capital. Further, to the extent one accepts the notion that employees are financial investors, and to the extent one agrees with OECD's Corporate Governance principles (as a lot of people throughout the world do), I propose Organizational Compensation Ethics should include the five moral obligations listed below:

First, firms have the moral obligation to make decisions that are consistent with long-term employee interests. For example, firms have the moral obligation to ensure sufficient funding for any deferred compensation they have (explicitly or implicitly) promised employees such as post-retirement health insurance and pension benefits.

Second, firms have the moral obligation to inform employees in a timely and accurate fashion about conditions and situations likely to affect their investment in the firm. For example, firms that offer Employee Stock Ownership Programs and/or Savings plans based on the firm's stock have the obligation to keep employees abreast of external developments or strategic plans that may affect the price of the firm's stock shares.

Third, firms have the moral obligation to avoid policies and decisions affecting managers' compensation that contradict the corresponding policies and decisions affecting other employees' compensation. For example, firms should not offer "golden parachute" benefits to executives that they are not willing to offer to rank-and-file employees.

Fourth, firms have the moral obligation to share the firm's financial success with its employees. For example, firms in financial trouble that ask for and get employee wage concessions have the moral obligation to redress such concessions when the firm gets out of its financial crisis.

Fifth, firms have the moral obligation to ensure employees recover (at least part of) their deferred compensation and/or firm-specific human capital investments when the employment relationship ends. For example, firms have the moral obligation to offer fair severance compensation to employees dismissed for causes other than inappropriate behavior.

The reader may conclude the five moral obligations proposed here are naïve philosophical dreams. Alternatively and to the extent the reader agrees with the foundational premises for this chapter – prevailing Economics theory and the value of

OECD's Corporate Governance principles – the reader may also conclude that the fact that the obligations proposed here appear so extreme, even irrational, reflects the ethical deficiency in prevailing compensation scholarship and practice.

This chapter also proposes one can understand a business firm's moral obligations towards its employees in terms of a hierarchy comprised of universal, national and firm-specific norms in which norms at each level must be compatible with norms at higher levels. Seeking to provide an example, and to motivate a conversation regarding the important topic addressed in this chapter, I use data reported by Holzmann *et al.* (2003) to analyze country legislation around the world, and to provide initial and tentative support for the existence and validity of universal and national norms applicable to severance pay – a compensation practice related to the fifth obligation listed above. I find evidence to support a (somewhat) universal norm that firms owe severance compensation to workers dismissed for reasons other than inappropriate behavior. However, the poorest and richest countries in the world do not seem to endorse this norm. I also find wide differences across regions and between countries in each region when it comes to the magnitude of this benefit. These findings reinforce the importance of considering country-specific features when discussing Organizational Compensation Ethics.

I hope this chapter motivates a fruitful debate about the substance and scope of Organizational Compensation Ethics that involves practitioners and scholars. Possible lines for further scholarly inquiry may include: (1) the premises and conclusions in this chapter; (2) the financial consequences of the proposed obligations for the financial performance of firms at various financial health stages and/or across various industries; and (3) the extent to which various participants (employees, capital investors and managers) agree with these obligations.

References

Barker, R.A. 2002. An examination of organizational ethics. *Human Relations*, 55: 1097–16.

Barth, E. 1997. Firm specific seniority and wages. *Journal of Labor Economics*, 15: 495–506.

Boatright, J.R. 2002. Ethics and corporate governance: Justifying the role of shareholder. In N. E. Bowie (ed.), *The Blackwell Guide to Business Ethics*: 38–60. Malden, MA: Blackwell.

Budd, J.W. 2004. *Employment with a human face: Balancing efficiency, equity, and voice.* Ithaca, NY: Cornell University Press.

Dickens, W.T., Götte, L., Groshen, E.L., Holden, S., Messina, J., Schweitzer, M.E., Turunen, J. and Ward, M.E. 2006. How wages change: Microevidence from the International Wage Flexibility Project. European Central Bank, Working Paper Series No. 697.

Donaldson, T. and Dunfee, T.W. 1999. *Ties that bind: A social contracts approach to business ethics.* Boston, MA: Harvard Business School Press.

Ehrenberg, R.G. and Smith, R.S. 2003. *Modern labor economics and public policy* (8th edition). Boston, MA: Addison-Wesley.

Goodpaster, K.E. 2001. Business Ethics. In L.C. Becker and L.B. Becker (eds), *Encyclopedia of Ethics* (2nd edition): 170–5. New York: Routledge.

Hartman, L.P., Shaw, B. and Stevenson, R. 2003. Exploring the ethics and economics of global labor standards: A challenge to Integrated Social Contracts Theory. *Business Ethics Quarterly*, 13: 193–220.

Heugens, P.P.A.M.R., van Oosterhout, J. and Kapstein, M. 2006. Foundations and applications for contractualist business ethics. *Journal of Business Ethics*, 68: 211–28.

Holzmann, R., Iyer, K. and Vodopivec, M. 2003. Severance pay programs around the world. Rationale, status, and reform. Unpublished paper presented at the Workshop on Severance Payments jointly organized by the World Bank and the Institute for Applied System Analysis, November 4, 2003.

Hutchens, R.M. 1989. Seniority, wages and productivity: A turbulent decade. *Journal of Economic Perspectives*, 3(4): 49–64.

James, H.S. Jr. and Johnson, D.M. 2000. Just cause provisions, severance pay, and the efficiency wage hypothesis. *Managerial and Decision Economics*, 21: 83–8.

Jensen, M.C. and Meckling, W.H. 1994. The nature of man. *Journal of Applied Corporate Finance*, 7(2): 4–19.

Jesover, F. and Kirkpatrick, G. 2005. The revised OECD Principles of Corporate Governance and their relevance to non-OECD countries. *Corporate Governance: An International Review*, 13(2): 127–36.

Klein, K.J., Dansereau, F. and Hall, R.J. 1994. Level issues in theory development, data collection, and analysis. *Academy of Management Review*, 19: 195–229.

Lazear, E.P. 1998. *Personnel Economics for Managers*. New York: Wiley.

McAfee, R.B. and Anderson, C.J. 1995. Compensation dilemmas: An exercise in ethical decision-making. *Developments in Business Simulation and Experiential Exercises*, 22: 156–9.

McClelland, P.D. 1990. *The American search for economic justice*. Cambridge, MA: Blackwell.

Macneil, I.R. 1980. *The new social contract: An inquiry into modern contractual relations*. New Haven, CT: Yale University Press.

Morris, D. 2004. Defining a moral problem in business ethics. *Journal of Business Ethics*, 49: 347–57.

Orlando, J. 1999. The fourth wave: The ethics of corporate downsizing. *Business Ethics Quarterly* 9: 295–314.

Phillips, R.A. and Margolis, J.D. 1999. Towards an ethics of organizations. *Business Ethics Quarterly*, 9: 619–38.

Reynolds, L.G., Masters, S.H. and Moser, C.H. 1998. *Labor Economics and Labor Relations* (11th edition). Upper Saddle River, NJ: Prentice-Hall.

Roe, M.J. 1998. Comparative corporate governance. In P. Newman (ed.), *The New Palgrave Dictionary of Economics and the Law*. New York: Stockton Press.

Rousseau, D.M. 1985. Issues of level in organizational research: Multi-level and cross-level perspectives. *Research in Organizational Behavior*, 7: 1–37.

Shleifer, A. and Vishny, R.W. 1997. A survey of corporate governance. *Journal of Finance*, 52: 737–83.

Vodopivec, M. 2004. *Income support for the unemployed: Issues and opinions*. Washington, DC: The World Bank.

Welch, D.D. 1998. Social ethics, overview. In Ruth Chadwick (ed.), *Encyclopedia of Applied Ethics* 4: 143–51. San Diego, CA: Academic Press.

Performance measurement issues, incentive application and globalization

4

Monica Franco-Santos

Adopting an incentive pay scheme does not guarantee better organizational performance. The effectiveness of an incentive system is closely related to the appropriateness of its performance measures (Indjejikian, 1999). Thus, choosing which performance measures to use in an incentive system is a central issue for most organizations. The performance measures used for incentive purposes communicate strategic priorities and motivate employees to perform and behave as expected by the management team (Milkovich and Newman, 2008). That is in theory, but in practice the reality is somehow different. If the wrong performance measures are used in incentives, dysfunctional behaviors and distorted performance may be created (Austin, 1996; Ridgway, 1956).

The aim of this chapter is to review the research that has examined the use of performance measures in incentive systems in a global context. The chapter is structured in six sections. Section one looks at bedrock issues associated with performance measurement. Section two reviews the main theory underpinning the use of performance measures in incentive pay – that is agency theory. Section three summarizes the key characteristics that measures should meet in order to be appropriate for assessing performance and determining pay. Section four examines the impact that the use of different performance measures in incentive systems can have on individual behavior and firm performance. Section five discusses the implications that globalization is having on performance measurement and its application to incentives. Finally, section six presents a discussion of the topics presented in previous sections and some concluding remarks.

Performance measurement bedrock issues

Organizations see performance measurement as one of the key factors influencing their business results (Meyer, 2002). Most of today's managers seem to strongly believe in the expression: "if you can't measure it, you can't manage it" (Austin, 1996). They commonly assume that when progress toward organizational goals is measured, efforts and resources are more rationally managed and, as a result, organizational success is more likely to occur. However, several issues regarding performance measurement affect the validity of this assumption. Each of these issues is now reviewed in turn.

Perfect performance measures

The first and most important issue associated with performance measurement is the illusion that performance measures can be perfect representations of managerial performance. The key question that managers ask when they are designing an incentive system is "how should we measure managerial performance?" It is normally assumed that everything can be measured. However, managers soon realize that there is a big gap between what they want to measure and what they can measure (Meyer, 2002). Managerial performance has multiple dimensions, some of which are not observable (Feltham and Xie, 1994). The designers of incentive systems can only focus on those performance dimensions that are observable and therefore measurable either quantitatively or qualitatively. In addition to this, performance measures have an associated cost, which affects the probability of those measures being selected by the designers of incentive systems. As a result, the measures that are finally used in incentive systems tend to be imperfect representations of the complex actions that generate managerial performance, and these imperfect performance measures cannot be confused with the true managerial performance.

Multiple purposes of performance measures

A second issue associated with performance measurement occurs when performance measures are used for both informational and motivational purposes. Most organizations use the same performance measures for providing insights that facilitate decision-making and generate improvements (i.e. *informational purpose*) as well as for affecting the behavior of those employees that are being measured (i.e. *motivational purpose*). However, these two purposes of performance measures are not always compatible (Austin, 1996). When performance measures are used for informational purposes (e.g. for process improvement), their main objective is to help employees learn about whatever is being measured in order to be able to improve it. For instance, a manager using a lead time measure purely informationally just wants to understand how the process works and to what extent he/she can take any action to make it more effective. When performance measures are used for motivational purposes (e.g. in incentive plans), their main objective is to ensure that the interest of the organization is aligned with the interest of individuals (Eisenhardt, 1989; Jensen and Meckling, 1976).

Research has found that the more performance measures are used for motivational or control purposes the more subject they are to corruption pressures and the more apt they are to distort and corrupt the performance they are intended to monitor (Campbell, 1979). Organizations are social systems composed by people that have the desire to look good in front of their superiors when their performance is being measured and rewarded. This desire to be seen as a good performer provides an incentive for people being measured to distort the data that flow upward (Austin, 1996). This in turn makes it difficult for organizations to be able to use their performance measures for both motivational and informational purposes as the validity of the information delivered by the measurement system is compromised by the unintended reactions of those being measured (i.e. little can be learned from data that has been previously manipulated).

One of the reasons why people corrupt measurement systems is because, as seen earlier, performance measures are imperfect and they do not capture the true performance of individuals. Unless measures can be made perfect or some mechanism can be implemented for avoiding the distortion of data, dysfunction seems destined to accompany the use of performance measures for both informational and motivational purposes. This is why supporters of measurement systems such as Balanced Scorecards (e.g. Kaplan and Norton, 1996, 2001, 2004, 2006) are reluctant to recommend these performance measurement systems for evaluating or rewarding performance (Meyer, 2002). Of course, from a global perspective, the propensity for distorting the data may be affected by cultural, institutional and other national differences.

Correlation between performance measures

A third issue associated with performance measurement arises when several performance measures are employed and the correlation between measures is investigated. For example, an organization that annually rewards individuals based on the achievement of good results in measures such as customer satisfaction, employee turnover, innovation and profits, may find that investments in projects that generate more innovative products might not be correlated with higher profits in the same year. This phenomenon will generate dissatisfaction among employees as the problem is inbuilt in the measurement system and the results do not reflect their true performance. Consequently, employees may take special actions in order to influence the results, actions such as "window dressing" or "performance padding" (i.e. distorting information). Another issue may arise if multiple performance measures that are highly correlated are used in an incentive system. In principle, if two performance measures are highly correlated, one of them is not needed and could be discarded from the system. However, this rarely occurs, as has been shown in multiple research studies (Meyer and Gupta, 1994).

The diminished variance of performance measures

Last but not least, the diminished variance of performance measures is another issue associated with performance measurement that deserves mentioning. Over time, performance measures lose variability and thus the ability to differentiate good from bad performance. According to Meyer and Gupta (1994), this loss in variability can be caused by four factors: positive learning, perverse learning, selection or suppression. It can be due to positive learning as people learn how to improve their performance in whatever they are being measured on. It can be due to perverse learning or gaming as people learn how to meet the measure without improving the performance that is sought. It can be due to selection as organizations learn either positively or perversely and decide to replace low performers with high performers. Finally, it can be due to suppression of performance measures, which occurs when performance differences cannot be diminished by improvement, the appearance of improvement or selection.

What this shows is that the usefulness of a performance measure decays over time, as is shown by Meyer and Gupta (1994) using the evidence provided by a McKinsey and Co. (1982) study. They argue that this particular study shows how the use of Earnings per Share (EPS), which was a performance measure commonly used in executive incentive systems in the early 1970s, soon became obsolete and it was no longer effective in driving the expected behavior. In their own words, they suggest that

> towards the end of the 1970s, managers learned various techniques, including leverage, aimed at increasing EPS without otherwise changing the performance characteristics of the firm. Although not necessarily the wrong performance measure when first used, EPS became a wrong performance measure as managers adapted their decisions to it.
>
> (323)

Theoretical background: agency theory

Several organizational theories have addressed the phenomena associated with performance measurement (for further information on this point see Micheli, Franco-Santos *et al.*, 2004). Among them, agency theory has dominated the research on the use of performance measures in incentive pay systems (Bloom and Milkovich, 1998), although its applicability world wide is debatable due to cultural, institutional and other national differences. Agency theory is an economic theory that focuses on the relationship between two parties: *principals*, who are the owners or shareholders of a firm, and *agents*, who are the managers of a firm. Principals own the capital of the firm and bear the financial risks. Agents work on behalf of the principals, coordinating and controlling activities within the firm and making decisions (Eisenhardt, 1989). Both parties are assumed to be fully rational, with well-defined preferences, and motivated self-interest (i.e. willing to increase their own wealth with minimal effort). Agents in particular are assumed to be both effort-averse and risk-averse (i.e. they tend to avoid both work and risk) while shareholders are assumed to be risk-neutral since they can diversify their capital across several firms (Eisenhardt, 1989; Fama, 1980; Jensen and Meckling, 1976). Due to the nature of both parties two main problems arise from their relationship. One problem is known as *moral hazard* (hidden action or behavior). The other problem is known as *adverse selection* (hidden information).

A moral hazard problem arises due to the self-interest behaviors of principals and agents, and to the fact that it is difficult and expensive for principals to verify agents' actions. The principal cannot always observe if the agent is behaving in the best interest of the firm (i.e. the principal's best interest). An adverse selection problem arises due to the different levels of information the principal and the agents have regarding aspects such as agent's skills or capabilities and personal objectives. Assuming that both principals and agents have different attitudes towards risk, agents may choose to misrepresent their private information and take decisions that might not be aligned with the principal's objectives – for example receiving bonus or salary increases when the organization is underperforming according to the principal's expectations. If these two problems, moral hazard and adverse selection, are not solved they can negatively affect firm performance. As a result, most of the work of agency researchers looks at potential solutions to these two problems, which are normally referred to as agency costs (Baiman, 1982).

The main solution that agency theory proposes for reducing agency costs is the use of a contractual relationship between the principal and the agent (Baiman, 1982). In this contractual relationship the principal purchases information about the agents and designs a compensation mechanism for the agents which is contingent upon the information purchased (Lambert *et al.*, 1993). In practical terms, performance measures are the tools used to purchase information about agents. In agency theory, information is regarded as a commodity and it has a cost. Principals need to balance the cost of purchasing information with the benefits that this information will provide. For example, the cost of motivating misreporting through the use of a specific performance measure must be balanced against the benefit derived from choosing that specific measure in the first place (Lambert, 2001).

As seen earlier, performance measures tend to be incomplete representations of the consequences of managerial action. Agency theorists predict that the better principals' performance measurement systems (i.e. information system) report the effects of the actions taken by agents, and the better performance contingent incentive mechanisms motivate agents to focus on achieving principals' objectives, the more agency costs will be reduced. If these costs are reduced then principals' expected goals are more likely to be achieved and, in turn, firms' overall performance will improve (Jensen and Meckling, 1976).

Within agency theory, researchers looking at the relationship between performance measures and incentive systems have been particularly interested in finding the key characteristics of the "best" measures of managerial performance for incentive purposes. This area is further discussed in the next section.

Key characteristics of performance measures: lessons from agency theory

One of the major concerns of agency theorists has been, and still is, how to select the most appropriate measures of performance. Two key principles – the informativeness and controllability principles – and several other factors have been proposed by agency researchers in order to guide the selection of the "best" performance measures for evaluating and rewarding managerial performance. These performance measurement principles and the other key factors investigated by agency researchers are summarized as follows.

Performance measures' informativeness

According to agency theorists, the most important aspect to take into account when selecting measures of performance is the informativeness principle (Holmstrom, 1979). This principle states that additional performance measures should potentially increase the expected utilities of the principal and the agent in order to be used to increase agents' incentives or improve the risk sharing of the contract (Lambert, 2001). In other words, a measure should be included in the firm's performance measurement or compensation system if it provides information about the dimensions of managerial action that the owner wishes to motivate (Ittner *et al.*, 1997). According to this principle, the question is not what is the best measure of organizational performance but what combination of performance measures most appropriately reflects an agent's contribution to the organization (Indjejikian, 1999).

Performance measures' controllability

Agency theorists have also suggested what is known as the controllability principle (e.g. Demski and Feltham, 1978). This principle suggests that an individual should be evaluated and rewarded by a performance measure, if he or she can control or significantly influence that measure (Indjejikian, 1999). Antle and Demski (1988) and Demski (1994), relying on the informativeness principle, provide a more precise notion of the controllability principle by arguing that managerial performance evaluation should be based on the concept of conditional controllability.

> A performance measure is conditionally controllable if the information content of the measure is controllable conditional on whatever other information is being observed (e.g. an index computed from the performance of competitors' firms is not controllable by a manager in the traditional sense, but may be informative – i.e. conditionally controllable – and hence useful for relative performance evaluation purposes).
>
> (Indjejikian, 1999: 150)

Performance measures' relative weights: sensitivity and precision

Due to the fact that measures tend to be aggregated in order to assess and reward managerial performance, agency researchers have been particularly interested in the investigation of the relative weight or importance placed on a pair of performance measures. Scholars such as Banker and Datar (1989) suggest that the weight of a performance measure should be based on its sensitivity and precision. The sensitivity of a measure refers to the degree to which the result of a performance measure changes with the agent's actions. The precision of a measure refers to the lack of noise in a measure or, in other words, the ability of a measure to be consistent and accurate.

In statistical terms and as suggested by Banker and Datar (1989), sensitivity is calculated by the change in the mean of a performance measure in response to a change in the agent's action. Precision is calculated as the inverse of the variance of a performance measure. The noisier a measure is, the smaller its weight should be. The more sensitive to changes of managerial action a measure is, the greater the weight on that measure should be. For instance, when an accounting-based measure and a price-based measure are used for determining an incentive contract, then the relative weight of both measures can be calculated as a ratio of the "sensitive-times-precision" of the accounting-based measure relative to the "sensitive-times-precision" of the price-based measure (Indjejikian, 1999).

Numerous agency researchers have examined the sensitivity and precision concepts through empirical studies (e.g. Bushman and Indjejikian, 1993; Kim and Suh, 1993; Lambert, 1993). As an extension, some researchers have found that firm- and manager-specific characteristics also have an influence on the relative weight placed on two measures of performance. Lambert and Larcker (1987), for example, found evidence suggesting that firms place relatively more weight on market performance (and less weight on accounting performance) in compensation contracts for situations in which (1) the variance of the accounting measure of performance is high relative to the variance of the market measure of performance, (2) the firm is experiencing high growth rates in assets and sales and (3) the value of the manager's personal holdings of his or her firm's stock is low.

Performance measures' congruence

Another aspect that has been examined by agency theory is the importance of performance measures' congruence. Performance measures and incentive schemes are designed to align agents' interests with principals' interest. In agency-based research, alignment is achieved when the value agents assign to the different dimensions of their work is similar to the value principals assign to the dimensions of agents' work (Schnedler, 2005). This notion of alignment is also referred to as goal congruence between principal and agent (Anthony and Govindarajan, 1995).

Performance measures can be employed in order to create goal congruence (Schnedler, 2005). However, not all measures of performance can be used for aligning the interests of both agents and principals. Some agency theorists have focused on the search for alternative methods of creating congruent performance measures. Others have paid more attention to alternative sets of performance measures that might be used to deal with the problems of goal congruence. The work of Feltham and Xie (1994) is crucial in this latter area of research as they find that the use of a non-congruent performance measure (e.g. profit) will induce suboptimal effort allocation across tasks and that this non-congruity can be reduced with the use of additional measures of performance (e.g. non-financial measures).

Performance measures' diversity

Agency-based research has traditionally been concerned with the use of financial measures of performance in incentive pay. In recent decades, the work of authors such as Johnson and Kaplan (1987) or Anthony and Govindarajan (1995) on the practical use of multi-criteria performance measures has had a great influence on agency research. Several extensions to the theory have been developed (e.g. Feltham and Xie, 1994; Sliwka, 2002) and a number of empirical studies have been conducted in order to test the new theory developments.

Analytical research conducted by Feltham and Xie (1994) has actually found that financial measures alone may not provide the most efficient means to motivate agents to act in the manner desired by the principal. Hemmer (1996), through a mathematical model, argues that given that financial measures are not completely effective, they should be supplemented or replaced by non-financial measures, which are more informative. Holmstrom and Milgrom's (1991) research adds a different perspective to the use of diverse measurement since they find that the use of financial and non-financial metrics may direct agents' efforts to tasks that are easily measured at the expense of tasks that are harder to measure. In summary, the true benefit of having multi-criteria measures of performance is still unclear (Ittner and Larcker, 1997).

In general, the impact of using performance measures in incentive systems is far from being understood. Many researchers have concentrated their efforts on trying to find whether performance measures linked to incentive pay can generate positive results on individual behavior and on firm performance. A summary of this research stream is presented in the next section.

The impact of using performance measures for incentive purposes

The empirical research looking at the impact of using performance measures for determining pay can be classified according to the type of performance criteria used in a particular incentive system – that is, single or multiple. The category of *single performance criteria* refers to the situations in which performance is assessed taking into consideration only financial information (e.g. profit, revenues, etc.). The category of *multiple performance criteria* refers to those situations in which performance is evaluated according to financial as well as non-financial information (e.g. customer satisfaction, quality, employee absenteeism).

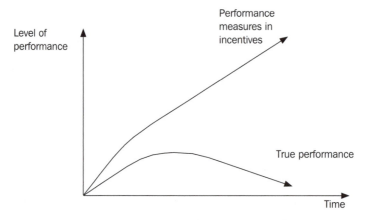

Figure 4.1 Impact over time of using performance measures in incentives

Source: Adapted from Austin (1996).

At this point, it is important to introduce the definitions of both financial and non-financial information. There seems to be little misunderstanding when the term financial information is used. However, the concept of non-financial information generates confusion and misinterpretation in numerous situations, as suggested by Morissette (1996) in his doctoral dissertation. Morissette argues that there is "anecdotal evidence suggesting that managers who are asked to identify non-financial information often confound qualitative information (i.e. information that is not expressed in terms of numerical metrics) with non-financial numerical expressions" (12). Morissette defines non-financial information as "any quantitative measure, (1) expressed in a metric other than a monetary unit, or (2) that results from mathematical manipulations or ratios of pieces of information expressed in metrics other than monetary unit" (13). He defines financial information as "(1) a piece of information expressed as a monetary unit; (2) ratios resulting from mathematical manipulations of information expressed in monetary units; and (3) a piece of information resulting from a ratio that includes a piece of information expressed in a monetary unit and a non-monetary unit" (12).

Going back to the review of the impact of using performance measures in incentive systems, it is interesting to note that the use of either single or multiple performance criteria in incentives communicate to the employees what are the key priorities of the organization, and make employees focus their attention on those actions that can have a direct influence on the performance measures being evaluated. In the literature there is evidence of how performance measures help management teams to translate the business strategy into operational terms that can then be easily communicated to the rest of the employees (e.g. Malina and Selto, 2002). Performance measures transmit information to the people that use them and they are very useful when communicating priorities (Austin, 1996).

Besides their communication effect, the performance measures used in incentive plans influence employees' decision-making. This effect can be beneficial as it will help management to coordinate their efforts towards achieving the performance targets associated with the measures. However, as discussed earlier in the chapter, it can also be detrimental as evidence suggests that the level of the performance measures used will improve over time regardless of the level of the true performance of the organization, group or individual that the measures are aiming to evaluate (see Figure 4.1) (Austin, 1996; Meyer and Gupta, 1994). This outcome is usually reflected in the common expression "you get what you measure and reward." People will focus their efforts on affecting the results of the performance measures they are being rewarded for. However, if the performance measures used in the incentive system are not perfect (i.e. they do not reflect all the different aspects of people's true performance), which is what normally occurs (as suggested earlier in the chapter), then the results of the performance measures used in the individual's incentives will improve, although this improvement might not represent an improvement of the true performance of the individuals.

Effects of using single performance criteria in incentive systems

The use of financial performance measures only in incentive systems has been found to have an impact on individual behavior, even if it is not exactly the expected behavior. For instance, Healy (1985) found evidence of earnings manipulation in response to incentive plans that were entirely based on corporate-wide earning-based financial performance measures. Years later Gaver and colleagues (1995) and Holthausen and colleagues (1995) replicated Healy's study addressing different methodological issues and they found similar results to those found by Healy. More recently Guidry and colleagues (1999) conducted a replication of Healy's study but focusing on incentive plans that use business-unit earning-based financial performance measures. They found evidence consistent with Healy's.

The use of financial performance measures only in incentive systems has also been found to reinforce firms' short-termism. When incentive plans are linked to short-term measures of financial performance (e.g. accounting-based measures such as profit) rather than to long-term measures of value (e.g. customer loyalty), individuals tend to behave according to the measures. They will only focus on actions that can deliver results within the incentive plan period (Coates et al., 1995; Hayes and Abernathy, 1980; Kaplan, 1983; Wallace, 1997). Long-term decisions such as investments in research and development or employee wellbeing will be overlooked as their effects on the financial performance measures being used for determining pay are not directly observable and they may take longer than the bonus period.

Since the early nineties, organizations have started to use multiple performance criteria (i.e. a combination of financial and non-financial information) in their incentive plans. This change has mainly been due to the promoted detrimental effects of using single performance criteria for determining incentive pay – misreporting and short-termizing – and to the implementation of performance measurement frameworks such as the Balanced Scorecard (Kaplan and Norton, 1992, 1993, 1996, 2001, 2004, 2006). Researchers are still uncertain of the full effects of using multiple performance criteria in corporate, team and individual incentive plans (Ittner and Larcker, 1997; Ittner *et al.*, 2003). Empirical evidence has started to emerge but further investigations are still required. This evidence is described below.

Effects of using multiple performance criteria in incentive systems

It must be noted that the use of multiple performance criteria in incentive systems is not an idea that was first introduced in the research arena in the nineties. For instance, as suggested by Ridgway (1956), investigators in the Soviet Union

> had concluded by 1940 that no single measure of success of a firm [e.g. profit] is adequate in itself and that there is no substitute for genuine analysis of all the elements entering into a firm's work [e.g. financial as well as non-financial aspects of performance].
>
> (243)

In the fifties, operation researchers were already concerned with the right choice of multi-criteria performance measures in manufacturing settings (Hitch and McKean, 1954); and management consultants such as Peter Drucker (1954) were stressing the importance of multi-criteria measures for evaluating managerial performance. However, it is from the late eighties and early nineties that empirical research into the adoption and consequences of diverse measurement at all organizational levels had a significant increase (Neely, 1999).

The majority of work investigating the effects of using multiple performance criteria in incentive systems has focused on the effects of this type of measure on overall firm performance, and the results have been inconclusive. Researchers such as Chenhall and Langfieldsmith (1998) and Sim and Killough (1998) have found evidence suggesting that the use of non-financial performance information in addition to financial performance information in incentive systems is associated with higher firm performance. However, other researchers such as Ittner and Larcker (1995) have found no support for the proposition that the use of multiple performance criteria in incentives is associated with better firm performance. Furthermore, Ittner and colleagues (2003) actually question the usefulness of using multiple performance criteria for determining pay as it increases subjectivity and favoritisms.

Some researchers have further investigated the relationship between the use of multiple performance criteria in incentives and firm performance by exploring the influence of several contextual factors. For instance, Franco-Santos (2007) recently conducted a study in the United Kingdom that looked at the impact of business risk (defined as volatility in a firm's income stream (e.g. Bloom and Milkovich, 1998)) and organizational culture (Cameron and Quinn, 2005) on how effective the use of financial and non-financial performance measures in executive incentives was.

Franco-Santos (2007) found that the use of financial and non-financial performance measures in executive incentive systems was only beneficial (1) for firms that operated in very high or low business risk environments – as opposed to those firms with moderate business risk environments – and (2) for firms with clan and adhocracy corporate cultures – as opposed to those firms with market or hierarchy corporate cultures. These results suggest that the investigation of the direct effect of using multiple performance criteria in incentives on firm performance may be pointless. A more fruitful avenue to pursue when looking at this relationship would be to search for those idiosyncratic conditions in which the use of multiple performance criteria as opposed to single performance criteria in incentives works best.

Globalization and the use of incentives

One condition that is now of great importance to organizations is their degree of globalization. Many organizations are now operating in global markets and require specific mechanisms that can help them be more efficient and effective across countries. The use of a consistent set of performance measures in incentives is one of the mechanisms global organizations tend to employ as performance measures increase the level of comparability that exists among different locations. However, the use of a consistent set of performance measures throughout the different locations of the global organization should not be a mandate.

Global organizations need to review the unique stakeholder profile and business model of each of the locations where they operate. If an organization creates value to its stakeholders by excelling on a single business model throughout its entire network of operations, then the set of performance measures used for incentive purposes should be largely consistent. Alternatively, if an organization has different business models and creates value to its stakeholders through a range of diverse business units, then a variable set of performance measures will be required in order to effectively assess its business success and reward their employees.

When using performance measures in incentives as a management mechanism, global organizations should also take into consideration contextual factors such as national culture. National culture influences the way in which people perceive performance measurement and incentives (e.g. Chow et al., 1999; Chung et al., 2002). In collective cultures such as the ones of China and Japan, performance measures tend to be seen as a mechanism for improvement rather than for control (Chow et al., 1994). In this type of culture the theoretical premises suggested by agency research in previous sections may not hold (Chang and Taylor, 1999; Ekanayake, 2004). For instance, it has been found that if organizations rely heavily on performance measures to assess individual performance and reward employees in countries with collective national cultures, this policy may generate unexpected behaviors that will negatively affect organizational performance (e.g. Awasthi et al., 2001).

In research terms, little investigation has been conducted about the use of performance measures for incentive purposes in global organizations. For example, little evidence exists about the extent to which single performance criteria would be better than multiple performance criteria in global environments. We also know very little about what would be the best method to follow for identifying key performance measures and for deploying these measures along the organization in its different locations or how variables such as national culture and country-specific business strategies could affect the use of global measures for incentive purposes. These are all fascinating research questions, relevant for both academics and practitioners, which urgently demand further research.

Conclusions

The purpose of this chapter was to review the research looking at performance measurement issues and at the use of performance measures for incentive purposes. There are at least four key issues associated with performance measurement. The most important one refers to the fact that performance measures alone are unable to reflect the full complexity of the actions that generate managerial performance. They are always "second-best" options (Holmstrom, 1979). If they are well designed and selected they will capture the most important dimensions of performance but there are always aspects of managerial performance that will not be included in the measurement system – either because they are not observable and thus measurable or because there is only a certain number of measures that can be included in an incentive system. The work of Miller (1956) has been used to argue that an incentive system should include a reduced number of performance measures – seven plus/minus two – if it is to be effective, as individuals can remember, recall and work creatively with seven bits of information. With ten or more bits of information, individuals suffer from information overload. Moreover, if people are asked to focus on too many things concurrently, no single initiative will receive enough attention to assure success.

The other three issues associated with performance measurement relate to the problems that appear when the same performance measures are used for motivational and informational purposes; the lack of correlation that exists among the different measures of performance; and the fact that the usefulness of performance measures decreases over time. The issues related to performance measurement generate dysfunctional behaviors (e.g. data distortion), which need to be addressed during their design, implementation and management processes if the benefits of using performance measures (i.e. increased communication, motivation and focus) in incentives are to be realized.

Most of the critical aspects associated with the use of performance measures in incentives have been tackled in agency theory research. Agency theorists have been particularly interested in understanding the main characteristics performance measures should have in order to be suitable for compensation purposes. In summary, according to agency researchers performance measures should be informative (i.e. provide insights about the dimension of performance the principal wishes to motivate); they should be controllable (agents' actions must be able to influence the results of the performance measures); they should have weight according to their sensitivity and precision (these weights will help to communicate their importance to employees); they should be congruent (i.e. designed to aligned the interest of both principals and agents); and finally, they should be not only financial but also non-financial in order to be more effective.

Agency-based research has also been concerned with the impact of using performance measures for incentive purposes. Agency researchers together with other organizational researchers have investigated the effects that performance measures linked to compensation plans have on managerial and organizational performance. In general, the use of performance measures for determining pay has been found to produce positive but also negative effects on organizations. On the one hand, when performance measures are used in incentive systems they help organizations to communicate business goals and to motivate and focus their employees in pursuing those goals. On the other hand, when performance measures are used in incentive systems they can generate dysfunctional behaviors such as data manipulation or short-termism. As a result, it is difficult to suggest that the use of this management tool will always be effective. In fact, the expression "one size fits all" does not seem to apply to the use of performance measures in incentive systems.

In certain contexts the benefits obtained from the use of performance measures in incentives (i.e. communication, motivation and focus) will exceed the cost of using this management mechanism (i.e. dysfunctional behaviors). However, in other contexts the cost will be greater than the benefits (e.g. some public sector organizations (Ingraham, 1993); global organizations operating in locations with national cultures that do not support the use of performance related pay) and thus the link between compensation and performance measures might not be recommended. The most important aspect in this area of research seems to be the search for those idiosyncratic conditions in which the application of performance measures to incentives is effective. To date many studies have taken into consideration this contingency approach (e.g. Franco-Santos, 2007) but more research is still needed until we can clearly identify which is the profile of those companies that will see benefits out of this management mechanism and which is the profile of those companies that will see their true performance diminish as a result of this management mechanism.

References

Anthony, R. and Govindarajan, V. 1995. *Management Control Systems* (8th edition). Chicago, IL: Irwin.
Antle, R. and Demski, J.S. 1988. The Controllability Principle in Responsibility Accounting. *The Accounting Review*, 63(4): 700–18.
Austin, R.D. 1996. *Measuring and Managing Performance in Organizations*. New York: Dorset House.
Awasthi, V.N., Chow, C.W. and Wu, A. 2001. Cross-Cultural Differences in the Behavioral Consequences of Imposing Performance Evaluation and Reward Systems: An Experimental Investigation. *The International Journal of Accounting*, 36(3): 291–309.
Baiman, S. 1982. Agency Research in Managerial Accounting: A Survey. *Journal of Accounting Literature*, 2: 154–213.
Banker, R.D. and Datar, S.M. 1989. Sensitivity, Precision, and Linear Aggregation of Signals for Performance Evaluation. *Journal of Accounting Research*, 27(1): 21–39.
Bloom, M. and Milkovich, G.T. 1998. Relationships Among Risk, Incentive Pay, and Organizational Performance. *Academy of Management Journal*, 41(3): 283–97.
Bushman, R.M. and Indjejikian, R.J. 1993. Accounting Income, Stock Price, and Managerial Compensation. *Journal of Accounting and Economics*, 16(1–3): 3–23.

Cameron, K.S. and Quinn, R.E. 2005. *Diagnosing and Changing Organizational Culture: Based on the Competing Values Framework*. San Francisco, CA: Jossey-Bass.

Campbell, D. 1979. Assessing the Impact of Planned Social Changed. *Evaluation and Program Planning*, 2: 67–90.

Chang, E. and Taylor, M.S. 1999. Control in Multinational Corporations (Mncs): The Case of Korean Manufacturing Subsidiaries. *Journal of Management*, 25(4): 541–65.

Chenhall, R. and Langfieldsmith, K. 1998. The Relationship between Strategic Priorities, Management Techniques and Management Accounting: An Empirical Investigation Using a Systems Approach. *Accounting, Organizations and Society*, 23(3): 243–64.

Chow, C.W., Kato, Y. and Shields, M.D. 1994. National Culture and the Preference for Management Controls – an Exploratory-Study of the Firm Labor-Market Interface. *Accounting, Organizations and Society*, 19(4–5): 381–400.

Chow, C.W., Shields, M.D. and Wu, A. 1999. The Importance of National Culture in the Design of and Preference for Management Controls for Multi-National Operations. *Accounting, Organizations and Society*, 24(5–6): 441–61.

Chung, L.H., Gibbons, P.T. and Schoch, H.P. 2002. Performance Metrics, Parenting Style and Control: A Study of MNC Subsidiaries in Four Countries. In M.J. Epstein and J.-F. Manzoni (eds), *Performance Measurement and Management Control: a Compendium of Research*: 119–28. Oxford, UK: Elsevier Science.

Coates, J., Davis, T. and Stacey, R. 1995. Performance Measurement Systems, Incentive Reward Schemes and Short-termism in Multinational Companies: A Note. *Management Accounting Research*, 6(2): 125–35.

Demski, J. 1994. *Managerial Uses of Accounting Information*. Boston, MA: Kluwer.

Demski, J.S. and Feltham, G.A. 1978. Economic Incentives in Budgetary Control Systems. *Accounting Review*, 53(2): 336–59.

Drucker, P.F. 1954. *The Practice of Management*. New York: Harper & Row.

Eisenhardt, K.M. 1989. Agency Theory: An Assessment and Review. *Academy of Management Review*, 14(1): 57–74.

Ekanayake, S. 2004. Agency Theory, National Culture and Management Control Systems. *Journal of American Academy of Business*, 4(1/2): 49–54.

Fama, E. 1980. Agency Problems and the Theory of the Firm. *Journal of Political Economy*, 88: 288–307.

Feltham, G.A. and Xie, J. 1994. Performance-Measure Congruity and Diversity in Multitask Principal-Agent Relations. *Accounting Review*, 69(3): 429–53.

Franco-Santos, M. 2007. *The Performance Impact of Using Measurement Diversity in Executives' Annual Incentive Systems*. Unpublished doctoral dissertation, Cranfield University, Cranfield School of Management, Cranfield, UK.

Gaver, J.J., Gaver, K.M. and Austin, J.R. 1995. Additional Evidence on Bonus Plans and Income Management. *Journal of Accounting and Economics*, 19(1): 3–28.

Guidry, F.J., Leone, A. and Rock, S. 1999. Earnings-Based Bonus Plans and Earnings Management by Business-Unit Managers. *Journal of Accounting and Economics*, 26(1–3): 113–42.

Hayes, R.H. and Abernathy, W.J. 1980. Managing Our Way to Economic Decline. *Harvard Business Review*, July–August: 67–77.

Healy, P.M. 1985. The Effect of Bonus Schemes on Accounting Decisions. *Journal of Accounting and Economics*, 7: 85–107.

Hemmer, T. 1996. On the Design and Choice of Modern Management Accounting Measures. *Journal of Management Accounting Research*, 8: 87–116.

Hitch, C. and McKean, R. 1954. Suboptimization in Operations Problems. In F.J. McCloskey and F.F. Trefethen (eds), *Operations Research for Management*. Baltimore, MD: The Johns Hopkins University Press.

Holmstrom, B.R. 1979. Moral Hazard and Observability. *Bell Journal of Economics*, 10: 74–91.

Holmstrom, B. and Milgrom, P. 1991. Multitask Principal-Agent Analyses: Incentive Contracts, Asset Ownership, and Job Design. *Journal of Law, Economics and Organization*, 7: 24–52.

Holthausen, R., Larcker, D.F. and Sloan, R. 1995. Annual Bonus Schemes and the Manipulation of Earnings. *Journal of Accounting and Economics*, 19: 29–74.

Indjejikian, R.J. 1999. Performance Evaluation and Compensation Research: An Agency Perspective. *Accounting Horizons*, 13(2): 147–57.

Ingraham, P.W. 1993. Of Pigs in Pokes and Policy Diffusion: Another Look at Pay. *Public Administration Review*, 53(4): 348–56.

Ittner, C.D. and Larcker, D.F. 1995. Total Quality Management and the Choice of Information and Reward Systems. *Journal of Accounting Research*, 33: 1–40.

—— 1997. *Performance, Compensation, and the Balanced Scorecard*. Working paper, Wharton Business School, PA.

Ittner, C.D., Larcker, D.F. and Meyer, M.W. 2003. Subjectivity and the Weighting of Performance Measures: Evidence From a Balanced Scorecard. *Accounting Review*, 78(3): 725–58.

Ittner, C.D., Larcker, D.F. and Rajan, M.V. 1997. The Choice of Performance Measures in Annual Bonus Contracts. *The Accounting Review*, 72(2): 231–55.

Jensen, M.C. and Meckling, W.H. 1976. Theory of the Firm: Managerial Behaviour, Agency Cost and Ownership Structure. *Journal of Financial Economics*, 3: 305–60.

Johnson, H.T. and Kaplan, R.S. 1987. *Relevance Lost: The Rise and Fall of Management Accounting*. Boston, MA: Harvard Business School Press.

Kaplan, R.S. 1983. Measuring Manufacturing Performance: A New Challenge for Accounting Research. *The Accounting Review*, 58: 686–705.

Kaplan, R.S. and Norton, D.P. 1992. The Balanced Scorecard – Measures That Drive Performance. *Harvard Business Review*, 70(1): 71–9.

—— 1993. Putting the Balanced Scorecard to Work. *Harvard Business Review*, 71(5): 134–42.

—— 1996. *The Balanced Scorecard – Translating Strategy into Action*. Boston, MA: Harvard Business School Press.

—— 2001. *The Strategy-Focused Organization: How Balanced Scorecard Companies Thrive in the New Business Environment*. Boston, MA: Harvard Business School Press.

—— 2004. *Strategy Maps: Converting Intangible Assets into Tangible Outcomes*. Boston, MA: Harvard Business School Press.

—— 2006. *Alignment: Using the Balanced Scorecard to Create Corporate Synergies*. Cambridge, MA: Harvard Business School Press.

Kim, O. and Suh, Y. 1993. Incentive Efficiency of Compensation Based on Accounting and Market Performance. *Journal of Accounting and Economics*, 16(1–3): 25–53.

Lambert, R.A. 1993. The Use of Accounting and Security Price Measures of Performance in Managerial Compensation Contracts. *Journal of Accounting and Economics*, 16: 101–23.

—— 2001. Contracting Theory and Accounting. *Journal of Accounting and Economics*, 32(1–3): 3–87.

Lambert, R.A. and Larcker, D.F. 1987. An Analysis of the Use of Accounting and Market Measures of Performance in Executive Compensation Contracts. *Journal of Accounting Research*, 25(Supplement): 85–125.

Lambert, R.A., Larcker, D.F. and Weigelt, K. 1993. The Structure of Organizational Incentives. *Administrative Science Quarterly*, 38(3): 438–61.

Malina, M.A. and Selto, F.H. 2002. Communicating and Controlling Strategy: An Empirical Study of the Effectiveness of the Balanced Scorecard. *Journal of Management Accounting Research*, 13: 47–90.

Meyer, M.W. 2002. *Rethinking Performance Measurement: Beyond the Balanced Scorecard*. Cambridge, UK: Cambridge University Press.

Meyer, M.W. and Gupta, V. 1994. The Performance Paradox. *Research in Organizational Behavior*, 16: 309–69.

Micheli, P., Franco-Santos, M., Marr, B. and Bourne, M. 2004. Business Performance Measurement: An Organisational Theory Perspective. In A. Neely (ed.), *Performance Measurement and Management: Public and Private*: Cranfield, UK: Centre for Business Performance.

Milkovich, G.T. and Newman, J.M. 2008. *Compensation* (9th edition). New York: McGraw Hill.

Miller, G.A. 1956. The Magic Number Seven, Plus or Minus Two: Some Limits in Our Capacity for Processing Information. *The Psychological Review*, 63: 81–97.

Morissette, R. 1996. *Toward a Theory of Information Choices in Organisations: An Integrative Approach*. Unpublished doctoral dissertation, University of Waterloo, Waterloo, Ontario, Canada.

Neely, A.D. 1999. The Performance Measurement Revolution: Why Now and What Next? *International Journal of Operations and Production Management.* 19(2): 205–28.

Ridgway, V.F. 1956. Dysfunctional Consequences of Performance Measurements. *Administrative Science Quarterly*, 1(2): 240–47.

Schnedler, W. 2005. *Performance Measure Congruence and Goal Congruence.* Unpublished working paper, Heidelberg University.

Sim, K.L. and Killough, L.N. 1998. The Performance Effects of Complementarities Between Manufacturing Practices and Management Accounting Systems. *Journal of Management Accounting Research*, 10: 325–46.

Sliwka, D. 2002. On the Use of Nonfinancial Performance Measures in Management Compensation. *Journal of Economics and Management Strategy*, 11(3): 487–511.

Wallace, J.S. 1997. Adopting Residual Income-Based Compensation Plans: Do You Get What You Pay for? *Journal of Accounting and Economics*, 24(3): 275–301.

5

Contracting for success in the era of globalization

Aligning the supply chain manager's compensation contract with the company's supply chain strategy

Björn Claes

Research into compensation strategy has aimed at identifying the relationship between compensation design and firm performance. The relationship between CEO compensation and firm performance has been among the most widely investigated. Barkema and Gomez-Mejia (1998) have identified over 300 studies analyzing top management compensation, spanning more than 70 years of research. However, relatively little attention has been dedicated to the compensation of other managers (Barkema and Gomez-Mejia, 1998; Tosi *et al.*, 2000) and its link to functional performance. Our chapter attempts to address this knowledge gap by focusing on compensation design at the functional management level and how it impacts a firm's functional performance. Because of its growing importance our analysis will be centered on the functional area of supply chain management.

Once considered a minor area of concern, an efficient and responsive supply chain capability is no longer a mere contributor to organizational success in today's increasingly competitive global markets; rather, it has become one of the major factors behind a firm's long-term survival (Aitken *et al.*, 2002; Christopher and Towill, 2000). The company's supply chain is ultimately concerned with getting the right product, at the right price and at the right time to the consumer. This task is becoming increasingly complex and challenging due to continuing trends of expanding product variety, shortening product life cycles, increased outsourcing, the globalization of businesses and advances in information technology (Lee, 2002).

Despite increasing academic interest in the field of supply chain management, there has been little systematic investigation into the relationship between a company's supply chain performance and the design of compensation mechanisms applied to supply chain managers. The extant research has focused primarily on optimizing material and information flows within the firm and throughout the supply chain and on investigating the relationships between supply chain partners. However, some authors claim that the human factor, that is the people who manage the supply chains, is equally if not more important in the design of supply chain strategies than "harder" factors such as the physical, information and communication infrastructure (Van Hoek *et al.*, 2002). Indeed, studies on the relationship between compensation design and company performance argue that there is a positive association between these two factors (Gomez-Mejia and Balkin, 1992).

This chapter addresses the above gap and examines the following research questions: What are the appropriate compensation designs for managers responsible for the efficient operation of different types of supply chains? Does an appropriately designed (i.e. theory-grounded) compensation for supply chain managers result in superior supply chain performance?

By applying an agency theory perspective, we propose a relationship between the choice of different compensation mechanisms for the supply chain manager and the company's supply chain performance. The motivation for this chapter, therefore, is to provide a theoretical framework that would guide future research in this critical domain.

Background

The relationship between supply chain managers and their superiors is an appealing venue in which to pursue our research question for three main reasons. First, the prominence of supply chain management is underscored by the magnitude of supply chain related costs. In the United States in 2002, these costs equaled US$910 billion, which was equivalent to 8.7 percent of the GDP (Federal Highway Administration, 2005). In recent years, the supply chain costs have continued to increase, reaching 9.5 percent of US GDP (US$1.183 trillion in 2005). This trend has brought supply chain costs perilously close to the 10 percent of GDP mark, a long-accepted demarcation separating reasonable and excessively high costs (Cooke, 2006). The increasing outsourcing of production to low-wage countries has reduced manufacturing costs but, at the same time, has led to a rise in supply chain costs. Aging infrastructure, increased cargo security, rising fuel prices and interest rates have put additional upward pressure on supply chain costs. In this environment, the efficient management of supply chain within each company becomes ever more important. In other words, the economic stakes are getting higher as the supply chain function itself gains greater strategic importance.

Second, there is no one easy way to effectively manage supply chain capabilities. Different products/markets require different supply chain designs. What might be key success factors for some markets might imply high risk factors for others.

Finally, the incentive system is increasingly and consistently recognized as an important management tool in numerous surveys conducted by management consultants (Rigby, 2001). Different studies (e.g. Avery, 2006; Rigby, 2001; Business Wire, 2001; Bernstein, 2000) estimate that 60 to 80 percent of firms use some form of variable pay for performance remuneration for their employees across different functional areas. The average bonus received in the supply chain area ranges between 10 percent and 15 percent of annual salary across different surveys. In over 60 percent of the firms surveyed bonuses were awarded for meeting company financial goals, and close to 20 percent for meeting the cost targets (Avery, 2006). As supply chain management moves higher on the management agenda, companies are paying closer attention to goal alignment so that the supply chain can make the business as effective as possible.

Given the increasing importance of supply chain management function within firms due to globalization, the appropriate design of compensation packages for supply chain professionals becomes imperative. Studies on compensation design show that well-designed incentives which recognize employee's effort that are aligned with firm objectives do indeed influence the desired behaviors (Eisenhardt, 1988; Gerhart and Rynes, 2003).

Research into the choice of employee compensation has provided valuable insights into the factors that explain compensation choices. These factors relate to the nature of the relationship between employers and employees and are grounded in agency theory (Eisenhardt, 1988; Gomez-Mejia, 1992; Mahony, 2005; Tremblay *et al.*, 2003), institutional theory (Eisenhardt, 1988), transaction cost perspective (Gomez-Mejia, 1992; Tremblay *et al.*, 2003), contingency (Gomez-Mejia, 1992) and resource-based view (Tremblay *et al.*, 2003) arguments.

The empirical research on the compensation design of employees below the top management level has been restricted to a few contexts, including sales and marketing (Eisenhardt, 1988; Fuentalsaz and Gomez, 2000; Joseph and Thevaranjan, 1998; Tremblay *et al.*, 2003), the high-tech industry (Balkin and Gomez-Mejia, 1987) and university faculty (Gomez-Mejia and Balkin, 1992). Our study looks into the under-researched relationship between supply chain managers and their general managers and the role played by incentives as a control mechanism.

For organizations, the topic of this chapter is highly relevant because effective management of this human side of logistics and supply chain management is complicated by the fact that over 90 percent of all work in this area takes place outside of the vision of any supervisor (Bowersox *et al.*, 2000). In such environments, thorough understanding of the effective control and motivation of individuals managing the supply chain will be instrumental in countering costs caused by agency problems.

Theoretical framework

Supply chain management, as defined by the Council of Supply Chain Management Professionals, encompasses the planning and management of all activities involved in sourcing and procurement, conversion and all logistics management activities.

An important problem that plagues many supply chains is the mismatch between the type of products and the supply chain strategies (Fisher, 1997). Products differ in terms of their demand pattern, with functional products at one extreme of the continuum and innovative products at the other. Functional products are staple products that satisfy basic human needs and tend to have a stable and predictable demand and long life cycles. Groceries and basic apparel are the extreme examples of functional products. Innovative products on the other hand, are novel products, such as high-end computers, fashion apparel or toy fads, with an uncertain market and a hard-to-predict demand.

In addition to different demand patterns, products may also have different supply processes (Lee, 2002). A stable supply process is one where the required manufacturing process and the underlying technology are mature and the supply base is well established. An evolving supply process is where manufacturing procedures and technology are still in early development and are subject to rapid changes. Consequently, the supply chain base may be limited in both size and experience.

Functional products are likely to have a more stable supply chain process, although this is not always the case. For example, some food stuffs may have a very stable demand pattern, yet their supply may depend on weather conditions in any given year. Similarly, certain pharmaceutical products may enjoy relatively predictable demand, yet their supply stability might be compromised due to limited availability of key components. Likewise, some innovative products may have stable rather than evolving supply processes. Although fashion apparel has short selling seasons and unpredictable demand, the supply base is usually very reliable and stable, with mature manufacturing and technological processes. It follows, therefore, that there may be many combinations of products with different degrees of functionality and supply certainty. However, for the sake of simplicity, in this chapter we shall focus on functional products with stable supply processes and innovative products with evolving supply processes.

Clearly, different demand and supply patterns and the combinations thereof require different supply chain strategies. Much debate during the last decade has been dedicated to the relative merits of the so-called lean and agile strategies. *Lean* strategies focus on developing a supply chain geared towards elimination of waste so as to ensure a level schedule (i.e. avoiding peaks and troughs in production or orders) (Aitken *et al.*, 2005; Naylor *et al.*, 1999). In the lean supply chain context, waste refers to buffer stocks and inefficient use of time.

In other words, lean strategies are about doing more with less, through, most notably, optimization techniques and scale economies directed at achieving optimal capacity utilization in production and distribution. Lean strategies resonate with the concept of *efficiency* of operations (Mentzer and Konrad, 1991). Research has shown that level scheduling, combined with an elimination of waste, has resulted in successful delivery of a wide range of products to markets where low cost is the primary competitive advantage (Aitken *et al.*, 2002). Therefore, supply chains with stable supply processes designed to deliver functional products to the market call for the application of lean strategies.

However, there are many markets where demand is volatile and where availability rather than low cost is key to securing customer loyalty. These markets require supply chain strategies aimed at being flexible and responsive to customer needs (Evans and Lindsay, 2008). In these environments, given high profit margins, lost sales due to product unavailability have a greater impact on the company's bottom line than higher supply chain costs. Fad-sensitive toys are an example of innovative products for which an agile supply chain strategy is required. While margins for these products tend to be high, the market uncertainty represents a major challenge. Demand can explode overnight and then suddenly evaporate when another new hot product arrives in the market. Constant product innovation, short life cycles with sales concentrated in brief selling seasons and high cannibalization rates characterize the toy industry (Johnson, 2001). Additional supply chain uncertainty is created by the fact that supply chains extend to many far-flung emerging markets (where products are produced), implying longer lead times and potential supply disruptions. Industry-wide, November and December alone represent nearly 45 percent of annual toy sales, with many companies generating more than 70 percent of their sales during this time (Johnson, 2001). Not being able to ensure sufficient supply of the right type of a fashionable toy during such highly concentrated sales season may lose a company a large part of its yearly revenues.

To facilitate agility, firms need to maintain close relationships with supply chain partners both upstream and downstream (including clients) to understand their emerging needs and requirements, empowering employees as decisions makers and utilizing effective manufacturing and information technology (Evans and Lindsay, 2008).

Within the supply chain division, main operational performance drivers relate to the management of inventory, transportation, facilities and information. Chopra and Meindl (2000) describe these four drivers as follows (see Figure 5.1):

(1) *Inventory*. Inventory level is a powerful tool that influences the supply chain's efficiency and responsiveness. Reducing the inventory makes a company more efficient by lowering inventory carrying costs. However, maintaining minimum inventory levels may compromise the company's ability to respond to sudden increases in demand. Likewise, increasing inventories improves the company's responsiveness to demand fluctuations but increases overall costs by locking up capital in inventory carrying costs. It also increases the risk of damage and product obsolescence.

(2) *Transportation*. One of the metrics of transportation efficiency is a minimum order size. Reducing minimum order size might benefit sales and marketing but it will decrease transport efficiency and increase costs.

(3) *Facilities* refer to the places in the supply chain network where inventory is stored, assembled or fabricated. A higher density of facilities will enhance responsiveness but reduce efficiency by increasing costs.

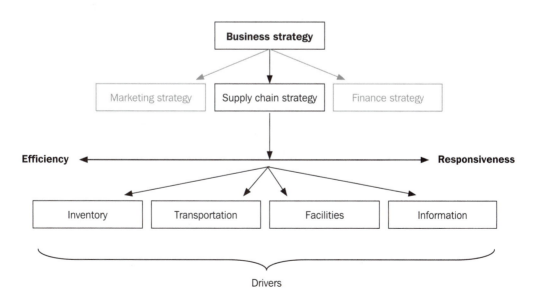

Figure 5.1 Performance drivers in the supply chain strategy

Source: Based on Chopra and Meindl (2000).

(4) *Information* consists of data and analysis regarding the inventory, transportation, facilities and customers throughout the supply chain. Information is potentially the biggest driver of performance in the supply chain as it directly affects each of the other drivers.

Table 5.1 shows how the application of leanness and agility approaches influences a company's supply chain performance drivers. To make its supply chain leaner, a supply chain manager would attempt to reduce its inventory levels and increase its minimum order size, thereby reducing transportation costs. A lower density of facilities would also contribute to the elimination of waste. Gaining more accurate information on the requirements of members of the supply chain would help the supply chain manager to optimize the other supply chain performance drivers, regardless of whether the company aims to have lean or agile operations.

Table 5.1 Application of lean and agile strategies to the supply chain performance drivers

	Lean	*Agile*
Inventory levels	Decrease	Increase
Transportation costs (minimum order quantity)	Increase	Decrease
Facilities density	Decrease	Increase
Information	Increase	Increase

A supply chain manager's responsibility is to enhance the organization's competitiveness by managing the supply chain drivers such as to ensure elimination of waste and assure responsiveness to demand fluctuations. In other words, supply chain managers have to minimize costs associated with operating the supply chain while at the same time avoiding erroneous deliveries, undesired supply delays or full stock-outs. An important question, therefore, is whether a well-designed incentive system motivates better performance on the part of supply chain managers. Furthermore, what is a well-designed compensation structure that best aligns the supply chain manager's interests with the company's strategy of operating lean or agile supply chains? One theoretical lens for examining these issues is agency theory.

Agency theory

An agency relationship is said to exist between two parties when one, designated as the principal, engages another, designated as the agent, to perform some service on their behalf which involves delegating decision-making authority (Eisenhardt, 1989; Jensen and Meckling, 1976; Levinthal, 1986). In the context of this chapter, the supply chain manager acts as an agent on behalf of the company's general manager, the principal.

Agency models incorporate two basic features of organizations: *uncertainty* and *goal conflict* between the agent and the principal (Levinthal, 1986). The first of these, *uncertainty*, manifests itself in two phenomena – *moral hazard* and *adverse selection*. *Moral hazard* refers to the lack of effort or opportunistic behavior on the part of the agent as a result of the principal's inability to costlessly verify this agent's endeavors. For instance, in the fashion industry, agility in the supply chain is a key success factor as it insures that the variety of products reaching the market match what consumers want to buy. Moral hazard occurs when a supply chain manager consciously fills the supply chain with excessive product to avoid stock-outs leading to potentially high losses when these products remain unsold. In a lean environment a supply chain manager might maintain needlessly high stock levels to avoid production interruptions being attributed to stock-outs. For example, the supply chain manager of an automobile assembly plant might maintain more tires in stock to avoid having to exert tighter stock management or avoid having to negotiate more frequent deliveries from tire suppliers.

Bowersox and colleagues (2000) observe that effective management of supply chain processes are complicated by the fact that over 90 percent of all work in that area takes place outside of the vision of any supervisor. Moreover, continuing trends of expanding product variety, shortening product life cycles, increased outsourcing, globalization of businesses and continuous advances in information technology increase the uncertainty of the supply chain environment (Lee, 2002). The more decision-making autonomy the agent has and the greater the specialized knowledge required for performing the task, the more significant moral hazard issues become (Holström, 1979; Tosi and Gomez-Mejia, 1989).

Adverse selection refers to agents' misrepresentation of their abilities or of certain information available to the agents that is of interest to the principals (Barney and Hesterly, 1996; Levinthal, 1986). Illustrations of adverse selection tend to be similar to the ones presented for moral hazard. Yet, in the case of adverse selection reasons for sub-optimal result are not caused by the agent's conscious avoidance of exerting the utmost effort, but rather by the agent's inability to perform up to the requirements for the job. The relevance of the adverse selection problem within the firm's internal supply chain is further illustrated by the fact that supply chain management ranks among the topics for further education that are requested most frequently by supply chain executives, if given the opportunity (Ginter and La Londe, 2002; La Londe and Ginter, 2004).

The second basic component of agency models is the *goal conflict* between the principal and the agent. If two parties have the same goals, uncertainty will not result in incentive problems (Levinthal, 1986). The goal conflict in a supply chain context concerns the agents' reluctance to introduce improvements that would enhance the companies' competitiveness but which, at the same time, might make it more difficult for the supply chain managers (the agents) to achieve their performance targets. These changes relate to improvements in efficiency (such as reducing supply chain costs), or in responsiveness (e.g. improving service rendered to customer). Supply chain managers' maintaining higher stock levels or lower standards of service (in terms of product availability, delivery times and flexibility) harm companies' competitiveness, but reduce their risk of bad performance. In order words, sub-optimal performance would allow for a larger margin of error.

An important assumption of agency theory, aside from individuals being boundedly rational, self-interested and prone to opportunism, is that agents and principals differ in their risk emphasis. Agents tend to be more risk-averse than principals (Eisenhardt, 1989) because a significant part of their livelihood depends on the compensation which is awarded by the principal. The supply chain manager's livelihood largely depends on their successful performance in a well-defined area, the company's supply chain. Principals, on the other hand, are in a position to diversify their means of achieving positive performance ratings over all of the organization's departments. Therefore, the more risk-averse agent will try to reduce his or her risks by behaving opportunistically, that is in a way that may not be optimal for the principal (Eisenhardt, 1989; Jensen and Meckling, 1976).

Because agents do not always act in the best interests of principals, principals can establish mechanisms for monitoring or incentivizing the agents to limit the divergence from principals' goals (Jensen, 1983; Jensen and Meckling, 1976). These mechanisms are termed behavior-based contracts and outcome-based contracts (Eisenhardt, 1989), respectively. In our research context, behavior-based contracts refer to contracts that remunerate supply chain managers based on objective, observable performance measures. Outcome-based contracts are based on the outcomes of agents' behavior. The underlying argument is that whenever it is difficult to verify agents' behavior using objective performance measures, principals have the option to reward agents based on the results of their efforts, in other words the agents' contribution to the company's financial bottom line. The drawback of the latter strategy, however, apart from the agent's behavior, is that outcomes may be affected by a host of other factors, such as economic climate, competitors' actions and regulatory or technological changes, that are beyond agents' immediate control. If agents' remuneration is based on outcomes, they bear risk due to inherent outcome uncertainty and hence would want to be compensated for bearing this risk. Much of the agency research is concerned with determining whether behavior-based contracts are more efficient (i.e. more cost effective) than outcome-based contracts in resolving particular agency problems.

The choice of compensation

The principal has several options to mitigate possible agency problems. If the agent's behavior is known, behavior-based contracts are most efficient. In this case, a contract based on outcomes would needlessly transfer the risk to the agent. If principals have little visibility over agents' behavior, they may (1) discover the agent's behavior by investing in information (Eisenhardt, 1989; Holström, 1979) or (2) contract, at least partially, on the basis of the outcomes of the agent's behavior (Eisenhardt, 1988; Eisenhardt, 1989; Jensen and Meckling, 1976). In these circumstances, outcome-based contracts motivate the agent to behave in the principal's interests, albeit at a price of transferring risk to a risk-averse agent.

To illustrate the typical metrics for behavior- and outcome-based contracts let us consider a simplified example of a pizza delivery business. The market conditions may require it to be either lean or agile. Suppose that the demand for pizzas in general and for each pizza variety is stable and predictable and there are a number of competitors with similar product offerings in the same geographical area. A winning supply chain strategy under these conditions would be focused on lean operations as they facilitate a low price strategy. Typical performance evaluation metrics would be minimizing ingredient inventory levels (as they deteriorate quickly and occupy kitchen space), idle oven time (as it lowers capacity utilization rate and hence increases investment payback time) and waiting pizza delivery staff (who tend to be paid by the hour and are a non-productive cost when not out on the street delivering pizzas). The trade-off for the customers is less product variety and longer delivery times.

If the pizza business were to operate in an environment where variety and service time are key (i.e. an environment requiring an agile strategy), performance measures would focus on the outcomes of the supply chain manager's behavior. These include measures of firm financial performance and of customer service such as on-time delivery (late vs on-time delivery), fill rate (products delivered over products ordered) and product rejection rate (in our example, rejection of cold pizzas). The manner in which a particular level of service is achieved is mostly at the discretion of the supply chain manager. For instance, to minimize the number of cold pizzas, several measures and the combinations thereof can be applied – reduce the number of pizzas per delivery person (i.e. increase the number of delivery staff or implement flexible working hours), reduce the waiting time between pizzas being baked and picked up for delivery and optimize the delivery routes.

The challenge in implementing the agile supply strategy, however, is not to disregard the efficiency of operations as it would negatively impact the firm's financial performance. Hence, in order to achieve optimal performance in a dynamic market environment, the trade-off between responsiveness and the costs thereof needs to be reviewed on an on-going basis. In an agile environment, a misplaced emphasis on efficiency in the supply chain manager's incentive system might lead to loss of business due to uncompetitive delivery times and mismatches between demand and supply for different product varieties.

In contrast, lean strategies, applied in stable market environments, can focus more exclusively on efficiency, with little need to provide for additional buffers in case of unexpected changes in demand. An example of inefficient incentive design in lean environment would be placing too much emphasis on secondary issues such as accommodating for sudden changes in demand, thus diverting supply chain manager's attention from the strive for efficiency, the real issue at play.

The supply chain manager, being the agent, is assumed to be more risk-averse than the principal, the company's general manager. Here, the agency theory argument referring to the agents' limited possibility to diversify their earnings applies. In contrast, the general manager is responsible for the overall performance of the company. Poor supply chain efficiency may be, at least partially or in the short term, offset by strong sales or successful R&D efforts. In contrast, the success of the supply chain manager depends mostly on the performance of this specific department. To compensate for risk related to outcome uncertainty, already risk-averse supply chain managers would demand a premium over their regular remuneration.

The choice of the type of contract depends on the trade-off between the cost of measuring an agent's behavior and the cost of measuring outcomes and transferring risk related to outcome uncertainty to the agent (Demsky and Feltham, 1978). If it is relatively inexpensive to monitor behavior or expensive to place risk on the agent, behavior-based contracts are most efficient.

One factor that influences the feasibility of evaluating agents' performance is their job programmability (Eisenhardt, 1985, 1988). Programmable jobs are ones where behaviors can be defined relatively precisely in advance (i.e. they tend to be more predictable). Lean supply chains are characterized by an overarching striving for efficiency given both low supply uncertainty (i.e. stable processes) and low demand uncertainty (functional products). Performance indicators of efficiency can be defined in a relatively objective fashion as they include cost levels, delivery times and conditions, stock levels and so on.

Such metrics can be compared with those of competitors and with the industry average for the purposes of evaluating supply chain managers' behaviors.

Because supply chain performance measures are relatively easy to define in lean supply chains, behavior-based contracts will appear to be the most cost effective way of contracting in this environment. The reason for this is that the cost of measuring the agents' behavior is likely to be lower than the premium that would have to be paid to compensate for assuming risk related to outcome uncertainty risk. Thus the goals of both the firm as well as the supply chain managers are best aligned through a behavior-based contract. Based on this argument we conclude that supply chain managers responsible for lean supply chains tend to be remunerated based on a behavior-based contract.

Conversely, agile supply chains are characterized by high need for responsiveness and adaptability. These supply chains tend to face high supply as well as high demand uncertainty. Supply uncertainty occurs because many of the processes used to bring products to the market are still evolving and are subject to change. This increases the difficulty of determining appropriate performance indicators through which agents' behaviors can be inferred. Demand uncertainty is related to the difficulty of forecasting the demand for companies' products in the market. When bringing new and innovative products to the market, the emphasis in the supply chain tends to be on product availability rather than on minimizing the costs. Potentially, the cost of lost sales due to shortages, the risk of obsolescence and the cost of excess supplies is much greater than lower sales due to higher supply chain-related costs (the focus in lean supply chains).

The volatility inherent to agile supply chains makes evaluation using traditional performance metrics very costly due to the required investment in information. Furthermore, given the high level of uncertainty, there is a risk of using the wrong measure for performance evaluation, which would be counter-productive. Indeed, a study by Bain and Company has identified that although 85 percent of senior executives state that improving their supply chain performance is their top priority, only 33 percent correctly measure supply chain performance (Business Wire, 2002).

In agile supply chains the investment that has to be made in acquiring and interpreting the information required to make an objective and fair evaluation of the supply chain manager's performance is likely to exceed the cost of the premium that will have to be paid to compensate for transferring risk from the company to the supply chain manager. We therefore conclude that supply chain managers responsible for agile supply chains tend to be remunerated based on outcome-based contracts. In summary, when behaviors are easy to evaluate, general managers will use fixed remuneration. When it is difficult to evaluate behaviors, general managers will use more variable pay.

Compensation design and performance

A critical question in the compensation design area is whether efficient compensation design that adequately aligns principals' and agents' incentives actually relates to better organizational outcomes.

As argued previously, when supply chain performance metrics can be easily and objectively defined, behavior-based contracts will prove to be most cost-efficient. On the other hand, in agile supply chains, firms have the option of either investing in more information or transferring outcome uncertainty-related risk to the agents, both of which come at an additional cost. The need for additional information would require an investment in more elaborate, often real-time information systems that would enable the general manager to verify the optimality of supply chain manager's behavior. Aside from the potentially high price of such systems, the interpretation of such additional information would put extra strain on the general manager's time resources. Incentivizing the supply chain manager on the basis of firm performance implies that his or her bonus would partially depend on issues beyond their control, such as manufacturing and marketing-related problems (e.g. failing production equipment or the composition of the company's product offering).

In contrast to lean supply chains where cost minimization drives the competitive advantage, in an agile supply chain environment, higher supply chain costs are more tolerable. This is because new and innovative products tend to have higher initial profit margins and it is the product availability in the right quantity at the right moment that enables the companies to establish and maintain their market share.

The lower relative costs of behavior-based contracts in a stable supply chain environment are congruent with the cost minimization and efficiency focus in a lean supply chain. In contrast, in agile supply chains, allowing greater decision-making discretion to supply chain managers facilitates quicker response to the changing market requirements. Moreover, rewarding supply chain managers based on outcomes is likely to be less costly than investing in information to be able to evaluate their behavior by other means. We therefore conclude that aligning the organization's supply chain requirements with the personal incentives of the supply chain managers will lead to superior performance. Specifically, the use of behavior-based contracts to remunerate supply chain managers responsible for lean supply chains and the use of outcome-based contracts to remunerate supply chain managers responsible for agile supply chains will be associated with better supply chain performance. A graphical representation of these conclusions is presented in Figure 5.2 overleaf.

It should be noted that there might additional factors that would influence the choice of compensation design. One such factor is the managerial span of control that influences the observability of agent's behavior. When their span of control is low, general managers can maintain close supervision and have good information to be able to evaluate the supply chain managers' behavior. When behavior is known, behavior-based contracts are the most efficient as there is no need to discern behaviors from the outcomes.

Discussion

Research into compensation design has demonstrated that incentive systems have an impact on company performance. As firm performance becomes increasingly more dependent on the efficient operation of its supply chains, the examination of the impact of the incentive systems on supply chain performance becomes more and more relevant. Whereas most research within the supply chain literature has been dedicated to the relationships between the companies in the supply chain, we argue that there is need to examine the incentive systems within internal supply chains. We suggest that the

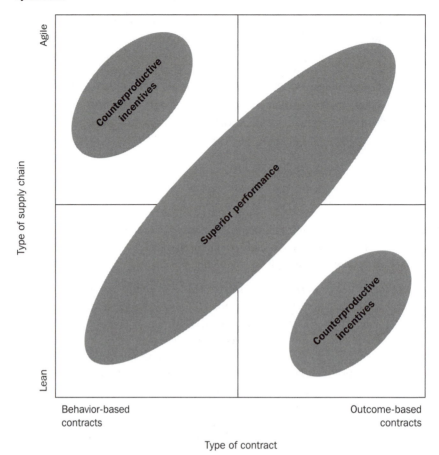

Figure 5.2 Graphical representation of the views presented in the chapter

implementation of an appropriate internal supply chain strategy (lean or agile, depending on the market environment) by supply chain members is a prerequisite of ensuring effective operation of the supply chain as a whole.

Local vs global supply chain

The alignment between compensation and supply chain strategy is particularly relevant in view of increasing globalization of production and sourcing. When a company decides to transfer its sourcing overseas, partially or entirely, it needs to take into consideration not only the potential cost savings, but also the additional complexity such business models bring. The complexity brought about by the globalization of supply chains is related to different market and labor conditions, business cultures and security and regulatory pressures. Let us consider the example of the toy industry outlined earlier. When the manufacturing function was transferred to the Far East, the companies' flexibility in managing the supply chain diminished. Longer transit times, customs delays, quota restrictions, political instability and communications barriers make managing the supply of products from far away sources (such as Asia) a significant challenge (Johnson, 2001).

In this environment, traditional supply chain practices and procedures that have proven effective for managing the localized supply chains are no longer sufficient. Depending on a company's particular sourcing strategy, extra emphasis might have to be given to a set of measures that tackle a particular risk or complexity. For example, a company may try to diversify its supplier base across countries to mitigate the risk of supplier failure caused by the consequences of political instability in or around the sourcing country, or by misunderstandings brought about by cultural differences or communication barriers. In addition, sourcing from distant, low cost regions might also call for alternative shipping strategies that make smaller but more frequent deliveries more efficient, such as the use of shipment consolidation with others and resorting to third party logistics service providers.

Whether or not a supply chain manager is implementing the strategy that best secures the company's competitive position and its long-term survival however, is something that might prove difficult to evaluate using objective measures. Indeed, one can only infer whether a set of suppliers have been chosen well by examining their subsequent performance, particularly under uncertain market conditions. Likewise, the adequacy of the supply chain manager's choice of shipping arrangements is difficult to measure and can best be inferred through the resulting performance. Has a decision to use alternative ports to avoid congestion or a more expensive air-freight paid off or led to higher costs without solving the problem? Therefore, the more global and hence, complex a company's supply chain becomes, the more the supply chain manager's performance might have to be evaluated using outcome-based measures.

Concluding remarks

In this chapter we have attempted to provide a framework for further research into the alignment of supply chain managers' incentives through their compensation design with the supply chain environment in which the company operates. Agency theory represents a powerful theoretical tool for defining the type of compensation contract appropriate for inducing optimal behavior, congruent with the company's supply chain strategy. Drawing on agency theory, we propose that the choice of either behavior-based or outcome-based contract depends on the supply chain context the company operates in. A match between the type of compensation and the type of supply chain context should result in superior supply chain performance. Further research should define correct performance indicators that enable performance evaluation under lean and agile strategies.

References

Aitken, J., Christopher, M. and Towill, D. 2002. Understanding, Implementing and Exploiting Agility and Leanness. *International Journal of Logistics*, 5(1): 59–74.

Aitken, J., Childerhouse, P., Christopher, M. and Towill, D. 2005. Designing and Managing Multiple Pipelines. *Journal of Business Logistics*, 26(2): 73–95.

Avery, S. 2006. 2006 Salary Survey, Purchasing Paychecks get Fatter. *Purchasing Magazine*, 135(18): 36–40.

Balkin, D.B. and Gomez-Mejia, L.R. 1987. Toward a Contingency Theory of Compensation Strategy. *Strategic Management Journal*, 8(2): 169–82.

Barkema, H. R. and Gomez-Mejia, L. R. 1998. Managerial Compensation and Firm Performance: A General Research Framework. *Academy of Management Journal*, 41(2): 135–45.

Barney, J. B. and Hesterly, W. 1996. *Organizational Economics: Understanding the Relationship between Organizations and Economic Analysis*. Thousand Oaks, CA: Sage.

Bernstein, C. 2000. Refashioning Supply-Chain Management's Role. *Electronic Buyer's News*, 1231 (October 2nd): E4.

Bowersox, D., Closs, D. and Cooper, M. 2000. Ten Mega-trends that will Revolutionize Supply Chain Logistics. *Journal of Business Logistics*, 21(2): 1–16.

Business Wire. 2001. Synygy Survey: Use of Incentives Moving Beyond Sales – and Beyond Employees – to Customers, Partners, and Suppliers. *Business Wire*, 23 (October).

—— 2002. Bain & Company Survey Shows Supply Chain Still Mismanaged By Most Companies. *Business Wire*, 28 (May).

Chopra, S. and Meindl, P. 2000. *Supply Chain Management – Strategy, Planning and Operation*. Upper Saddle River, NJ: Prentice Hall.

Christopher, M. and Towill, D. 2000. Supply Chain Migration from Lean and Functional to Agile and Customized. *International Journal of Supply Chain Management*, 5(4): 206–13.

Cooke, J. A. 2006. Costs under Pressure. *Logistics Management*, (July): 34–8.

Demsky, J. and Feltham, G. 1978. Economic Incentives in Budgetary Control Systems. *Accounting Review*, 53: 336–59.

Eisenhardt, K. 1985. Control: Organizational and Economic Approaches. *Management Science*, 31: 134–49.

—— 1988. Agency- and Institutional Theory Explanations: The Case of Retail Sales Compensation. *Academy of Management Journal*, 31(3): 488–511.

—— 1989. Agency Theory, an Assessment and Review. *Academy of Management Review*, 14(1): 57–74.

Evans, J.R. and Lindsay, W.M. 2008. *Managing for Quality and Performance Excellence*. Mason, OH: Thompson South-Western.

Federal Highway Administration. 2005. Logistics Costs and US Gross Domestic Product. In US Dept. of Transportation (ed.). Washington: United States Federal Highway Administration.

Fisher, M. 1997. What is the Right Supply Chain for your Product. *Harvard Business Review*, 75(2): 105–16.

Fuentalsaz, L. and Gomez, J. 2000. Remuneration Policies in the Marketing Area: Behavioral vs Performance Measures. *Journal of Marketing Management*, 16(8): 937–57.

Gerhart, B. and Rynes, S. L. 2003. *Compensation: Theory, Evidence and Strategic Implications*. Thousand Oaks, CA: Sage.

Ginter, J. and La Londe, B. 2002. *The Ohio State University 2002 Survey of Career Patterns in Logistics*. The Ohio State University Max M. Fisher College of Business Supply Chain Management Research Group, Columbus, Ohio.

Gomez-Mejia, L.R. 1992. Structure and Process of Diversification, Compensation Strategy, and Firm Performance. *Strategic Management Journal*, 13(5): 381–97.

Gomez-Mejia, L.R. and Balkin, D.B. 1992. The Determinants of Faculty Pay: An Agency Theory Perspective. *Academy of Management Journal*, 35(5): 921–55.

Holström, B. 1979. Moral Hazard and Observability. *The Bell Journal of Economics*, 10(1): 74–91.

Jensen, M.C. 1983. Organizational Theory and Methodology. *Accounting Review*, 58(2): 319–39.

Jensen, M.C. and Meckling, W.C. 1976. Theory of the Firm: Managerial Behavior, Agency Costs and Ownership Structure. *Journal of Financial Economics*, 3(4): 305–60.

Johnson, E. 2001. Learning From Toys: Lessons in Managing Supply Chain Risk from the Toy Industry. *California Management Review*, 43(3): 106–24.

Joseph, K. and Thevaranjan, A. 1998. Monitoring and Incentives in Sales Organizations, an Agency Theoretic Perspective. *Marketing Science*, 17(2): 107–23.

La Londe, B. and Ginter, J. 2004. *The Ohio State University 2004 Survey Of Career Patterns in Logistics*. The Ohio State University Max M. Fisher College of Business Supply Chain Management Research Group, Columbus, Ohio.

Lee, H.L. 2002. Aligning Supply Chain Strategies with Product Uncertainties. *California Management Review*, 44(3): 105–19.

Levinthal, D. 1986. A Survey of Agency Models and Organizations. *Journal of Economic Behavior and Organizations*, 9(2): 153–85.

Mahony, J.T. 2005. *Economic Foundations of Strategy*. Thousand Oaks, CA: Sage.

Mentzer, J.T. and Konrad, B.P. 1991. An Efficiency/Effectiveness Approach to Logistics Performance Measurement. *Journal of Business Logistics*, 12(1): 33–62.

Naylor, J.B., Naim, M.M. and Berry, D. 1999. Leagility, Integrating the Lean and Agile Manufacturing Paradigms in the Total Supply Chain. *International Journal of Production Economics*, 62(1–2): 107–18.

Rigby, D. 2001. Management Tools and Techniques: A Survey. *California Management Review*, 43(2): 139–60.

Tosi, H.L. and Gomez-Mejia, L.R. 1989. The Decoupling of CEO Pay and Performance: An Agency Theory Perspective. *Administrative Science Quarterly*, 34: 169–89.

Tosi, H.L., Werner, S., Katz, J. and Gomez-Mejia, L.R. 2000. How Much Does Performance Matter? A Meta Analysis of CEO Pay Studies. *Journal of Management*, 26(2): 301–39.

Tremblay, M., Côté, J. and Balkin, D.B. 2003. Explaining Sales Pay Strategies Using Agency, Transaction Cost and Resource Dependence Theories. *Journal of Management Studies*, 40(7): 1651–82.

Van Hoek, I., Chatham, R. and Wilding, R. 2002. Managers in Supply Chain Management, the Critical Dimension. *Supply Chain Management: An International Journal*, 7(3): 119–25.

Incentives to stimulate innovation in a global context

6

Marianna Makri

> Firms can no longer view the domestic and foreign spheres as separate and different but must see the whole – how to conceive and implement overall strategies for competing globally.
>
> Michael Porter

Given today's focus on innovation, it should come as little surprise that research and development spending is on the rise. According to a recent survey by *Business Week*, in 2005, the 1,000 companies from around the world with the biggest R&D budgets spent a combined total of $407 billion – $20 billion more than the top 1,000 of 2004 (Scanlon, 2006). Innovation lies at the heart of the issue of the growth of firms, domestically and internationally, and firms compete on the basis of the superiority of their information and know-how, and their ability to generate new knowledge. Put differently, firm growth is contingent upon firms' ability to exploit and expand their technology platforms and foreign direct investment is a pivotal expression of the growth of the firm. The evolutionary process of firm growth often begins with the establishment of exporting facilities where the firm transfers the knowledge acquired in its home market while gradually accumulating new knowledge in the foreign market. Next, the recombined knowledge from the foreign market is transferred internationally throughout the network of subsidiaries, including the home market.

Several studies suggest that the recent rapid growth of foreign direct R&D investment, particularly in the United States, reflects corporate efforts to harness external scientific and technological capabilities and generate new technological assets (see Dunning and Narula, 1995; Kummerle, 1997). While a few years ago, companies were off-shoring for cost reasons, the shift is now driven by strategy and the need to build out global innovation networks and move closer to fast growing foreign markets (Scanlon, 2006).

The foreign direct investment (FDI) literature emphasizes the role of demand-side factors in motivating FDI in R&D, such as exploitation of the home base firm's technology to offshore markets by adapting products for foreign markets and providing technical support to offshore manufacturing operations (Abernathy and Utterback, 1978; Utterback, 1989). Some more recent studies however, note the importance of science and technology factors or supply-side factors in motivating FDI in R&D. Several studies note that foreign R&D investment represents a strategy to maintain competitive advantage by generating new technological assets and capabilities (see Cantwell, 1989; Casson, 1991; Kummerle, 1997; Mowery, 1997). Put differently, gaining access to scientific and technical talent and exploring new knowledge lacunae is a pivotal motive for foreign direct R&D investment (Florida, 1997). These two strategies of exploring and exploiting are discussed next.

Home base exploration vs exploitation strategies

> The way you will thrive in this environment is by innovating – innovating in technologies, innovating in strategies, innovating in business models.
>
> IBM CEO Samuel J. Palmesano

As Teece and colleagues (1997) note, because the value of resources constantly changes, competitive advantage stems from the firm's capability to continually create, integrate and reconfigure new resources. Creating new capabilities entails the creation of new knowledge and recombination of existing knowledge. Simply put, in high technology markets firms ought to constantly learn, continuously search for and acquire knowledge to continuously reconfigure their resource portfolio and build new capabilities (Sirmon *et al.*, 2007).

There are two general types of organizational learning: exploration and exploitation (March, 1991) that lead to the creation and reconfiguration of knowledge. Exploratory learning often involves experimentation with new alternatives and acquiring major additions of knowledge to an organization's knowledge stock. Alternatively, exploitative learning involves the extension of existing capabilities. Such learning is likely to be more incremental, whereas exploratory learning is likely to be more innovative and radical (Ahuja and Lampert, 2001). Both exploratory learning and exploitative learning can occur simultaneously and the global firm can use *home base exploration* and *home base exploitation* strategies to engage in the two types of learning.

A home base exploration strategy involves adding to a firm's knowledge stocks through experiencing new contexts. It often entails building tacit knowledge through learning by doing. It involves exploratory learning when the knowledge created is new and unrelated to the firm's current knowledge stocks. Alternatively, a home base strategy is exploitative when the knowledge added is more incremental and helps the firm exploit its current knowledge stocks.

A home base exploration strategy can include collaboration with partners or it can involve the firm learning through its own experiences. A home base exploitation strategy can also be implemented either in cooperation with a local firm or alone. Put differently, a *home base exploration cooperative strategy* involves building new knowledge that is largely or wholly unrelated to the firm's current knowledge stocks by working with partners to jointly create the new knowledge. *A home base exploitation cooperative strategy* involves enriching a firm's current knowledge stocks through transfers of knowledge between partners in ways that allow a firm to exploit its current knowledge.

Whether a company seeks to pursue home base exploration or exploitation strategies would affect the capabilities required by R&D executives. For instance, to build an effective home base exploration site (Kummerle, 1997), R&D executives need to invest in strategies that absorb knowledge from the local scientific community by exchanging researchers with local university laboratories and transferring it to the home base lab central R&D site. R&D executives need to be able to attract junior scientists with high potential, and target the right university institutes and scholars for joint research projects. On the other hand, a home base exploitation strategy calls for commercializing knowledge by transferring it from the home base to the laboratory site abroad and from there to local manufacturing and marketing where it can be used to adapt products to local needs.

A home base exploration strategy requires that R&D firms are present at the most advanced locations and that they engage in option-seeking activities in R&D, exploratory marketing and advanced manufacturing. Further, a home base exploration strategy involves the offshore R&D site becoming a "generating station" which generates new scientific and technical knowledge. Developments in science and technology have led to the transition to a polycentric structure of national research and innovation systems where R&D firms need to have a presence in more than one center of R&D and innovation and establish strong centers of science and technology in order to increase their "absorptive capacities" (Cohen and Levinthal, 1990).

Additionally, an exploration strategy needs to be complemented by efficiency in internally transferring knowledge across subsidiaries and transforming options into new products. Fast changing consumer demands, global outsourcing and open-source software make speed to market paramount today. Put differently, an exploitation strategy is also needed in order to speed up the conversion of knowledge into marketable products and such strategy calls for the offshore R&D site to become a "listening post," the primary function of which is to monitor the scientific and technical capabilities of domestic firms and universities.

While both strategies are important, home base exploration activities are, on balance, more so. Put differently, gaining access to new science and technology and attracting high quality scientific and technical talent are more vital to long term success than customizing products, or supporting offshore markets.

Managing global R&D

As more and more sources of potentially relevant knowledge emerge across the globe, companies must establish a presence at an increasing number of locations to access new knowledge and to absorb new research results from foreign universities and competitors into their own organizations. As Kogut and Zander (1992) put it, globalization calls for an expansion of a firm's "combinative capability," that is its ability to recombine knowledge from different sources. Firms pursuing a home base exploration strategy are critically dependent on excellent R&D resources and talent pools. Also, companies competing around the world must move new products from development to market at an ever more rapid pace. Consequently, companies must build R&D networks that excel at tapping new centers of knowledge and at commercializing products in foreign markets with the speed required to remain competitive (Kummerle, 1997).

Incentive schemes play a pivotal role in stimulating R&D managers to engage in activities that support the firm's global R&D strategy whether that is a home base exploration or exploitation strategy. Indeed, a properly designed pay scheme can stimulate R&D executives to link corporate strategy to R&D strategy by effectively implementing either an exploration or exploitation strategy, pick the most appropriate mode of growth for each country and integrate the activities of the different foreign sites so that the entire network is a coordinated whole. This last part, integration, is pivotal and an incentive system should match the characteristics and needs of the global knowledge network. As Kummerle (1997) notes, managers of R&D networks must be global coordinators, not local administrators. More than being managers of people and processes, they must be managers of knowledge and they should be incentivized to be so.

Building a global R&D network requires that multinational corporations locate R&D in the most dynamic markets. Managing a global R&D network requires that CEOs and top-level managers build a team of people who have technical expertise and in-depth organizational knowledge. They need to team up people from across the organization and link rewards to innovation because successful innovative companies build innovation cultures. Such teams need to integrate scientists, engineers, marketing and manufacturing executives and need to be able to mobilize resources, set research agendas, monitor results and create direct ties between sites. These central R&D managers need to continuously inform R&D scientists and engineers about the entire company's current state of technical knowledge and capabilities as well as trends in current and potential future markets. They need to determine timelines and resource requirements for specific projects as well as create direct links among researchers across different sites. Finally, this central R&D team needs to constantly monitor new regional pockets of knowledge as well as the company's expanding network of manufacturing sites to determine whether the company will need additional R&D locations.

Procter & Gamble Co. has been very effective in creating a global innovation network by making it a goal that 50 percent of the company's new products come from outside P&G's labs. To do that P&G had to restructure much of its research organization. It created new job classifications, such as 70 worldwide "technology entrepreneurs," or TEs, who act as scouts, looking for the latest breakthroughs from places such as university labs. TEs also develop "technology game boards" that map out where technology opportunities lie and help P&G'ers get inside the minds of its competitors.

An effective compensation system for globalizing R&D should reward the behaviors outlined above. More specifically, firms pursuing a home base exploration strategy need to link rewards for R&D executives to the behaviors they expect them to exhibit. R&D executives need to be rewarded for their ability to tap into local centers of excellence in terms of scientific and technological knowledge and their ability to integrate such knowledge across global R&D sites. Put differently, pay in this scenario should be linked to the executive's ability to access, integrate and recombine critical scientific and technological knowledge. On the other hand, in the case of firms pursuing a home base exploitation strategy, R&D executives should be rewarded for commercializing knowledge by transferring it from the home base to the laboratory site abroad and from there to local manufacturing and marketing where it can be used to adapt products to local needs. These ideas are discussed in more detail next.

Incentives for global R&D

Because of the complexity surrounding the R&D process, R&D executives often hold information about the firms' technical abilities that is not available to shareholders, thus exacerbating principal–agent information asymmetries (Milkovich *et al.*, 1991). For this reason,

> behavioral monitoring is more costly than measuring outcomes, and managers'
> behaviors cannot be as readily observed or controlled in R&D firms due to the very
> nature of the innovative process . . . [therefore] according to agency theory R&D
> intensive firms are more likely than others to make use of higher ratios of bonuses to
> base pay to focus managers' decisions on outcomes rather than bear the costs of
> monitoring managers' interim behaviors.
>
> (Milkovich *et al.*, 1991: 137)

Thus, as Wiseman and Gomez-Mejia (1998: 145) argue, under subjective monitoring, "the use of judgmental criteria is likely to increase agent risk bearing, resulting in greater preferences for lower risk strategic options."

On the other hand and again using an agency rationale, one could argue that relying on financial outcomes to reward R&D executives could be just as ineffective (e.g. Duysters and Hagedoorn, 2000; Hoskisson *et al.*, 1993) because assuming managers are risk-averse, linking their pay to financial results when innovation-related decisions are inherently risky, may lead to conservative decisions that smother innovation, as well as a focus on short term results. As Balkin and colleagues (2000: 1119) note,

> emphasis on innovation implies a greater variability of outcomes and a greater
> probability of failure . . . because the relationship between senior managers' actions
> and firm performance is very uncertain in high technology firms, executive
> compensation packages should be loosely linked to observed performance results.

One of the biggest mistakes companies may make is linking executives' incentives too closely to specific innovation metrics. Linking pay too closely to hard innovation measures such as number of patents may tempt managers to game the system. Linking pay to measures such as the number of patents granted or the percentage of sales from new products, can lead to incremental innovations rather than true breakthroughs. A key question that arises is based on the criteria on which R&D executives should be evaluated and compensated.

Makri and colleagues (2006) offer a complementary approach where R&D firms can simultaneously foster incentive alignment and manage risk aversion by rewarding executives using multiple performance criteria which include both financial results and behavioral indicators. They find that high technology firms that use more holistic outcome based and behavior based performance criteria to reward executives, exhibit better market performance than those that do not.

Building on this idea, it is reasonable to suggest that in the case of R&D firms pursuing home base exploration strategies executive pay should be linked to the innovation *processes* necessary to support such strategy, that is accessing critical knowledge and integrating with the network as opposed to innovation *outcomes* such as number of new patents or new products. On the other hand, in the case of R&D firms pursuing home

Table 6.1 Exploration vs exploitation strategy

Home base exploration strategy	Home base exploitation strategy
Integration and global coordination of knowledge	Integration and global coordination of knowledge
Locate critical centers	Mobilize resources
Set research agendas	Commercialize knowledge
Mobilize resources	Mobilize knowledge from home base to local labs, manufacturing and marketing

base exploitation strategies executive pay should be linked to the ability to commercialize new knowledge and adapt it to local markets. In this case, pay should be more strongly tied to innovation outcomes than when an exploration strategy is followed (see Table 6.1). As will be discussed in the next section, some institutional contexts call for a *cooperative* exploration/exploitation strategy and executives should be rewarded for pursuing alliances with local partners.

Susan Schuman, CEO of Stone Yamashita Partners, who works with CEOs on innovation and change, says that besides quantitative innovation measures some firms are including behavioral measures related to innovation, such as a manager's risk tolerance. For instance, General Electric Co. has begun evaluating its top 5,000 managers on "growth traits" that include innovation-oriented themes such as "external focus" and "imagination and courage." Simply put, global R&D firms need to build an innovation culture that rewards innovation quantity as well as innovation quality and evaluates managers based on innovation-related behaviors. For instance, Nokia Corp. inducts engineers with at least ten patents into its "Club 10," recognizing them each year in a formal awards ceremony hosted by the CEO, Jorma Ollila, while 3M has long awarded "Genesis Grants" to scientists who want to work on outside projects.

A global perspective involves deep understanding of the social, political and cultural contexts of the worldwide markets. Institutional environment, national cultures, political systems and market conditions can act as barriers or facilitators in defining a firm's technological priorities and ultimately its survival. As a result, compensation packages for global R&D executives need to account for these influences. These ideas are discussed next.

Institutional environment

Strong institutions have strong legal systems that clearly elaborate legal rights and responsibilities and provide a set of standards against which to measure actions within a society. When the institutional environment is underdeveloped, inefficient legal frameworks and weak intellectual property rights pose significant problems for foreign firms. Thus, in technology driven economies, legal systems are of paramount importance as they protect those who develop new products and useful innovations. For instance, a strong legal system can facilitate innovation by accelerating the patenting process. It can also establish intellectual property rights statutes and antitrust laws to offer support and protection for innovation through trademarks, copyrights and patents, which may allow strategic licensing. A well established legal system often encompasses a court system that can better handle claim cases and litigations, which may be used to deter infringement and thus stimulate innovation. In other words, firms would not assume the investments required to develop innovation if they cannot count on a system that protects them from those who want to copy them (Berrone *et al.*, 2008).

Take China as an example. In an effort to promote R&D, China has a legal system that encourages exploration but also does not shield from imitation. While in the late 90s, China spent less than 1 percent of gross domestic product on research and development, that figure is now up to 1.5 percent, and the government wants to raise it to 2.5 percent by 2020 by promoting cutting edge innovation. For instance, biotech startups are offering experimental therapies unavailable or prohibited in the West. Shenzhen Beike Biotechnology Co. is implanting adult stem cells in patients to treat conditions such as autism, Lou Gehrig's disease and strokes. Further, in terms of exploitation, China accounted for 130,000 patent applications in 2004. That makes it number five globally, according to figures released on October 16 by the World Intellectual Property Organization, a UN agency. Although China was still far behind number one, Japan (with 450,000 patents in 2004) and number two USA (with 403,000), its 2004 patent applications were six times the number in 1995.

India's goals are no less ambitious, and reflected in the slogans used to promote the 2005 and 2006 national R&D trade fairs in New Delhi: "Think Innovation, Think India," "Mind to Market," and best of all, "The World's Knowledge Hub of the Future." In support of such ambitious goals, India has 380 universities and 11,200 higher education institutions churning out around 6,000 PhDs and 200,000 engineers, 300,000 science graduates and post-graduates annually and R&D investment has been growing at a compounded annual growth rate of more than 40 percent (Sirkin, 2006).

As suggested earlier, one of the risks in including innovation criteria in compensation packages is that managers may manipulate them (Makri *et al.*, 2006). This risk of gaming becomes larger within weak legal systems as they not only add uncertainty to the environment faced by executives but also increase managerial leeway to manipulate innovation criteria to enhance rewards at the expense of principals. But a stable legal system stifles the agent's attempts to act opportunistically since systems of punishments and rewards are enforceable and well known, which makes innovation criteria more appealing. Therefore, it becomes more appropriate to reward R&D managers based on innovation outcomes when the firm is pursuing a home base exploitation strategy and when the legal system is strong.

Relatedly, a strong legal system can act as a useful external monitoring mechanism for principals since it can deter managers from opportunistic actions. That is, well developed legal institutions help tame managerial perverse intentions as they can face lawsuits in court in case of transgressions. For instance, Cisco Systems Inc. sued the Chinese company Huawei in 2002 for allegedly stealing Cisco's router technology, and General Motors Corp. took Chery to court in 2004 for allegedly copying a GM design for Chery's popular QQ compact. Further, strong legal institutions often entail sophisticated normative bodies that can curb the manager's attempt to "game" with innovation criteria to increase their pay since the vigilance of governmental examiners routinely control the patenting process (Meyer, 2002). A solid legal system also provides reliable information about the true value of innovation. As a result, more sophisticated measures are likely to be used as compensation criteria than simple innovation quantity measures such as patent counts.

Despite the potential benefits that innovation criteria may entail for firms within solid legal systems, it may not fully preclude managers taking advantage of the information asymmetries that characterize high-technology sectors, which may be particularly severe in the short term (Milkovich *et al.*, 1991). Innovation development and the legal processes that accompany it are often outlined in multi-year frames. Thus, innovation measures are unlikely to be a wise assessment of managerial actions, at least in the short term. Neither does a strong legal system guarantee that managers will respond successfully to commercial pressures of highly innovative sectors. That is, inventions may be of little value unless the firm is able to commercialize and obtain a profit from them. Linking short term bonuses to financial results focuses executives' attention on the profitability consequences of innovation efforts. Thus, high-technology firms in strong legal systems will exhibit greater weight of financial measures in short term pay (e.g. bonuses) and greater weight of innovation measures in long term pay as well as lower use of internal monitoring to control for innovation activities.

However, legal systems may be perniciously manipulated by political regimes interfering with their functioning. For instance, the Indian government has implicitly allowed local pharmaceuticals to produce generic versions of patented drugs. This generated strong complaints from companies like Novartis. But the Indian government argued that these actions are needed to secure access to these drugs for a larger portion of underprivileged people. While this issue clearly poses an ethical dilemma, this example also shows that governmental intervention can seriously influence current and future innovation efforts of firms.

Oftentimes, strong governmental intervention is characterized by frequent changes of policies and unanticipated alterations in the current and future economic landscape that adds uncertainty to the challenges faced by managers. For example, political pressure in some countries on pharmaceutical companies to reduce their prices will lower revenues and ultimately lower returns to shareholders. As a result, political intervention exacerbates executives' personal risk by making performance outcomes more unpredictable and less dependent on their own efforts (Gregorio, 2005; Shrader *et al.*, 2000). The increased uncertainty is particularly severe in technology intensive environments distinguished for being highly volatile. For that reason, it is reasonable to expect that for high-technology firms, compensation is to be largely decoupled from innovation criteria and even more decoupled from financial measures. Instead, we would expect pay criteria to consider a more complex set of issues such as governmental influence abilities or political acquiescence since CEOs can exert more influence over these criteria.

National culture

Cultural factors have been held responsible for hindering management development and performance (Roney, 1997) and for even placing limits on knowledge transfer (Jankowicz, 2001) among firms. Perhaps the most renowned and comprehensive study on national culture is the work by Hofstede (1980), where he identified four primary dimensions of culture, namely power distance (the acceptance of social stratification), individualism–collectivism (the desire to promote one's self-interest over the interest of the group), masculine–feminine (task oriented versus relation oriented) and uncertainty avoidance (the need for rules and procedures to counter ambiguity and uncertainty). See Chapters 1 and 11 for a more in-depth discussion on the topic.

Using patents as a proxy for innovation, Shane (1992) examined the influence of culture on knowledge transfer and innovation and found that non-hierarchical and individualistic societies are more inventive than others. He later (Shane, 1993) tested the effect of other cultural dimensions on national rates of innovation by using trademarks per capita as a proxy for innovation, and found that low power distance, high individualism and weak uncertainty avoidance were positively related to higher innovative capacity.

This suggests that the compensation package of R&D managers needs to be designed with country-specific cultural issues in mind. Put differently, compensation schemes are likely to be influenced by the national culture in which firms operate (Conyon and Murphy, 2000; Tosi and Greckhamer, 2004). When the cultural distance between the foreign firm's home country and the emerging market country is high, the foreign firm may sometimes struggle to understand how to navigate effectively in that culture (Shimizu and Hitt, 2004). Understanding the culture is important in all relationships in the emerging market (e.g. customers, suppliers, government officials, competitors, etc.). Foreign entrants also need to learn with whom they need to build social capital in the local market (Hitt *et al.*, 2002). The way these factors influence compensation is twofold. First, some societies and certain institutional contexts might have a cultural advantage in inventiveness which, if true, would suggest that innovation is held in high esteem and is considered very valuable for that society (including firms). For instance, China's goal is to become an "innovation-oriented society" by the year 2020 and a global leader in science and technology by mid-century.

Second, the same values that operate on the national level are also likely to mirror those that operate at the firm level, so that companies in innovation-supporting cultures tend to place greater merit in inventiveness than others. Specifically, we would expect high-tech firms located in nations with the "culture of innovation" (i.e. those that sustain innovation) to place greater emphasis on innovation measures as criteria to reward their executives than to financial measures because innovation has value in itself regardless of the potential pay-offs it may produce.

Moreover, if innovation is highly valued by society members, then it is reasonable to expect that compensation schemes reward more creative developments and processes that highlight the concept of newness rather than the raw number of innovations. One way to measure the relevance of the innovation is through the economic impact these innovations have on the profitability of the company. Thus, we expect the use of a combination of innovation and financial measures in incentive schemes. At the same time, however, individuals and groups that innovate are likely to find other benefits beyond the economic rewards (such as high reputation, personal pride, social acceptance) if society places great merit in inventiveness. This may entail peer-monitoring and intrinsic motivations to pursue innovation activities, reducing the need for controlling mechanisms. As such, high-tech firms facing innovation-supporting national cultures (i.e. those with low power distance, high individualism and weak uncertainty avoidance) will exhibit a combination of innovation and financial criteria in compensation packages, both in the short and long term, and lower use of internal monitoring to control for innovation activities.

The challenge of emerging markets

According to Hoskisson and colleagues (2000), emerging markets include economies in Latin America, the Middle East, Southeast Asia and Africa, and also transition economies such as China, Central and Eastern Europe and the former Soviet Union. While emerging markets offer growth opportunities for firms, they also impose challenges for firms' competitive behavior due to their weaker institutional infrastructure that increases political and economic risks to firms that contemplate investments in those markets. Not all emerging markets are alike (Hoskisson *et al.*, 2000) in terms of their economic growth maturity, cultural context and institutional stability. Some emerging markets are more mature economically and have more stable institutional environments. For this reason, foreign entrants in emerging markets need to use different learning approaches in different institutional contexts. For example, in mature and institutionally stable emerging markets, foreign entrants may focus more on a home base exploration strategy where in an emerging market with a weak institutional environment a home base cooperative exploitation strategy may be more appropriate.

Because in emerging markets the informal institutions sometimes are more important than formal institutions (Rodriguez *et al.*, 2005), foreign entrants may need the help of local partners because they have knowledge of the culture and how it relates to the customers, they understand the distribution networks, and have relationships with important government entities (Zahra *et al.*, 2000). Simply put, in emerging markets, firms may need to be able to engage in cooperative learning, exploratory in addition to exploitative. Because emerging markets differ from developed markets in infrastructure and in ways of doing business, foreign entrants cannot simply transfer or adapt their technologies to the local markets. For example, while new computing and Internet technologies have been embraced in developed markets, the diffusion of these technologies is much slower in many emerging markets where people are poor and the literacy level is lower. Thus, foreign entrants need to learn how to develop new technologies to satisfy idiosyncratic demands from emerging markets via exploratory and exploitative learning.

Hitt *et al.* (2004) compared the institutional environments of two more mature emerging markets, China and Russia, and noted their differences in terms of stability. While China evolved over time, making gradual changes in its institutional arrangements while maintaining central control by the government, Russia followed decentralized political control that led to many different local policies that changed frequently. This situation led to institutional chaos and substantial uncertainty for firms operating there which led to a short term orientation in terms of strategy. In contrast, Chinese firms were more long term oriented and strategic in their actions. Put differently, the stability in the Chinese environment supports the investment in learning the skills and capabilities that can be used to compete effectively over the long term. Alternatively, Russian firms focused on obtaining the resources needed to survive in the short run as opposed to learning the capabilities that they might need in the future to compete in global markets. In addition, the Chinese government encouraged and provided incentives to learn certain types of knowledge, especially new technologies. But, there was no such support from and incentives provided by the Russian government (Hitt *et al.*, 2004). Thus, while exploratory learning is likely to be used in both countries, Russian firms largely focus on short term exploitative learning while Chinese firms strongly emphasize exploratory learning to develop capabilities that facilitate the achievement of their long term goals.

Foreign firms entering relatively stable environments can take a longer term approach to learning and they are more likely to engage in exploratory learning. However, when the institutional environment is highly unstable, firms seek to learn what is needed to survive in the short term and thus exploitative learning is likely to be more common. Further, foreign entrants have an even greater need for local partners in highly unstable environments because in these environments, even more transactions are conducted in the informal market and are based on relationships. On the other hand, an unstable environment also increases the likelihood of opportunistic behavior by partners. Thus, while uncertainty in the institutional environment presumably increases the need for a local partner, local firms in relatively unstable environments (e.g. Russian firms) may provide less value as partners. Therefore, in these environments, foreign entrants are more likely to engage in exploitative learning by collaborating with local firms.

In contrast, learning about the culture, institutions and relations is more valuable for foreign entrants in relatively stable institutional environments. In these environments, foreign entrants are likely to devote greater investment and effort into learning and exploring new knowledge and new opportunities. Also, local firms from stable environments should be more productive sources of learning the tacit knowledge desired by foreign partners. These conditions encourage foreign entrants to engage in exploratory learning by collaborating with local entrants.

Simply put, the institutional stability in emerging markets affects the learning behaviors of foreign entrants and most foreign entrants need local partners in emerging markets for reasons explained earlier. For this reason, the compensation scheme of R&D executives should account for the differences in the stability across these markets and reward risks taken in joint ventures and alliances. Firms entering Russia for instance may want to consider reducing risk bearing by executives by only loosely coupling their pay to financial and innovation performance, while rewarding them for their ability to form relationships with the local government or other firms. Firms entering a more stable environment such as China can afford to link pay to more objective measures of innovation performance such as new products developed.

Concluding remarks

As Gerybadze and Reger (1999: 262) note, the new paradigm of globalized R&D is characterized by

> intense market and technology interaction, multiple centers of knowledge at several geographical locations, cross-functional learning, integrating several functions and segments along the value chain, a combination of inward and outward learning, as opposed to one-way information transfer, and reverse and interactive technology transfer, both between different geographical locations, as well as between organizational units.

Thus, it is imperative that managers of R&D networks are global coordinators, able to integrate key capabilities worldwide including technology, people, knowledge and processes.

Properly designed incentive schemes can align R&D managers' actions with the firm's global R&D strategy whether that is a home base exploration or exploitation strategy. More specifically, in firms pursuing home base exploration strategies executive pay should be linked to the innovation processes necessary to support such strategy, that is accessing critical knowledge and integrating it with the global network, while in firms pursuing home base exploitation strategies executive pay should be linked to the ability to commercialize new knowledge and adapt it to local markets.

When firms venture into countries with weak legal systems, executives are not only faced with uncertainty but also with greater opportunity for gaming in terms of manipulating innovation criteria to enhance their pay at the expense of principals. For that reason, it becomes more appropriate to reward R&D managers based on quantitative innovation outcomes when the legal system is strong. On the other hand, when legal systems are weak and governmental intervention is strong it is reasonable to expect compensation for R&D managers to be largely decoupled from innovation criteria and even more decoupled from financial measures. Instead, expected pay criteria should encompass a more complex set of issues such as governmental influence abilities or political acquiescence since executives can exert more influence over these criteria.

Additionally, pay criteria should consider the impact of national culture on R&D executives' ability to execute the firm's strategy. For R&D executives facing innovation-supporting national cultures (i.e. those with low power distance, high individualism and weak uncertainty avoidance) pay should be contingent on a combination of innovation and financial criteria and lower use of internal monitoring to control for innovation activities. Finally, the institutional stability in emerging markets calls for a cooperative exploration/exploitation strategy since foreign entrants are more likely to need local markets. For this reason, the compensation scheme of R&D executives should account for the differences in the stability across these markets and reward risks taken in joint ventures and alliances.

References

Abernathy, W. and Utterback, J. 1978. Patterns of Innovation in Technology. *Technology Review*, 80(7): 40–7.

Ahuja, G. and Lampert, C.M. 2001. Entrepreneurship in the Large Corporation: A Longitudinal Study of How Established Firms Create Breakthrough Inventions. *Strategic Management Journal*, 22: 221–38.

Balkin, D.B., Markman, G.D. and Gomez-Mejia, L.R. 2000. Is CEO Pay in High-Technology Firms Related to Innovation? *Academy of Management Journal*, 43: 1118–29.

Berrone, P., Makri, M. and Gomez-Mejia, L.R. 2008. Executive Pay in High-technology Firms: A Contextual Approach. *International Journal of Human Resource Management*, forthcoming.

Cantwell, J. 1989. *Technological Innovation and Multinational Corporations*. Oxford, UK: Basil Blackwell.

Casson, M. (ed.). 1991. *Global Research Strategy and International Competitiveness*. Oxford, UK: Basil Blackwell.

Cohen, W.M. and Levinthal, D.A. 1990. Absorptive Capacity: A New Perspective on Learning and Innovation. *Administrative Science Quarterly*, 35: 128–52.

Conyon, M.J. and Murphy, K.J. 2000. The Prince and the Pauper? CEO Pay in the United States and United Kingdom. *Economic Journal*, 110: 640–71.

Dunning, J. and Narula, R. 1995. The R&D Activities of Foreign Firms in the United States. Unpublished paper.

Duysters, G. and Hagedoorn, J. 2000. Core Competences and Company Performance in the World-Wide Computer Industry. *Journal of High Technology Management Research*, 11: 75–91.

Florida, R. 1997. The Globalization of R&D: Results of a Survey of Foreign Affiliated R&D Laboratories in the USA. *Research Policy*, 26: 85–103.

Gerybadze, A. and Reger, G. 1999. Globalization of R&D: Recent Changes in the Management of Innovation in Transnational Corporations. *Research Policy*, 28: 251–74.

Gregorio, D. 2005. Re-Thinking Country Risk: Insights from Entrepreneurship Theory. *International Business Review*, 14: 209–26.

Hitt, M., Lee, H. and Yucel, E. 2002. The Importance of Social Capital to the Management of Multinational Enterprises: Relational Networks among Asian and Western Firms. *Asia Pacific Journal of Management*, 19(2/3): 353–72.

Hitt, M.A., Ahlstrom, D., Dacin, M.T., Levitas, E. and Svobodina, L. 2004. The Institutional Effects on Strategic Alliance Partner Selection in Transition Economies: China versus Russia. *Organization Science*, 15: 173–85.

Hofstede, G. 1980. *Culture's Consequences: International Differences in Work-Related Values*. Beverly Hills, CA: Sage.

Hoskisson, R.E., Hitt, M.A. and Hill, C.W. 1993. Managerial Incentives and Investment in R&D in Large Multiproduct Firms. *Organization Science*, 4: 325–41.

Hoskisson, R.E., Eden, L., Lau, C.M. and Wright, M. 2000. Strategy in Emerging Economies. *Academy of Management Journal*, 43: 249–67.

Jankowicz, D. 2001. Limits to Knowledge Transfer: What they Already Know in the Post-command Economies. *Journal of East–West Business*, 7(2): 37–51.

Kogut, B. and Zander, U. 1992. Knowledge of the Firm, Combinative Capabilities, and the Replication of Technology. *Organization Science*, 3: 383–97.

Kummerle, W. 1997. Building Effective R&D Capabilities Abroad, *Harvard Business Review*, March–April: 61–70.

Makri, M., Lane, P.J. and Gomez-Mejia, L.R. 2006. Ceo Incentives, Innovation, and Performance in Technology-Intensive Firms: A Reconciliation of Outcome and Behavior-Based Incentive Schemes. *Strategic Management Journal*, 27: 1057–80.

March, J.G. 1991. Exploration and Exploitation in Organizational Learning. *Organization Science*, 2: 71–87.

Meyer, G. 2002. The "First" First Inventor Defense vs. The "Second" First Investor Defense. *Intellectual Property & Technology Law Journal*, 14: 1–9.

Milkovich, G.T., Gerhart, B. and Hannon, J. 1991. The Effects of Research and Development Intensity on Managerial Compensation in Large Organizations. *Journal of High Technology Management Research*, 2: 133–45.

Mowery, D. 1997. Technological Innovation in a Multipolar System: Analysis and Implications for US Policy. Prepared for the Council on Foreign Relations Study Group on the Globalization of Industrial R&D, New York.

Rodriguez, P., Uhlenbruck, K. and Eden, L. 2005. Corrupt Governments Matter: How Corruption Affects the Entry Strategies of Multinationals. *Academy of Management Review*, 30: 383–96.

Roney, J. 1997. Cultural Implications of Implementing TQM in Poland. *Journal of World Business*, 32(2): 152–64.

Scanlon, J. 2006. How to Turn Money into Innovation, Innovation, Nov 14. The World's Most Innovative Companies. *Business Week*, April 24.

Shane, S.A. 1992. Why Do Some Societies Invent More Than Others? *Journal of Business Venturing*, 7: 29–46.

—— 1993. Cultural Influences on National Rates of Innovation. *Journal of Business Venturing*, 8: 59–73.

Shimizu, K. and Hitt, M.A. 2004. What Constrains or Facilitates Divestitures of Formerly Acquired Firms? The Effects of Organizational Inertia. *Journal of Management*, 31(1): 50–62.

Shrader, R., Oviatt, B. and Mcdougall, P. 2000. How New Ventures Exploit Trade-Offs among International Risk Factors: Lessons for the Accelerated Internationalization of the 21st Century. *Academy of Management Journal*, 43: 1227–47.

Sirkin, H. 2006. India and China Wise Up to Innovation. *Business Week*, April 24.

Sirmon, D.G., Hitt, M.A. and Ireland, R.D. 2007. Managing Firm Resources in Dynamic Environments to Create Value: Looking Inside the Black Box. *Academy of Management Review*, 32(1): 273–92.

Teece, D.J., Pisano, G. and Shuen, A. 1997. Dynamic Capabilities and Strategic Management. *Strategic Management Journal*, 18: 509–33.

Tosi, H. and Greckhamer, T. 2004. Culture and CEO Compensation. *Organization Science*, 15: 657–70.

Utterback, J. 1989. Innovation and Industrial Evolution in Manufacturing Industries. In B. Guile and H. Brooks (eds), *Technology and Global Industry*: 16–48. Washington, DC: National Academy Press.

Wiseman, R.M. and Gomez-Mejia, L.R. 1998. A Behavioral Agency Model of Managerial Risk Taking. *Academy of Management Review*, 22: 133–53.

Zahra, S.A., Ireland, R.D., Gutierrez, I. and Hitt, M.A. 2000. Privatization and Entrepreneurial Transformation: Emerging Issues and a Future Research Agenda. *Academy of Management Review*, 25: 509–24.

Executive compensation in an international context

The role of informal and formal institutions

Katalin Takacs Haynes

In 2002, US CEOs made 23 times as much as CEOs in mainland China, ten times as much as CEOs in India, nine times as much as CEOs in Taiwan, five times as much as CEOs in Japan and two to four times as much as their counterparts in Spain, the United Kingdom, France, Italy, the Netherlands, Germany and Switzerland (Towers Perrin, 2002). Why does CEO pay vary so much across countries? Exploring the individual, firm and industry determinants of CEO pay has led to a rich research stream on CEO pay, yet even CEOs who manage similarly sized firms and compete in the same global industries often have different pay. As examples, in 1998 the CEO of Dutch Unilever received $2.4M in compensation, while the CEO of US-based Colgate Palmolive received $52.7M; in 1999 the CEO of Eriksson received $1.1M, compared to the CEO of Motorola who received $58.9M (Anderson *et al.*, 1999). Clearly, the answer to the question "what contributes to the disparity in executive pay across countries?" is not merely individual, firm or industry variables.

Rather, as several scholars suggest, institutional level determinants are also important. For example, Randoy and Nielsen (2002) and Barkema and Gomez-Mejia (1998) suggest that cultural factors influence CEO compensation, whereas Zajac and Westphal (1995) argue that executive pay practices are embedded in societal contexts. However, despite these research calls, systematic modeling of the contextual factors leading to CEO pay are lacking. While multiple country comparisons of pay practices exist (e.g. Abowd and Bognanno, 1995; Conyon and Schwalbach, 1997), little attempt has been made to theoretically explain why CEO pay variance exists. As a first step to do so, it is helpful to set the foundation for such an inquiry by describing macro-level institutions and their effect.

The impact of macro-level institutions on various aspects of firm behavior has been widely recognized within the strategy literature. Examples include the relationships between country environment and corporate diversification strategies (Wan and Hoskisson, 2003), entry mode (e.g. Brouthers, 2002; Kogut and Singh, 1988), corporate political strategies (Hillman and Keim, 1995), the actions of CEOs (Lau, 1998), business strategy (Peng, 2002) and corporate governance (Pedersen and Thomsen, 1999). The common thread among these studies is the emphasis on the macro-level institutional dimensions, such as culture, the legal system or country-level endowments that affect strategic management and decision-making. The impact of institutional variance on governance systems has also been in a series of studies by La Porta and colleagues, who find that country effects affect minority shareholder protection, as well as various other governance mechanisms (La Porta *et al.*, 1997, 1998, 2000; La Porta *et al.*, 1999; Pedersen and Thomsen, 1997; Schleifer and Vishny, 1997).

However, studies on the macro-level determinants of CEO pay using an institutional model are absent from strategic management research. A notable exception is Pennings (1993) who suggests that the informal institutions of individualism and masculinity (Hofstede, Neuijen, Ohayv and Sanders, 1990; Hofstede, 2001) affect CEO pay, yet falls short of providing a full multi-dimensional model of the formal and informal institutional determinants of CEO pay.

Dimensions of the institutional environment influencing CEO pay

North's (1990) institutional economics framework presents institutions and organizations as structural elements of human interaction intended to reduce uncertainty. Uncertainty stems from the complexity of the problems requiring attention, individuals' limitations of information processing and insufficient information (North, 1990). Formal and informal institutions remove some of the uncertainty from human interactions, provide a degree of predictability (Kasper and Streit, 1998), and reduce the cost of transactions within a society (North, 1990). The price paid for the benefits of an institutional framework is a limited set of choices for the actors (North, 1990). (See Chapter 15 for another perspective on national differences in CEO pay.)

North (1990) segments the institutional framework into formal and informal institutions emphasizing the preeminence of social and cultural traditions that form informal institutions. Informal institutions are socially transmitted information and part of a nation's heritage or culture and include customs, social norms, rules and usages accepted by a community. Informal institutions are pervasive and provide a framework for repeated interactions, among others, by sanctioning socially accepted behavior, values and norms, thus reducing the uncertainty inherent in human transactions. Repeated interactions over time result in a set of informal, unwritten rules that eventually become social norms dictating individual and organizational choice (North, 1990). In other words, the importance of certain societal values determines which informal norms are institutionalized. In line with North's thesis, naming uncertainty reduction as a fundamental reason for the existence of institutions, I argue that uncertainty avoidance is an important informal institution affecting CEO pay. Other informal dimensions that affect CEO pay are time horizon and egalitarianism. I discuss each in more detail below.

According to North, formal institutions are extensions of informal institutions that either complement and support informal institutions by lowering the cost of information and monitoring, or modify and replace them (North, 1990). Formal institutions include, among others, the legal tradition (common law or civil law) and dominant ownership patterns of firms examined in this study, as well as equity markets, the system of taxation, the political establishment, civil liberties and so on.

Together formal and informal institutions create a complex, "interconnected web" (North, 1990: 67) that defines the opportunity set of individual actors, giving rise to the incentives and disincentives of political, social and economic exchanges. The institutional complex varies across societies and across time but is relatively stable at any given time within a society (Kasper and Streit, 1998). In other words, as fundamental values differ across societies they give rise to a different set of informal and formal institutions, creating multiple, interdependent equilibria (Kasper and Streit, 1998; North, 1990) and varying incentives or disincentives to the actors (Clark, 1997).

Informal institutions

The five dimensions listed earlier (uncertainty avoidance, time horizon, egalitarianism, the legal system and dominant ownership pattern) form the institutional economics model of CEO pay (see Figure 7.1). This model, consisting of two formal and three informal dimensions, reflects North's (1990) notion of "complex of institutional constraints." Below, I explain each of the five institutions and how they connect to form a model to explain the disparity in CEO pay levels and the ratio of fixed to variable pay across home countries.

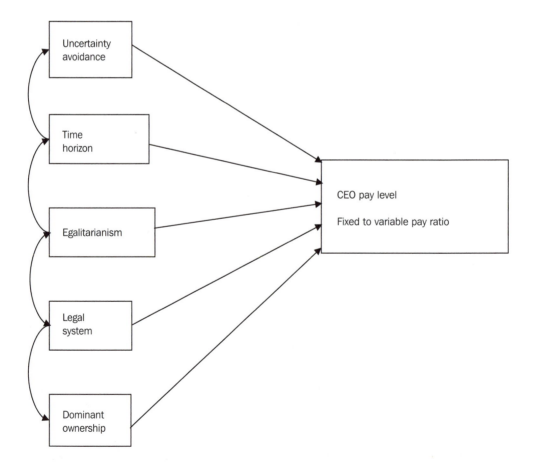

Figure 7.1 An institutional economics model of CEO pay

Two aspects of executive pay are investigated: CEO total pay and the ratio of fixed to variable pay. Fixed pay represents the full amount of the CEO pay package. Total pay consists of fixed pay, which is independent of performance, and variable pay, which may include performance bonuses and equity pay, such as stock, stock options and long-term incentive plans. CEO pay packages also include perquisites and benefits; however, these are beyond the scope of this study. My conclusions are based on the institutional system of the corporation's home country; however, implications for pay design in the multinational context are examined in the discussion section.

Uncertainty avoidance

According to North (1990), the reduction of uncertainty is the fundamental driver of the development of institutions. Uncertainty increases transaction costs and thus, institutions (both formal and informal) act to reduce uncertainty and render the exchange more secure for the parties involved. Berger and Calabrese (1975) and Kasper and Streit (1998) refer to the predictability associated with reductions in uncertainty as a fundamental human need, a correlate of which is the concept of uncertainty avoidance (Hofstede, 2001), defined as "the extent to which members of collectives seek orderliness, consistency, structure, formalized procedures and laws to cover situations in their daily lives" (Sully de Luque and Javidan, 2004: 603).

Uncertainty avoidance is a multi-level construct affecting CEO pay at both the home country institutional level and the organizational level. Uncertainty avoidance is a societal value orientation created as a coping mechanism to handle the anxiety produced by uncertainty (see Sully de Luque and Javidan, 2004: 602–8; also, Hofstede, 2001). However, the term "uncertainty avoidance" was originally coined by Cyert and March (1963) and applied to the organizational level to describe organizational procedures established to minimize uncertainty.

According to Wiseman and colleagues "different forms of compensation have different probabilities of award" (2000: 323). Namely, fixed pay has a very high probability of award, so in an environment with high uncertainty avoidance (low tolerance for uncertainty) a large portion of pay appears in the form of fixed pay, rather than variable pay. For example, Pennings (1993) notes the French have high uncertainty avoidance values, rendering bonus and other variable pay compensation unsuited for motivational purposes.

Beyond differences in the ratio of fixed to variable pay, the total amount of executive compensation also varies greatly across institutional environments. Conyon and Murphy (2000) show that base salaries compose a smaller percentage of total pay for US CEOs than for UK CEOs and that while 82 percent of both groups of CEOs receive variable pay in the form of a bonus, US CEOs receive three times as much as their British counterparts. The differences in option grants are also significant, with US CEOs receiving over 20 times the amount that British CEOs are granted. Conyon and Murphy's findings are in line with the reports of the Towers Perrin international executive surveys (2002, 2005) that indicate the source of the greatest disparity in total pay among CEOs across countries is in variable pay.

A significant stream of research has linked firm risk to CEO compensation levels theorizing a positive relationship (e.g. Beatty and Zajac, 1994; Eisenhardt, 1988; Gray and Cannella, 1997). Because firms face increased uncertainty, managers have less control over firm outcomes, and thus, CEOs must be compensated more. Managers must either take more risk, endangering their own employment, or adopt risk reduction techniques, damaging shareholders' and their own financial interests (Miller *et al.*, 2002). Managers in a high uncertainty avoidance environment will opt to reduce risk resulting in lower returns for the firm, the principals and themselves. Thus, higher uncertainty avoidance in the home country leads to higher ratios of fixed pay to variable pay and lower total CEO pay.

Time horizon

Long versus short-term horizon is an informal institution that refers to the length of the planning horizon (Trompenaars and Hampden-Turner, 1998). Trompenaars and Hampden-Turner (1998) measure an average of past, present and future orientation to see how far into the past, present and future societies' horizons extend. In their study, they find differences in the short- versus long-term horizon across 42 nations and a positive correlation between past, present and future time horizons. Similarly, Hofstede and colleagues (2002) asked MBA students from Anglo, Latin American, Latin European and Asian countries to evaluate the time focus of business "tycoons" and found "tycoons" from India, China and Hong Kong appear to focus on profits "ten years from now" whereas others focus on profits "this year."

While each remains a unique dimension, uncertainty avoidance and time horizon are related (Sully de Luque and Javidan, 2004), such that high levels of uncertainty avoidance at the country level are associated with long-term orientation in organizational practices (Zhao, 2000). The appreciation for building long-term relationships over time in societies with low tolerance for uncertainty explains this inter-relationship (Zhao, 2000). The link between time horizon and CEO compensation manifests itself in several ways. Gomez-Mejia (1994) suggests that the longer a CEO's time horizon, the higher the risk to his or her pay given the increased uncertainties and unpredictability of future events. In a society with a short-term horizon, CEOs whose bonuses are tied to "bottom line" performance measures (e.g. in the US) might be tempted to demonstrate profitability every quarter and show the highest possible earnings each time, regardless of the long-term welfare of the company and shareholders. Supporting this line of research are Grossman and Hoskisson (1998) who note that incentive plans may cause a short-term bias in executives decision-making processes, in particular when compensation is tied to performance.

A second time horizon-related concept, CEO tenure, also affects CEO pay. The necessity to improve performance on a short-term basis, motivated by the quarterly reporting requirements of US public corporations, poses a risk to the CEO's personal wealth and employment, as shown by the findings on CEO compensation and CEO tenure (Hill and Phan, 1991; Mangel and Singh, 1993; Rajagopalan and Prescott, 1990). The evidence on the relationship between CEO tenure and pay is mixed: while most scholars predict a positive relationship between CEO tenure and CEO pay, a few authors propose an inverted U-shaped relationship (e.g. Cordeiro and Veliyath, 2003; Hambrick and Finkelstein, 1995). The short- versus long-term horizon dimension might help reconcile these different predictions. In both short- and long-term horizon oriented societies, CEO tenure initially has a positive relationship to CEO pay as the CEO gains credibility, influence (Hill and Phan, 1991) and builds human capital (Cordeiro and Veliyath, 2003). However, in societies with a short-term time horizon (e.g. the US), long-tenured CEOs are viewed to "outlive their usefulness" after a certain point, becoming liabilities due to the perceived rigidity and limited range of their strategic vision (Cordeiro and Veliyath, 2003). Finally, over time, CEOs might find the pressure to improve performance each quarter exceedingly difficult, which might contribute to decrease in tenure. In long-term horizon oriented societies, the point of diminishing returns is not assumed to exist.

To summarize, in short-term time horizon societies, the combined effects of a focus on short-term goals and the increased risk of turnover force CEOs to maximize their wealth while they can, through negotiating for higher pay and for maximized value of their compensation. In countries with a longer-term horizon, however, CEOs are more likely to consider the long-term welfare of the firm and thus be less threatened by quarterly profit-reporting requirements. Consequently, their immediate wealth maximizing needs are reduced. Therefore, shorter time horizons in the home country lead to lower ratios of fixed pay to variable pay within the CEO pay package and higher total CEO pay.

Egalitarianism

A third key informal institution affecting CEO pay levels is cultural emphasis on hierarchy versus egalitarianism (Smith *et al.*, 2002). Hierarchy refers to the "legitimacy of an unequal distribution of power, roles and resources," while egalitarianism is "the transcendence of selfish interests in favor of voluntary commitment to promoting the welfare of others" (Smith *et al.*, 2002: 193). The egalitarianism versus hierarchy dimension is similar to the power distance dimension known from the work of Hofstede and colleagues (1990, 2001), which is defined as "the degree to which members of an organization or society expect and agree that power should be shared unequally" (Carl *et al.*, 2004: 517). Thus, power distance, like egalitarianism, reflects the extent to which a community accepts authority, power and status differences, and equality/inequality in areas like prestige, wealth and power. In this chapter, I use egalitarianism and the power distance interchangeably, due to their strong conceptual overlap.

Beteille writes that the conventions and rules of society are the "seedbed of what may be called social as opposed to natural inequality" (1977: 4). While inequality appears to be present in any society (Dahrenhof, 1969), what degree of inequality a society considers "fair" differs. For example, in societies where higher degrees of inequality are acceptable, (hierarchical or "high power distance" societies) the status of individuals with more power and authority is unquestioned. In more egalitarian (lower power distance), societies however, individuals enjoy upward mobility based on their unique contributions (Carl *et al.*, 2004).

CEOs are highly visible and powerful individuals in any society. In hierarchical (high power distance) societies, because unequal distribution of power and resources is accepted, levels of CEO pay are likely unquestioned. In highly egalitarian societies, however, cultural expectations pressure CEO pay to be within an "acceptable" level. In Norway, a strongly egalitarian country, legislative and tax policies penalize exceptionally high earners (*Economist*, January 21, 1999). Highly egalitarian Sweden also witnesses social pressures for CEO pay to conform to "acceptable levels," where a CEO's proposed $20M pay package was reduced to $1M due to public outcry (Randoy and Nielsen, 2002). In addition, with its fundamental purpose being to incentivize and reward exceptional performance, variable pay creates inequality and may introduce more uncertainty into the pay package, indicating that the variable pay component of the CEO pay package is likely to carry smaller significance in egalitarian countries. Thus, more egalitarian home countries have higher ratios of fixed pay to variable pay within the CEO pay package and the lower total CEO pay.

Formal institutions

The formal institutions of a country include legal tradition and dominant ownership pattern. Both of these appear to have an affect on the CEO's pay mix and pay level.

Legal tradition

Extensive research shows a country's legal tradition (civil versus common law) tightly linked with various aspects of governance (La Porta *et al.*, 1997, 1998, 1999). Civil law, the most common legal tradition in the world, uses statutes and legal code formulated by legal scholars and legislators. The tradition originally derives from Roman law and comprises the French, the German and the Scandinavian subsystems (La Porta *et al.*, 1998: 1118). Common law, on the other hand, develops via the precedent set by judicial decisions regarding specific cases. Common law originates in England and is predominant in "Anglo" countries (e.g. USA, Australia, United Kingdom) (La Porta *et al.*, 1997). Based on case law, in which past decisions become embedded in the structure of the law (North, 1990), common law evolves as new, previously unseen cases or new facts or from former cases emerge. Civil law, on the other hand, is codified law, created by legal scholars who write statutes.

As noted by North (1990) and Sully de Luque and Javidan (2004), nations institute legal systems to reduce uncertainty. Taking this further, the common law tradition appears to have emerged in countries that have a higher tolerance for uncertainty, indicated by the less prescriptive and emergent nature of this legal system. Conversely, the civil tradition prevails in countries that have somewhat higher societal uncertainty avoidance practices. Further, the relationship between the informal institution of uncertainty avoidance and the legal tradition works in both directions. Namely, common law tradition encourages risk taking by allowing members of the society to make changes on the margins of the institution (North, 1990), because additions to the body of law are created by precedent rather than by legal scholars. Thus, increased risk taking is indirectly encouraged under the common law system, and until a practice, act, product or service is deemed illegal, it will continue to exist.

Regarding matters of corporate governance, La Porta and colleagues' findings about the common law and civil law systems include that the former have better shareholder protection, including that of minority shareholders, while the latter, in particular French civil law countries, have the weakest shareholder protection as well as lowest firm performance. In support of La Porta and colleagues' findings, Hillman and Haynes

(2004) review the legal traditions of common law and civil law countries with respect to board monitoring and resource provision and suggest that they are differentially important across legal system dimensions.

The systematic country-level differences in corporate law, governance systems, investor protection and firm financial performance identified by La Porta and colleagues (1997, 1998, 1999) also affect CEO pay. Common law is less prescriptive than civil law. Consequently, in common law countries, there is more freedom to expand practices in a particular direction and as long as the practice is lawful, it will be tolerated. In civil law countries, conversely, what is acceptable is prescribed in the law, thus individual actors have significantly less opportunity to venture into previously uncharted legal territory. Thus, in common law countries, CEOs have fewer limitations on higher pay. In countries where civil law prevails, however, the legal experts often include sections in the civil code that limit CEO pay. For example, in Argentina and the Philippines (both civil law countries) legal limitations determine maximum CEO pay (Cheffins and Thomas, 2003). Similarly the legal code in some jurisdictions in Germany (German civil law tradition) specifies that executive pay must be "reasonable," implying a maximum upper limit.

Beyond the implications of the prescriptive nature of the civil tradition, the protection of shareholder rights also differs between civil and common law countries. La Porta and colleagues (1997, 1998) note that common law countries provide more and better legal protection to shareholders than do civil law countries. Bryan and colleagues (2002) suggest this added protection is likely to motivate managers to try to increase shareholder wealth and to incentivize the public to have wider equity holdings, eventually leading to larger and more efficient stock markets. Morck and colleagues (2000) indicate that poor protection of shareholder rights weakens the reliability and efficiency of information about stock prices. Thus, a common law legal tradition in the home country decreases the ratio of fixed pay to variable pay within the CEO pay package and exerts upward pressure on total CEO pay.

Dominant ownership pattern

Ownership pattern refers to the predominant type of institution that typically holds claims to firms in a country. According to Hoskisson and colleagues (2001) ownership patterns vary along a continuum of more or less developed economic and transaction environments with widely held public corporations (e.g. in the United States or United Kingdom), through holdings by financial institutions (e.g. Germany or Japan), through tightly held family controlled firms (e.g. Sweden, Spain and France) to business groups (e.g. Korea). The dominant ownership pattern in a country is closely linked to the legal system. Namely, in common law countries, protection of minority shareholders' property rights, well-developed capital markets and lively entrepreneurial activity (Hoskisson *et al.*, 2001) over time has led to the prevalence of widely held corporations. In civil law countries however, as shown by La Porta and colleagues (1997) due to poor investor protection, ownership is concentrated in the hands of either families or the state.

In a study of disciplinary mechanisms as a function of institutional settings, Moerland (1995) proposes a similar segmentation of corporate governance systems linking them to ownership structure and governance mechanisms. According to his terminology, in "network-oriented" systems such as Germany and Japan, banks and financial holding companies exert pressure on corporations through corporate holdings; in Spain, France and Italy, tight family and state ownership discipline managers. In "market-oriented" systems however, such as the USA and the United Kingdom, where 99 percent of large firms (Moerland, 1995) are publicly traded, disciplinary issues are resolved through the equity market.

Apart from base pay and bonus, equity-based compensation in the form of stock and stock options is one of the main components of CEO pay. The intent of the equity pay component of the CEO pay is to resolve agency conflicts by aligning CEO and shareholder interests. However, due to differences in ownership patterns across institutional settings, the amount and proportion of the equity portion of CEO pay also differs across countries. Towers Perrin's (2002) annual global report on executive compensation shows that in countries with widely held public corporations as the dominant ownership pattern, the equity portion of pay is significantly higher than in countries where family, state or bank ownership dominate.

In other words, the "agency conflict" at the heart of the CEO pay issue is resolved differently in countries that have differing ownership patterns. The alignment of CEO and shareholder interests in countries with widely held public corporations occurs through the equity portion of CEO pay, exerting upward pressure on total pay. In other institutional settings where ownership is more tightly held by banks, financial institutions, business groups or families, CEOs have significantly less equity pay in their total compensation or none at all.

Gomez-Mejia and colleagues (2003) note that in family-owned firms, family ownership and the CEO's family membership depresses CEO pay, such that the more concentrated the family ownership the more depressed the pay. The authors also show that over time, non-family member CEOs of family-controlled firms receive higher long-term incentive pay than family CEOs. Gomez-Mejia and colleagues imply that the family ownership structure is more risk averse than the widely held public corporation ownership structure, stating "investors will avoid paying the family executive with equity-based income, as this would give them greater ability to make conservative decisions in an already risk-averse family business context" (2003: 234).

Equity pay is the incentive alignment component of CEO pay, and often referred to as a substitute for monitoring: if strong monitoring mechanisms are in place, incentive alignment may be weaker, and vice versa (Tosi et al., 1997). To the extent that monitoring of the CEO is more difficult in widely held public corporations, the incentive alignment portion of pay (equity) is expected to be more significant in countries where this ownership structure dominates over others. Conversely, under ownership structures where close monitoring is more possible, (e.g. family ownership) the equity portion of pay is likely to be reduced or insignificant. Dominant ownership structure affects total CEO pay through the equity portion of pay, which is the most significant source of CEO pay variance across countries, and a major component of variable pay. Thus, the more dominant widely held public corporations are in the home country the lower the ratio of fixed pay to variable pay within the CEO pay package and the higher the total CEO pay.

Discussion and implications

I argue that certain informal and formal institutional variance across countries affects CEO pay by exerting upward or downward pressure on the level of pay. This argument takes the discussion on CEO pay away from the dominant arguments of individual, firm and industry predictors to consider the importance of country-level contextual variables. In doing so, I begin to fill an often noted and rarely addressed gap in the literature.

In addition, the model of informal and formal institutions that I present extends the mostly US-based and -centered CEO compensation literature to provide an overarching theoretical model to explain CEO pay variance across countries. Empirically, the mostly US-based CEO pay literature indicates firm size as the most significant factor in explaining the variance in CEO pay, with further individual level, firm level and contextual variables (e.g. industry) adding to the model. While these variables might explain some of the variance in CEO pay within one country they carry limited explanatory power across others. The variance in CEO pay across countries may be more readily explained by country-level institutional factors, such as those presented here.

The interconnectedness of informal and formal institutions and their impact on CEO pay has several implications. One of the most significant is whether the model can provide useful information to multinational companies setting executive pay while operating within multiple institutional frameworks (Murphy, 1999; Xu and Shenkar, 2002). There are contradictory theories in the literature regarding this matter. One stream of literature (e.g. Cheffins and Thomas, 2003) proposes that globalization will likely lead to CEO pay convergence, which they equate with the Americanization of pay (i.e. they predict that foreign firms will adopt US pay policies). In Cheffins and Thomas's perspective local institutions will likely yield to "global" institutions, US CEO pay being one of them. The granting of US style stock options for non-US executives in multinational corporations was a common practice pointing in the direction of pay convergence and in 2002 Towers Perrin found only 5 percent of US MNCs used a local pay scheme for executives.

Another stream of literature asserts that such convergence of CEO pay towards US levels and composition is unlikely to occur, due to the power of local, country-level institutions. (See Chapters 10 and 15.) Notable examples to the power of local institutions over convergence are common in egalitarian countries, such as Sweden where CEO pay is public yet social pressure forces it to remain at levels acceptable to the public. Randoy and Nielsen (2002) note that in 1999, the average compensation of S&P 500 CEOs was 475 times higher than the average employees' compensation, whereas for European CEOs of companies similar to the S&P 500, the multiples range from a high of 24 times average worker pay to a low of 11–12 times worker pay in Sweden and Norway. Due to the significant differences in CEO to average worker pay, it is difficult to perceive that convergence at the highest level will occur in the near future, regardless of globalization. Indeed, this is consistent with a recent survey by Towers Perrin (2005), showing 39 percent of MNCs are now shifting to local pay practices for their non-US executives, particularly in granting fewer stock options, which historically constitutes the largest portion of the international CEO pay variance. This move to "re-localize" pay reflects a shift in the US accounting requirements (a formal institution) in that companies will likely have to expense stock options in the future. Therefore, it is difficult to perceive convergence towards US levels in the near future.

Based on North's (1990) arguments, convergence to US pay is a significant change that would require changes in the underlying institutional structure. As North notes, the process of change is "overwhelmingly incremental" since stability is achieved by a set of formal and informal institutions that are nested together. These institutions are not only costly to change, at times tension might develop between formal and informal institutions that may be inconsistent. Informal institutions, being part of human behavior (North, 1990) have "tenacious survival ability," while formal rules are relatively easy to change. In other words, once local norms or rules become part of societal culture, a lock-in based on the interconnectedness of institutions, organizations and the individuals occurs. The lock-in leads to path dependence, dictating future decisions. North's arguments suggest that due to the path dependence present choices become an extension of past choices, all of which are embedded in the institutional environment. Consequently, a compensation model that reflects the institutional configuration of one country is not easily transferred to another. While the pay levels might converge and composition may transfer from US headquarters to local subsidiaries, the practice might clash with local informal institutions.

The imposition of foreign formal rules that collide with local informal institutions is illustrated by the example of the British Empire. In former British colonies, the common law system installed by the British still prevails. However, a legal system imposed on a country instead of organically emerging from its informal institutions is likely to be in conflict at least on some issues with the local culture (Licht *et al.*, 2004). An example is India, where CEO pay is regulated in spite of its common law system. CEO pay is linked to the pay of the President of India, and cannot exceed 11 percent of the company's net profit (Cheffins and Thomas, 2003).

To close, the contributions of this chapter are several. First, it takes a novel view on the area of CEO compensation by expanding the perspective on the determinants of CEO pay to macro-institutional or country-level variables. It brings into light several elements of the macro-institutional environment, performance orientation, time horizon, egalitarianism and legal tradition, which all exert significant up or downward pressure on the level of CEO pay and contribute to our understanding of the international CEO pay variance. The implications of the model presented are significant for multinational corporations subject to multiple country-level institutional pressures, following in the footsteps of Sanders and Carpenter (1998) in an attempt to address the previously "almost totally ignored" area (Barkema and Gomez-Mejia, 1998) of CEO pay and globalization. Finally, it opens the door to reconciling the applicability of the agency argument in the international context.

References

Abowd, J.M. and Bognanno, M. 1995. International differences in executive and managerial compensation. In R. Freeman and L. Katz (eds), *Differences and changes in wage structures*: 67–103. Chicago IL: The University of Chicago Press.

Anderson, S., Cavanagh, J. and Estes, R. 1999. A decade of executive excess: The 1990s. *Sixth Annual Executive Compensation Survey*. United for a Fair Economy, September 1.

Barkema, H.G. and Gomez-Mejia, L.R. 1998. Managerial compensation and firm performance: A general research framework. *Academy of Management Journal*, 41(1): 135–46.

Beatty, R.P. and Zajac, E.J. 1994. Managerial incentives, monitoring and risk bearing: A study of executive compensation ownership and board structure in initial public offerings. *Administrative Science Quarterly*, 39(2): 313–35.

Berger, C.R. and Calabrese, R.J. 1975. Some explorations in initial interaction and beyond: Toward a developmental theory of interpersonal communication. *Human Communication Research*, 1: 99–112.

Beteille, A. 1977. *Inequality among men*. Oxford, UK: Basil Blackwell.

Brouthers, K.D. 2002. Institutional, cultural and transaction cost influences in entry mode choice and performance. *Journal of International Business Studies*, 33(2): 203–22.

Bryan, S.H., Nash, R.C. and Patel, A. 2002. *The equity mix in executive compensation: An investigation of cross country differences*. EFA 2002 Berlin Meetings Presented Paper; EFMA 2002 London Meetings.

Carl, D., Gupta, V. and Javidan, M. 2004. Power distance. In R.J. House, P.J. Hanges, M. Javidan, P.W. Dorfman and V. Gupta (eds), *Culture, leadership and organizations*: 513–63. Thousand Oaks, CA: Sage.

Cheffins, B. and Thomas, R.S. 2003. *Regulation and the globalization (Americanization) of executive pay*. Working paper No. 02–05, Vanderbilt University Law School, Law and Economics, Nashville, TN.

Clark, A. 1997. Economic reason: The interplay of individual learning and external structure. In J.N. Drobak and J.V.C. Nye (eds), *The frontiers of new institutional economics*: 269–90. San Diego, CA: Academic Press.

Conyon, M.J. and Murphy K.J. 2000. The prince and the pauper? CEO pay in the United States and United Kingdom. *The Economic Journal*, 110(467): 640–71.

Conyon, M.J. and Schwalbach, J. 1997. *Pay for performance and board effectiveness in Britain and Germany*. Working paper.

Cordeiro, J.J. and Veliyath, R. 2003. Beyond pay for performance: A panel study of the determinants of CEO compensation. *American Business Review*, 21(1): 56–66.

Cyert, R.M. and March, J.G. 1963. *A behavioral theory of the firm*. Englewood Cliffs, NJ: Prentice Hall.

Dahrenhof, R. 1969. On the origin of inequality among men. In A. Beteille (ed.), *Social inequality: Selected readings*: 16–44. Baltimore, MD: Penguin.

Economist. 1999. Overworked and Overpaid – The American manager. (US edition) January 30: 55.

Eisenhardt, K.M. 1988. Agency and institutional theory explanations: The case of retail sales compensation. *Academy of Management Journal*, 31(3): 488–511.

Gomez-Mejia, L.R. 1994. Executive compensation: A reassessment and a future research agenda. *Research in Personnel and Human Resources Management*, 12: 161–222.

Gomez-Mejia, L., Larraza-Kintana, M. and Makri, M. 2003. The determinants of executive compensation in family-controlled public corporations. *Academy of Management Journal*, 46(2): 226–37.

Gray, S.R. and Cannella, A.A. Jr. 1997. The role of risk in executive compensation. *Journal of Management*, 23(4): 517–40.

Grossman, W. and Hoskisson, R.E. 1998. CEO pay at the crossroads of Wall Street and Main: Toward the strategic design of executive compensation. *Academy of Management Executive*, 12(1): 43–57.

Hambrick, D.C. and Finkelstein, S. 1995. The effects of ownership structure on conditions at the top: The case of CEO pay raises. *Strategic Management Journal*, 16(3): 175–93.

Hill, C.W.L. and Phan, P. 1991. CEO tenure as determinant of CEO pay. *Academy of Management Journal*, 34(3): 707–17.

Hillman, A. and Haynes, K. 2004. Institutional environments, board functions and firm performance. *Academy of Management Meeting*, New Orleans.

Hillman, A. and Keim, G. 1995. International variation in the business-government interface. *Academy of Management Review*, 20(1): 193–214.

Hofstede, G. 2001. *Culture's consequences* (2nd edition). Thousand Oaks, CA: Sage.

Hofstede, G., Neuijen, B., Ohayv, D.D. and Sanders, G. 1990. Measuring organizational cultures: A qualitative and quantitative study across twenty cases. *Administrative Science Quarterly*, 35(2): 286–316.

Hofstede, G., Van Deusen, C.A., Mueller, C.B. and Charles, T.A. 2002. What goals do business leaders pursue? A study in fifteen countries. *Journal of International Business Studies*, 33(4): 785–803.

Hoskisson, R.E., Johnson, R.A., Yiu, D. and Wan, W.P. 2001. Restructuring strategies of diversified business groups. In M.A. Hitt, R.E. Freeman and J.S. Harrison (eds), *The Blackwell handbook of strategic management*: 433–63. Malden, MA: Blackwell Publishers.

Kasper, W. and Streit, M.E. 1998. *Institutional economics*. Cheltenham, UK: Edward Elgar Publishing.

Kogut, B. and Singh, H. 1988. The effect of national culture on the choice of entry mode. *Journal of International Business Studies*, 19(3): 411–32.

La Porta, R., Lopez-de-Silanes, F. and Shleifer, A. 1999. Corporate ownership around the world. *Journal of Finance*, 54(2): 471–517.

La Porta, R., Lopez-de-Silanes, F., Shleifer, A. and Vishny, R. 1997. Legal determinants of external finance. *Journal of Finance*, 52(3): 1131–50.

—— 1998. Law and finance. *Journal of Political Economy*, 106(6): 1113–55.

—— 2000. Investor protection and corporate governance. *Journal of Financial Economics*, 58(1–2): 3–27.

Lau, C. 1998. Strategic orientations of chief executives in state owned enterprises in transition. In M. Hitt, J. Ricart i Costa and R. Nixon (eds), *Managing Strategically in an Interconnected World*: 101–17. Chichester, UK: Wiley.

Licht, A.N., Goldschmidt, C. and Schwartz, S.H. 2004. *Culture, law and corporate governance*. Working paper.

Mangel, R. and Singh, H. 1993. Ownership structure, board relationships and CEO compensation in large US corporations. *Accounting and Business Research*, 23(91): 339–50.

Miller, J.S., Wiseman, R.M. and Gomez-Mejia, L.R. 2002. The fit between CEO compensation design and firm risk. *Academy of Management Journal*, 45(4): 745–56.

Moerland, P.W. 1995. Alternative disciplinary mechanisms in different corporate systems. *Journal of Economic Behavior and Organization*, 26: 17–34.

Morck, R., Yeung, B. and Yu, W. 2000. The information content of stock markets: Why do emerging markets have synchronous stock price movements? *Journal of Financial Economics*, 58(1–2): 215–60.

Murphy, K. 1999. *Executive compensation*. Working paper.

North, D.C. 1990. *Institutions, institutional change and economic performance*. Cambridge, UK: Cambridge University Press.

Pedersen, T. and Thomsen, S. 1997. European patterns of ownership: A twelve-country study. *Journal of International Business Studies*, 28(4): 759–78.

—— 1999. Economic and systemic explanations of ownership among Europe's largest companies. *International Journal of the Economics of Business*, 6(3): 367–81.

Peng, M.W. 2002. Towards an institution-based view of business strategy. *Asia Pacific Journal of Management*, 19(2–3): 251–68.

Pennings, J. 1993. Executive reward systems: A cross-national comparison. *Journal of Management Studies*, 30(2): 261–80.

Rajagopalan, N. and Prescott, J.E. 1990. Determinants of top management compensation: Explaining the impact of economic, behavioral and strategic constructs and the moderating effects of industry. *Journal of Management*, 16(3): 515–38.

Randoy, T. and Nielsen, J. 2002. Company performance, corporate governance and CEO compensation in Norway and Sweden. *Journal of Management and Governance*, 6(1): 57–81.

Sanders, W.G. and Carpenter, M.A. 1998. Internationalization and firm governance: The roles of CEO compensation, top team composition and board structure. *Academy of Management Journal*, 41(2): 158–78.

Schleifer, A. and Vishny, R.W. 1997. A survey of corporate governance. *Journal of Finance*, 52(2): 737–83.

Smith, P.B., Peterson, M.F. and Schwartz, S.H. 2002. Cultural values, sources of guidance and their relevance to managerial behavior. *Journal of Cross-Cultural Psychology*, 33: 188–208.

Sully de Luque, M. and Javidan, M. 2004. Uncertainty avoidance. In R.J. House, P. Hanges, M. Javidan, P. Dorfman and V. Gupta (eds), *Culture, leadership and organizations*: 603–53. Thousand Oaks, CA: Sage.

Tosi, H.L., Katz, J.P. and Gomez-Mejia, L.R. 1997. Disaggregating the agency contract: The effects of monitoring, incentive alignment and term in office on agent decision making. *Academy of Management Journal*. 40(3): 584–602.

Towers Perrin. 2002. *Worldwide remuneration report*.

—— 2005. *Equity incentives around the world*.

Trompenaars, F. and Hampden-Turner, C. 1998. *Riding the waves of culture* (2nd edition). New York: McGraw-Hill.

Wan, W.P. and Hoskisson, R.E. 2003. Home country environments, corporate diversification strategies and firm performance. *Academy of Management Journal*, 46(1): 27–45.

Wiseman, R.M., Gomez-Mejia L.R. and Fugate, M. 2000. Rethinking compensation risk. In B. Gerhart and S. Rynes (eds), *The frontiers of industrial organizational psychology: Compensation in organizations*: 331–50. San Francisco, CA: Jossey-Bass.

Xu, D. and Shenkar, O. 2002. Institutional distance and the multinational enterprise. *Academy of Management Review*, 27(4): 608–18.

Zajac, E.J. and Westphal, J.D. 1995. Accounting for explanations of CEO compensation: Substance and symbolism. *Administrative Science Quarterly*, 40(2): 283–308.

Zhao, J.J. 2000. The Chinese approach to international business negotiation. *Journal of Business Communication*, 37: 209–37.

Shareholders' value maximization and stakeholders' interest

Is CEO long-term compensation the answer?

Carmelo Cennamo

The instrumental stakeholder view of the firm (e.g. Freeman, 1984; Jones, 1995; Jones and Wicks, 1999) maintains that stakeholders play a critical role in affecting a firm's behavior and eventually performance. Beyond providing the firm with the resources it needs, stakeholders are themselves important resources a firm can leverage to build a competitive advantage (Freeman, 1984). Establishing long-term idiosyncratic relationships with its stakeholders may benefit a firm's efficiency, reputation and ultimately performance (see for instance Jones, 1995). Strong and long-term oriented relationships with suppliers, for instance, will make a firm save on bureaucratic and monitoring costs while boosting cooperation. By managing stakeholder relationships, firms could also develop valuable and difficult to imitate capabilities, which are critical superior resources that can be further exploited in other firm activities and operations (Sharma and Vredenburg, 1998). Thereby, according to this view, managing stakeholders' interests and expectations is fundamental for the achievement of superior performance.

Despite the claimed theoretical superiority of the stakeholder management (SM) approach, in practice this model is still not fully implemented and only recently companies have started addressing some of the key stakeholders' claims. It has generally been thought that part of the reason is related to the short-term financial focus of managers. Hence, widening executives' horizon through long-term incentives may appear as a straightforward solution to the problem. Because compensation is one of the most central incentive mechanisms for managerial behavior, long-term compensation schemes (LTC) have indeed been proposed as an incentive and horizon alignment tool (see Kane, 2002). Having their compensation linked to a firm's long-term market value, executives would be induced to focus on strategies with the potential of creating or enhancing such value.

However, despite the mass adoption over the last decade of LTC, mainly in the form of stock option plans, SM has not become the competitive strategic "tool" executives think of to boost a firm's value. If SM increases or facilitates a firm's future prospects, executives should be receiving incentives to take actions toward the firm's stakeholders. Why then is this not the case? Do LTC, in particular stock option plans, provide executives with the incentive of balancing shareholders' and other stakeholders' interests?

This chapter tries to address these questions. In particular, it analyzes the "validity" of stock option plans – the major component of LTC – as the optimal incentive for promoting SM. Notwithstanding the potential benefits of LTC as an incentive alignment, it is argued here that stock option plans may rather fail to accomplish this target for the following reasons. First, because of existing ambiguity over SM linkage to a firm's market value, executives might prefer implementing alternative strategies which are more directly related to performance. Second, long-term compensation, in the form of stock option plans, may be a distortive incentive (for SM) because it might, on the one hand, increase management's discretion over short-term operations beyond alignment benefits, while on the other hand, making it more difficult for directors to assess management's responsibility and contribution to firm value. Third, this reward system may alter managers' risk tolerance, negatively affecting long-term firm value and stakeholders' wealth.

The instrumental stakeholder model

Within stakeholder theorists' conception of the firm as a center of pluralistic interests of individuals "who can affect or be affected by the achievement of the firm's objectives" (Freeman, 1984: 46), a stakeholder "must participate in determining the future direction of the firm in which it has a stake" (Evan and Freeman, 1988: 97). Managing the interdependence of a firm's stakeholders is not only a CEO's duty, but it also represents a potential strategic asset that the management can leverage in order to improve firm's operational efficiency and create value (e.g. Coombs and Gilley, 2005; Jones, 1995). Bureaucratic and transaction costs may, for instance, be lower under SM whereas cooperative effort may increase. The stakeholder-agency view suggests that organizational effectiveness is enhanced when organizations meet the needs of a wide variety of stakeholders (Coombs and Gilley, 2005; Hill and Jones, 1992; Waddock *et al.*, 2002). Accordingly, a CEO can be more generally viewed as a stakeholders' agent and be compensated for maximizing the aggregate value for all stakeholders (share-owning and non-share-owning).

Since managing conflicting stakeholders' interests is a complex task (Hall and Vredenburg, 2005) which involves a high degree of uncertainty, executives able to accomplish it would require to be rewarded for bearing such uncertainty and for their higher capabilities. In this line, Coombs and Gilley (2005: 829) predict that "CEOs simultaneously achieving superior financial performance and stakeholder performance would be compensated most highly." At the same time, executives and, in general, firms engaging in SM may develop valuable and hard to imitate capabilities that could be leveraged in other firm's activities and operations (Sharma and Vredenburg, 1998). On this ground, Freeman (1984) suggests that a firm considering systematically all stakeholders' interests will increase its efficiency and be more likely to outperform rivals. By the same token, Campbell (1997: 446) maintains that stakeholder theory is "fundamental to understanding how to make money in business."

However, defining who (relevant) stakeholders are and how they affect firm's performance remains a practical and major issue for SM implementation. Nonetheless, this ambiguity might be in part responsible for the superior value of SM as a strategic asset. According to the Resource-Based View (e.g. Barney, 1991; Peteraf, 1993; Wernerfelt, 1984), one of the characteristics of a resource being valuable and superior is its *causal ambiguous link* to firm performance. King (2007: 156) interprets causal ambiguity as a "continuum that describes the degree to which decision makers understand the relationships between organizational inputs and results." When this ambiguity is low, competitors might easily imitate and replicate the focal firm's strategy, offsetting its advantage (Barney, 1991; Reed and DeFillippi, 1990). On the other side, when rivals struggle to understand the source of such advantage, it is hard for them to decide what to imitate and how to do it. Idiosyncratic relationships with firm's stakeholders may represent such a resource that competitors struggle to imitate, providing the firm with a superior asset that might eventually enhance performance. However, this advantage comes at a cost, namely a wider managerial discretion. Managing this ambiguity is by definition a non-definable task and a highly uncertain process. Several options are available to the management of the firm, and the actions undertaken to implement SM policies rest ultimately on managers' vision and discretion (Jones and Wicks, 1999; McGuire *et al.*, 2003). In fact, defining and managing a firm's relevant stakeholders is not a standard and easy task.

Mitchell and colleagues (1997) propose to individualize salient stakeholders on the basis of three attributes: stakeholder power, legitimacy and urgency. Only when these three attributes are perceived by managers in stakeholders will salience be high and their claims be accommodated. Yet, this does not solve the trade-off associated with divergent groups of interests. Since stakeholders' salience relies on the perception of companies' managers, a specific stakeholder orientation strategy might fail in managing and meeting the interests and claims of "whoever really counts." Moreover, managers should have enough discretion to decide which claims must be accommodated and which interests must be pursued in particular phases and contingencies. The endogenous and changing form of stakeholders' salience makes management's task hardly definable ex-ante and the causal relation with firm's performance difficult to establish.

Frooman (1999:193) addresses the issue of "managing potential conflict stemming from divergent interests" with a resource dependence approach. The reliance on the external environment produces constraints and control of organizational behavior. The person able to control resources has the power and the ability to influence the strategies of the firm. SM is then a way to understand how stakeholders may influence the firm and a strategy to manage the resulting interdependence. Frooman (1999) develops possible scenarios according to the degree of interdependence existing between the firm and the stakeholder. Stakeholders control the resources through either *withholding strategies* – the stakeholder decides not to allocate the resource any longer – or *usage strategies* – the stakeholder continues to supply the resource but with strings attached. The firm, by knowing in which contingency it operates, should be able to react and contrast stakeholders' strategies accordingly.

SM could, consequently, be conceived as a strategy to react and cope with the changing conditions of the task environment and a way to guarantee to the firm the resources it needs (Pfeffer and Salancik, 1978; Thompson, 1967). In this view, though, it is still difficult to define the appropriate behavior of managers. The goal of SM is quite clear: avoiding disruptions (usually termed in the SM literature as mismanagement) in the process of resources exchange. Still, the causal ambiguity on the link between stakeholders' claims and firm's performance might impede managers understanding of (and decisions on) which factors and resources must be developed or leveraged to address the issue. Although the goal is clear, the way to reach it is highly ambiguous. Several options exist, but managers lack the information on the possible courses of action. Accordingly, reacting to stakeholders' claims and strategies might prove ineffective if managers of the focal firm cannot assess how those claims affect firm's operations and performance.

In a different vein, Jones (1995) posits that the advantage accrues to the firm from a reputational and efficiency effect. By establishing long-term contracts and cooperating with stakeholders, a firm may gain efficiency by saving on transactions and governance costs. Reputation is achieved through policies and decisions that give stakeholders the impression of the firm as a trustable partner. This will induce them to make firm-specific (long-term) investments and enhance cooperation and commitment, which will improve efficiency and flexibility in the firm's operations. Thus, relational contracts will be a substitute for more formal contracts, since trust is a better and more efficient governance form.

Notwithstanding the benefits of relational contracts, namely bureaucratic costs reduction and enhanced flexibility, scholars have documented the contingent limits of such contractual forms. In particular, Carson and colleagues (2006) find that relational contracting proves ineffective to constrain opportunism under ambiguity. In their words, "ambiguity reduces sanctions against opportunism (i.e. punishments), thereby increasing its likelihood of occurring. Similarly, under ambiguity, some cooperative acts will be incorrectly sanctioned as opportunistic, reducing incentives for cooperation" (2006: 1060).

Hence, on the one hand, the SM approach may be beneficial in terms of securing critical resources for the firm by gaining legitimacy in the operating environment or by enhancing reputation and efficiency through trustable relationships. On the other hand, the ambiguity surrounding this strategy also provides management with wider discretion and control over the firm. For this reason, an optimal compensation schedule should be more focused on limiting, or at best *disciplining* such discretion rather than providing further unconditioned discretion, as is likely to be the case under LTC.

This risk clearly emerges in the criticisms scholars have posed on stakeholder theory. According to Argenti (1993: 36–7), for instance, organizations trying to satisfy all stakeholders' claims "are not only at huge competitive disadvantage, they are also . . . literally unmanageable." To Sternberg (1997: 9), "a stakeholder approach would sacrifice not only property rights and accountability, but also the wealth-creating capabilities of business strictly understood." In general, scholars contrasting the instrumental stakeholder view of the firm see the politicization of the decision-making process as a primary outcome of this model and the major threat to value creation (see, for instance, Jensen, 2002).These criticisms of the validity of SM as a superior business model are relevant both from a theoretical and practical point of view, but are not the focus of this chapter. Here, the analysis is restricted to CEOs' incentives to engage in SM. In particular, under scrutiny are long-term compensation schemes (LTC), as this form has been suggested as an optimal mechanism for motivating executives' consideration and promotion of a stakeholder society (Kane, 2002).

SM and the (mis)alignment effects of long-term compensation

A stakeholder oriented firm should be concerned more about long-term value creation for stakeholders in general, rather than strictly focusing on short-term market value for financial investors. Accordingly, its board of directors may be induced to set a long-term compensation schedule, such as stock option plans, in order to align managers' interests with those of stakeholders. Notwithstanding the potential benefits of long-term plans as an alignment incentive, it is argued here that this may be rather a distortive mechanism for several reasons.

Stakeholder management and corporate social responsibility

First, while mismanaging key stakeholders' claims may negatively affect the market value of the firm, claims for the effect of pro-active ("good") SM on the financial value of the firm are rather spurious. Very few studies have analyzed the impact of governance structure on SM or more generally on the corporate social responsibility (CSR) propensity of a firm. However, the extant empirical evidence concerning the effect of LTC is quite clear. Long-term incentives are either associated with poor social performance or have no impact at all on strong social performance (Mahoney and Thorne, 2005; McGuire *et al.*, 2003), and this has been mostly attributed to the missing association of strong corporate social performance (CSP) with the firm's market value (McGuire *et al.*, 2003). Although research has also documented a positive relationship between some individual dimensions of CSR, mostly environmental management and market performance, here under inspection are the effects of the simultaneous management of *all* stakeholders, not a particular class.

Findings of recent studies suggest that the incentive effect of LTC on promoting SM policies beyond the simple avoidance of social wrongdoings is absent without an underlying link between strong actions towards stakeholders and market value (Mahoney and Thorne, 2005; McGuire *et al.*, 2003). The market value of SM may depend on the degree to which its impact on performance is communicated to outsiders (financial analysts, institutional investors and the like). If, in fact, the market is not able to recognize the long-term potential of a firm's SM strategy, its CEO, by documenting how the firm will benefit from SM, can make public critical information that investors need in order to correctly evaluate such strategy. Once this information is reflected in the stock price of the firm, its market value could eventually increase. However, a straightforward pitfall of such a mechanism is that the sustainability of a firm's competitive advantage on SM is jeopardized. Making public how the firm benefits from SM strategy will also allow rivals to discover the firm's source of superior performance. Once this information is released, imitation or counter strategic moves can effectively be put in place by competitors. Hence, if managers have an incentive to release critical information, this will ultimately be detrimental for a firm's competitive advantage. In the long run, the eventual value created through SM may indeed be destroyed.

It should be also noted that stock price, according to the market efficiency hypothesis, is supposed to correctly reflect the present value of future cash flows a firm is expected to generate. Hence, the value of a long-term strategy, if perfectly perceived by the market, is incorporated in the current market value of the firm and not on its future realization. Thereby also a short-term market value contingent pay could (theoretically) induce managers to engage in SM policies, provided that investors recognize its potential and then react positively to its adoption.

Stakeholder management and managerial discretion

The second motivation for arguing that stock options are a distortive mechanism stems from the effects of the greater discretion executives might enjoy. Long-term compensation plans will further increase the difficulty of assessing managers' contribution and responsibility for firm figures. This may widen their discretion on short-term operations as they will not be judged on the resultant contingent performance. Given that SM is a strategy that pays off in the long term, managers are "more free" in the short run to use firm resources according to their vision and expectations. Owing to the ambiguous correlation of this strategy to performance, it is very hard for the board of directors to set and challenge management's behavior (task programmability). Directors lack knowledge and information on the possible course of a management's action. Moreover, there are no objective measures of the impact of SM on firm performance (Tirole, 2001). This greatly complicates the already hard duty of directors to monitor and evaluate a CEO's performance.

Under SM strategy and LTC the board is completely dependent on the management's beliefs and discretion (McGuire *et al.*, 2003). A long-term compensation based on stock options is indeed likely to increase the ambiguity directors face, and consequently the CEO's power. Two main reasons apply here. First, under LTC, given the assumed interest alignment between a CEO and a firm's stakeholders, actions undertaken by the CEO are likely to be interpreted as having a long-term value orientation. In the short term these actions represent investment costs that reduce current performance. When short-term value is already expected to be depressed, CEOs may have unconditioned control over the use of firms' assets as they would not be under the pressure of the contingent low performance. On the other hand, when the exercising date of the holding options approaches, CEOs can be encouraged to take riskier and financially oriented decisions which positively affect the value of the stock options (Deyà-Tortella *et al.*, 2005; Sanders, 2001). Sanders (2001), for instance, argues that stock options induce managers to focus on riskier strategies with higher prospect gains, without paying attention to the potential losses. Managers, indeed, will not, or only in part, bear the cost of these eventual losses.

Moreover, the market value of the firm is influenced by several factors; among others, macroeconomic contingencies, investors' preferences, stochastic shocks or sectoral effects. Therefore such compensation plans do not gauge exclusively a CEO's contribution to the market value of the firm. A firm's stock value can then appreciate irrespective of or beyond a CEO's merit. Given that stock options granted to managers are seldom filtered by these extra factors (Boyer, 2005; Bebchuk and Fried, 2003; Conyon and Murphy, 2000), CEOs can be rewarded for aspects not related to the value created by their strategic decisions. This makes it difficult for a board to assess a CEO's contribution and eventually implement self-correcting mechanisms. Such implications, thus, cast doubts on the optimality (for SM) of this incentive compensation scheme.

More recently, in fact, many authors have started challenging the incentive alignment effect of stock option plans, pointing to the power and entrenchment effect they have generated over this last decade (Boyer, 2005; Bebchuk and Fried, 2003; Conyon and Murphy, 2000). Boyer (2005: 11), with respect to stock options, maintains that "what was supposed to be a rational method of generating value and wealth has become a 'casino economy' whereby everybody tries to get rich as quickly as possible, with little concern for the long-run viability of their strategy." The recent scandals of Enron and WorldCom are usually recalled as evidence of the high risk and pitfalls associated with this incentive scheme. Bebchuk and Fried (2003) argue that CEO compensation is also in part a product of the same agency problem it tries to solve. Though authors acknowledge the desirable incentives equity-based compensation could provide, they emphasize that "the devil, however, is in the details" (2003: 82). They in fact maintain that given the power and control a CEO usually exerts over her/his "controllers" (i.e. the board of directors), CEOs have a great ability to extract rents by obtaining arrangements that are substantially more favorable than what an optimal contract would suggest. The major conjecture of this view is therefore that stock options fail to provide alignment incentives because the details of these plans are highly influenced by the great bargaining power of the CEO. Tosi and colleagues (1999) have indeed suggested that CEOs attempt to acquire discretion and solidify their position through the process of negotiation of their contract.

Stakeholder management and risk allocation

The third reason why stock options are ineffective as an incentive for SM's promotion is related to risk allocation. The main argument stems from the Behavioral Agency Model's prediction that managers, whose compensation is linked to stock option plans, may take more than optimal risk when forecasting sure losses in their option value (Deyà-Tortella *et al.*, 2005; Sanders, 2001; Wiseman and Gomez-Mejia, 1998). The Behavioral Agency Model (BAM) developed by Wiseman and Gomez-Mejia (1998) challenges the widely held assumption that managers are risk averse, and instead proposes that they are in fact risk loving when they anticipate a scenario of sure losses. This is based on the *loss aversion* hypothesis of prospect theory (Kahneman and Tversky, 1979), which proposes that what drives decision making under risk is a psychological factor called *certainty effect*. The inclination of overweighting outcomes which are certain relative to those which are merely probable favors risk-aversion in the domain of gains and risk seeking in the domain of losses.

The BAM has been used, among different applications, to show that stock option plans, as a variable form of compensation, may fail to provide an incentive alignment and is rather a perverse incentive. For example, Deyà-Tortella and colleagues (2005) argue that agency problems will be more pronounced under stock option compensation plans, and the moral hazard of loss-averse managers more exacerbated. It should be noted that, in the spirit of prospect theory, managers would frame prospects as a loss or a gain according to their reference point (which in this case is a specific value-threshold of stock price they expect to realize). Thus, in this model, there is no relationship between executives' prospected losses and firm's actual economic losses. Managers may indeed forecast a loss in their compensation value with respect to what was previously expected when the firm is in fact realizing economic profits.

The model's prediction of managers being risk loving when a scenario of losses is in prospect represents a serious threat for a successful operation of SM strategy. Managers may take too risky decisions in order to recover losses on their stock options value. This perverse incentive can jeopardize the firm's stability, jeopardize the firm's relations with its risk-averse stakeholders, and reduce the potential benefits that could have been derived from a SM strategy.

This riskier posture is consistent with a SM approach. Stakeholders make specific investments in the corporation in expectation of a return going beyond the monthly compensation they receive (Etzioni, 1998). Many of these firm-specific investments may have little value outside the firm. Stakeholders may expect then to be rewarded for the high opportunity cost they bear. When managers take too risky decisions, not only are stakeholders' investments threatened, but also the viability of the firm. Thus, stakeholders' interests may be seriously compromised by the perverse incentive encompassed in stock option compensation plans.

On the cross-national differences of governance and other institutional systems

Several studies (e.g. Campbell, 2007; Gedajlovic and Shapiro, 1998; Schneper and Guillén, 2004) suggest that globally, many governance structures, compensation practices and stakeholder orientations differ from those of US firms. Campbell (2007: 947) maintains that "the tendency toward socially responsible corporate behavior varies across countries . . . the way corporations treat their stakeholders depends on the institutions within which they operate." Unfortunately, most of the research on CEO compensation and stakeholder management or corporate social responsibility is conducted in single country, mostly the USA. Some papers have undertaken such analysis for Canadian firms (e.g. Mahoney and Thorne, 2005), while others have analyzed cross-national differences in stakeholder rights and corporate governance (e.g. Schneper and Guillén, 2004). However, these studies, along with a few other exceptions, represent little empirical evidence of the phenomenon in non-US firms. This is at once surprising and disappointing. It is surprising because anecdotal evidence and existing academic research show that stakeholder orientation, compensation policies and their effects on CEO's incentives differ widely across countries, given the different national legislations and institutional systems companies are embedded into (see for instance Gedajlovic and Shapiro (1998) for a cross-national comparison of corporate governance; and Campbell (2007) for a discussion of the institutional conditions under which socially responsible corporate behavior is likely to occur).

This lack of research is then disappointing because most of the time findings of US-based studies about corporate governance dimensions are translated in codes of "good governance practices" and generalized to other contexts and countries without paying much attention to the different governance conditions and institutional characteristics firms, in countries other than the USA, are operating in. For instance, the governance structure of UK and US firms is usually presumed to be fairly similar, as well as the national mindset and culture. This implies that governance mechanisms are expected to be similar in those countries and exert effects in the same way. Nevertheless, differences exist; for example, in the United Kingdom boards of directors are more independent than in US firms, takeovers are not as frequent as in the USA, ownership is less dispersed in UK companies (though it is still high compared to average ownership dispersion of companies in other European countries), and stock option remuneration is not as dominant in CEOs' compensation as it is in the USA (Gedajlovic and Shapiro, 1998). See Table 8.1 for a cross-national comparison of corporate governance mechanisms.

The compensation schedule is but one incentive mechanism of the governance system. Using incentives might be heavily preferred and employed in companies characterized by dispersed and passive ownership, more independent boards (such as the American, and to a lesser extent the British corporations), and in countries (USA, United Kingdom and to a less degree Canada) where external monitoring by the market works quite efficiently. However, companies with high levels of ownership concentration and more independent boards (such as those of Japanese and German firms) might rely more on tight control and internal monitoring systems to effectively induce management towards a stakeholder orientation and less self-interested decisions.

When market control (e.g. takeovers) does not constitute a threat to effectively discipline management, ownership concentration is a natural answer to the principal–agent problem. Denis and McConnell (2003: 26), in reviewing studies on international corporate governance, notice that "without strong protection of investor rights, firms do not have the luxury of developing optimal firm-specific governance systems. Concentrated ownership is a *necessity*" (italic added). Corporate governance will then move from

Table 8.1 Cross-national comparison of corporate governance characteristics

Governance variables	US	UK	Germany and Japan	Italy and Spain
Ownership dispersion	Very high	High	Low	Very low
Ownership identity	Individuals, pension and mutual funds	Pension and mutual funds	Banks, corporate	Family, banks, corporate
Board of directors	Managers, outsiders	Managers, outsiders	Owners, workers	Family-owners, outsiders
Shareholders' power	Low	Low	High	Very high
Takeovers	High	High	Low	Low
Compensation				
Fixed salary	Relatively low	Moderate/high	Relatively high	Relatively high
Bonus	Moderate/high	Moderate/high	Moderate	Moderate/high
Stock options	High	Moderate	Low (increasing)	Very low
Stakeholder orientation	Low	Moderate	Very high	high

Source: The table is mainly drawn from Gedajlovic and Shapiro (1998: 537). Information on Japan, Italy and Spain has been added on the base of anecdotal and academic evidence. Data on CEO compensation structure across countries are re-elaborated mainly from Hamori and Kakarika (2007).

external to internal monitoring systems, with large shareholders and blockholders playing a central role. In line with this perspective, Schneper and Guillén (2004) consider hostile takeovers a function of legally institutionalized stakeholder power. In countries where shareholder rights are more protected, hostile takeovers increase in frequency, whereas they decrease in those systems where workers' and banks' rights are protected. In countries where institutions (legal and not) are centered more on stakeholders rather than simply shareholders,

> to discipline managers, corporations place greater emphasis on internal mechanisms such as boards of directors that exhibit broad stakeholder participation, including representation from labor, creditors and regulatory agencies. Countries labeled as stakeholder-oriented are characterized by the rare occurrence of hostile takeovers.
>
> (Schneper and Guillén, 2004: 268).

In Germany and Japan (and in other European countries) workers and banks play a central role in industrial relationships. For example, in Germany "strong labor participation in the supervisory board complements blockholders who actively monitor management" (Jackson, 2005: 422).

In institutional systems, firms rely more on internal governance mechanisms. Because external market monitoring is barely congruent with the institutions supporting the capitalist structure of the country, ownership concentration and stakeholder participation may represent a more efficient governance system. When corporate governance is structured this way, monitoring and alignment of interests are presumably higher than in that of the market-oriented governance system. As a consequence, compensation incentives are deemed not relevant and are required to a lesser extent. Both factors may explain the lower level of LTC in CEOs' compensation of European firms and their higher stakeholder orientation. Because incentive effects of compensation are limited, stakeholder policies and the orientation of European firms may generally be affected by other factors, such as institutional and powerful stakeholders' pressure, or owners' preferences.

Other countries have unique institutions. In Italy and Spain, for instance, family businesses represent the skeleton of the industrial system, with firm networks and clusters being the normal organizational production mode. Family-owners' preferences, interlocking positions and family reputation matter and may affect a firm's stakeholder orientation more than a formal governance system. Though Denis and colleagues (2006) in their US-based analysis of the relationship between incentive compensation (stock options) and securities fraud allegations found a positive association, they acknowledge that such a relationship is also influenced by the firm's ownership structure (and identity). They further found that the sensitivity of fraud and equity-based compensation is stronger in firms with large outside blockholders and institutional ownership. In the case of family-owned firms, because the reputation of the family and its legitimacy in the local operating environment is at stake (Roberts and Dowling, 2002), family-owners are willing to put effort into exerting tight control on management's activity and decisions in order to avoid the negative consequences to the family name (and business) derived from corporate irresponsible activity (Adams, Taschian and Shore, 1996; Dyer and Whetten, 2006). Moreover, this family concern may not only limit "negative" or socially irresponsible corporate actions, but may also be a driver for stakeholder oriented policies (SM). Berrone and colleagues (2007) have "surprisingly" found that the environmental performance of US family-controlled public corporations is higher than non-family firms. They also found that the relative sensitivity towards the environment increases with the degree of local embeddedness and family ownership, whereas long-term CEO pay incentives do not lead to an increase in environmental performance. In countries such as Italy and Spain (where firm embeddedness in local communities, networks and production clusters is a critical factor for the viability and success of the firm, and where family ownership and management is so central to the economic system), SM and more generally corporate social responsible behavior may represent the "new tool" for further establishing the family leadership and reputation within the network (business and social) in which it is embedded. In countries where family power and centrality are infused in the national culture and institutions, ownership identity and preferences may then be the underlying drivers of a firm's policies, strategy and behavior (Thomsen and Pedersen, 2000), irrespective or beyond other governance mechanisms.

Conclusion

The above discussion leads then to several questions. In countries where ownership concentration, and in particular family ownership, is prevalent, is a firm's stakeholder orientation *just* the result of owners' preferences? Does SM represent, to those owners (and their firms), a tool for gaining legitimacy and reputation in the operating environment and establishment? If this is so, how do they *induce* CEOs to take responsible actions? Stock option compensation seems to not be "in line" with this type of ownership-governance. Within firms with high ownership concentration or family control, the alignment of management's interests with those of the controlling shareholders is facilitated by the tighter control of those shareholders (Fama and Jensen, 1983a, 1983b) and/or by the clearer strategic visions and objectives infused and diffused into the firm by the controlling group (Jensen and Meckling, 1995). Moreover, given the general risk-aversion of family-owners and shareholders with large stakes, in those firms risky activity and incentives for risk-taking decisions are expected to be limited. What kind of compensation incentive do family and high concentrated firms use for motivating the CEO to act according to owners' preferences and the family reputation associated to the business they run? All the arguments presented suggest that for these firms/countries compensation alone is an insufficient explanatory variable for firm's posture towards stakeholders. How and which other factors influence CEOs' decisions is an open question requiring deeper inspection.

More research is needed on the intra-governance dimensions and institutional effects on CEOs' behavior and firms' stakeholder management. Concerning the strategic compensation system however, a potential solution to the incentive problem may rest on anchoring part of executive compensation to objective parameters reflecting a firm's strategic orientation to stakeholders. This could balance managers' exclusive attention to financial performance by forcing them to focus also on stakeholder indicators. Notwithstanding the multi-task problem highlighted by Tirole (2001), a well-structured compensation system of this form may indeed provide the management with the "right" discretion and incentive to consider both shareholder's value and other stakeholders' interests. Berrone and Gomez-Mejia (see Chapter 16) have proposed a framework in this direction. This is a good starting point and future research should explore forms of incentive mechanisms, and other institutions, that can correctly induce managers to consider the welfare of groups of firms' stakeholders beyond powerful shareholders and executives themselves.

References

Adams, J., Taschian, A. and Shore, T. 1996. Ethics in family and non family owned firms: An exploratory study. *Family Business Review*, 9: 157–70.
Argenti, J. 1993. *Your organization: What is for it?* New York: McGraw Hill.
Barney, J.B. 1991. Firm resources and sustained competitive advantage. *Journal of Management*, 17: 99–120.
Bebchuk, L.A. and Fried, J.M. 2003. Executive compensation as an agency problem. *Journal of Economic Perspectives*, 17(3): 71–92.
Berrone, P., Cruz, C., Gomez-Mejia, L. and Kintana, M.L. 2007. Governance and environmental performance in family-controlled public corporations. *Working paper*: 1–43.
Boyer, R. 2005. From shareholder value to CEO power: The paradox of the 1990s. *Competition & Change*, 9(1): 7–47.
Campbell, A. 1997. Stakeholders: The case in favor. *Long Range Planning*, 30: 446–49.
Campbell, J. L. 2007. Why would corporations behave in socially responsible ways? An institutional theory of corporate social responsibility. *Academy of Management Review*, 32: 946–67.
Carson, S.J., Madhok, A. and Wu, T. 2006. Uncertainty, opportunism, and governance: The effects of volatility and ambiguity on formal and relational contracting. *Academy of Management Journal*, 49(5): 1058–77.
Conyon, M. J. and Murphy, K.J. 2000. The prince and the pauper? CEO pay in the US and UK. *Economic Journal*, 110: F640–71.
Coombs, J.E. and Gilley, K.M. 2005. Stakeholder management as a predictor of CEO compensation: Main effects and interactions with financial performance. *Strategic Management Journal*, 26: 827–40.
Denis, D.J., Hanouna, P. and Sarin, A. 2006. Is there a dark side to incentive compensation? *Journal of Corporate Finance*, 12: 467–88.
Denis, D.K. and McConnell, J.J. 2003. International corporate governance. *Journal of Financial & Quantitative Analysis*, 38(1): 1–36.
Deyà-Tortella, B., Gomez-Mejia, L.R., DeCastro, J. and Wiseman, R. 2005. Incentive alignment or perverse incentives? A behavioral view of stock options. *Management Research*, 3: 109–20.
Dyer, G.W. and Whetten, D.A. 2006. Social responsibility: Preliminary evidence from the S&P500. *Entrepreneurship Theory and Practice*, 30: 785–802.
Etzioni, A. 1998. A communitarian note on stakeholder theory. *Business Ethics Quarterly*, 8: 679–91.
Evan, W.M. and Freeman, R.E. 1988. A stakeholder theory of the modern corporation: Kantian capitalism. In T. Beauchamp and N. Bowie (eds), *Ethical theory in business*: 75–93. Englewood Cliffs, NJ: Prentice-Hall.
Fama, E.F. and Jensen, M.C. 1983a. Separation of ownership and control. *Journal of Law and Economics*, 26: 301–25.
——— 1983b. Agency problems and residual claims. *Journal of Law and Economics*, 26: 327–47.
Freeman, R.E. 1984. *Strategic management: A stakeholder approach*. Boston, MA: Pitman.
Frooman, J. 1999. Stakeholder influence strategies. *Academy of Management Review*, 24: 191–205.
Gedajlovic, E.R. and Shapiro, D.M. 1998. Management and ownership effects: Evidence from five countries. *Strategic Management Journal*, 19: 533–53.
Hall, J. and Vredenburg, H. 2005. Managing stakeholder ambiguity. *MITSloan Management Review*, 47(1): 11–13.
Hamori, M. and Kakarika, M. 2007. External labor market strategy and career success. A comparison of CEO career paths in Europe and in the United States. *Working paper*: 1–30.
Hill, C.W.L. and Jones, T.M. 1992. Stakeholder-agency theory. *Journal of Management Studies*, 29: 131–54.

Jackson, G. 2005. Stakeholders under pressure: Corporate governance and labor management in Germany and Japan. *Corporate Governance: An International Review*, 13: 419–28.

Jensen, M.C. 2002. Value maximization, stakeholder theory, and the corporate objective function. *Business Ethics Quarterly*, 12: 235–56.

Jensen, M.C. and Meckling, W.H. 1995. Specific and general knowledge and organization structure. *Journal of Applied Corporate Finance*, 8(2): 4–18.

Jones, T.M. 1995. Instrumental stakeholder theory: A synthesis of ethics and economics. *Academy of Management Review*, 20: 404–37.

Jones, T.M. and Wicks, A. 1999. Convergent stakeholder theory. *Academy of Management Review*, 24(2): 208–21.

Kahneman, D. and Tversky, A. 1979. Prospect theory: an analysis of decision making under risk. *Econometrica*, 42: 262–91.

Kane, E.J. 2002. Using deferred compensation to strengthen the ethics of financial regulation. *Journal of Banking and Finance*, 26: 1919–33.

King, A.W. 2007. Disentangling interfirm and intrafirm causal ambiguity: A conceptual model of causal ambiguity and sustainable competitive advantage. *Academy of Management Review*, 32: 156–78.

Mahoney, L.S. and Thorne, L. 2005. Corporate social responsibility and long-term compensation: Evidence from Canada. *Journal of Business Ethics*, 57: 241–53.

McGuire, J., Dow, S. and Archgeyd, K. 2003. CEO incentives and corporate social performance. *Journal of Business Ethics*, 45: 341–59.

Mitchell, R.K., Agle, B.R.and Wood, D.J.1997. Toward a theory of stakeholder identification and salience: Defining the principle of who and what really counts. *Academy of Management Review*, 22: 853–86.

Peteraf, M.A. 1993. The Cornerstones of Competitive Advantage: A Resource-Based View. *Strategic Management Journal*, 14: 179–91.

Pfeffer, J. and Salancik, G.R. 1978. *The external control of organizations*. New York: Harper & Row.

Reed, R. and DeFillippi, R.J. 1990. Causal ambiguity, barriers to imitation, and sustainable competitive advantage. *The Academy of Management Review*, 15: 88–102.

Roberts, P.W. and Dowling, G.R. 2002. Corporate reputation and sustained superior financial performance. *Strategic Management Journal*, 23: 1077–93.

Sanders, W.G. 2001. Behavioral responses of CEO's to stock ownership and stock option pay. *Academy of Management Journal*, 44: 477–92.

Schneper, W.D. and Guillén, M.F. 2004. Stakeholder rights and corporate governance: A cross-national study of hostile takeovers. *Administrative Science Quarterly*, 49: 263–95.

Sharma, S. and Vredenburg, H. 1998. Proactive corporate environmental strategy and the development of competitively valuable organizational capabilities. *Strategic Management Journal*, 19: 729–53.

Sternberg, E. 1997. The defects of stakeholder theory. *Corporate Governance: An International Review*, 5: 3–10.

Thompson, J. 1967. *Organizations in action*. New York: McGraw-Hill.

Thomsen, S. and Pedersen, T. 2000. Ownership structure and economic performance in the largest European companies. *Strategic Management Journal*, 21: 689–705.

Tirole, J. 2001. Corporate governance. *Econometrica*, 69(1): 1–35.

Tosi, H.L., Gomez-Mejia, L.R., Loughry, M.L., Werner, S., Banning, K., Katz, J., Harris, R. and Silva, P. 1999. Managerial discretion, compensation strategy, and firm performance: The case for the ownership structure. In G.R. Ferris (ed.), *Research in Personnel and Human Resources Management*, vol. 17: 163–208. Stanford, CT: JAI Press.

Waddock, S., Bodwell, C. and Graves, S. 2002. Responsibility: The new business imperative. *Academy of Management Executive*, 16: 132–48.

Wernerfelt, B. 1984. A resource-based view of the firm. *Strategic Management Journal*, 5: 171–80.

Wiseman, R. and Gomez-Mejia, L.R. 1998. A behavioral agency model of managerial risk taking. *Academy of Management Review*, 25: 133–52.

A global perspective on executive compensation

9

Pascual Berrone and Jordan Otten

Executive compensation research has a long tradition. Indeed, top management pay issues have attracted both researchers and popular press for at least 80 years (e.g. Taussig and Baker, 1925) and have generated an enduring debate across different fields (Barkema and Gomez-Mejia, 1998; Gomez-Mejia and Wiseman, 1997; Werner and Ward, 2004).

The dominant paradigm in this line of inquiry is the perfect contracting thesis as introduced by Jensen and Meckling (1976). This approach, most often simply referred to as agency theory, is based on an economic framework in which contracting and pricing mechanisms serve as the mechanisms by which executive pay is set. Executive pay is set on the basis of arm's length contracting between shareholders, or their representatives, and management. A positive relationship between executive compensation and firm economic performance is one of the standard predictions of agency theory. Pay-for-performance rewards to managers are meant to align the interest of the manager with that of the shareholder since these rewards provide incentives to managers to initiate strategies that boost future economic performance (Eisenhardt, 1989; Fama and Jensen, 1983; Jensen and Meckling, 1976). This line of research is more popularly known as "pay-performance-sensitivity" research (Gomez-Mejia and Wiseman, 1997).

However, the large body of empirical literature surrounding this relationship has only provided weak support for this link at best. For instance, the authors of what is perhaps the biggest study in the field (Jensen and Murphy, 1990b), which considered a total of 10,400 CEO years of compensation and performance data, indicated disappointment for the low pay for performance sensitivity found. Their finding indicated that for every $1,000 change in firm value, the CEO's salary changes by 2 cents. More recently, Tosi and colleagues (2000) conducted a meta-analytic review (137 articles or unpublished manuscripts) to test the relationship between firm size, performance and CEO compensations. Results of this study indicated that firm size accounted for more than 40 percent of the variance in total CEO pay, while firm performance only explained less than 5 percent of the variance. As a whole, firm economic performance has appeared as a weak determinant of executive compensation. Not surprisingly, the failure to identify a robust relationship between executive compensation and firm performance led Gomez-Mejia (1994) to compare this relationship to the search for the "Holy Grail."

Given this damning evidence, some scholars have cast doubts about the true value of agency theory as a valuable framework to understand executive pay (see Gomez-Mejia and Wiseman, 2007; Lubatkin *et al.*, 2005 for a related discussion on the topic) while others have made a call for a contextual and contingency analysis of executive compensation in order to make relevant contributions to the field (Barkema and Gomez-Mejia, 1998; Gomez-Mejia, 1994; Gomez-Mejia and Wiseman, 1997).

As an answer to this call, this chapter offers a global analysis of the internal and external influences on executive pay. More specifically, we discuss influences at three levels. First, we investigate influences at the individual level (or the impact of managerial discretion on pay). We follow Bebchuk and Fried (2004) and others (Finkelstein and Boyd, 1998; Finkelstein and Hambrick, 1989; Grabke-Rundell and Gomez-Mejia, 2002; Hallock, 1997; Jensen and Murphy, 2004) to argue that managerial discretion plays an important role in pay setting practices. This must be seen in sharp contrast with the dominant perfect contracting approach, as in this paradigm managerial discretion is theoretically ruled out as real possible behavior (Grabke-Rundell and Gomez-Mejia, 2002).

Second, we describe influences at the organizational level (or the definition of the organizational goals and role of board of directors in setting pay policies). In this sense, we argue that the setting of organizational goals may go well beyond the maximization of shareholder value (which is the sole corporate purpose under the agency perspective) since the interests of *all* stakeholders should be taken into account to achieve the long term success of the firm. Moreover, we question the *altruistic* role of board of directors as a trustworthy representative of shareholders' interests. In the same way as managers have discretion, board members enjoy leeway to pursue other goals than those of shareholders, thus the board of directors can influence the pay setting process.

Third, we account for the influences at the institutional level (or the importance of national context in the pay setting process). We take up the issue of the observable variance in pay levels and structures that exist not only between firms in the same national context, but also across these contexts. When adhering to the dominant paradigm, rooted in neoclassical economic theory, ultimately market forces are argued to lead to similar pay levels and structures for similar executives employed by similar firms. This market clearing is however not supported by observable pay practices. Executive pay levels and structures differ greatly within and across countries. These differences do not seem to disappear over time and still exist when controlling for known firm-level indicators of executive pay, such as firm size, performance and executives' human capital (Abowd and Bognanno, 1995; Conyon and Murphy, 2000; Kaplan, 1994; Tosi *et al.*, 2000; Tosi and Greckhamer, 2004; Zhou, 1999).

The problems of the classical approach to executive compensation

Executive pay is a central issue in the debate on corporate governance. Observing executive pay means observing the fundamental governance processes of an organization (Hambrick and Finkelstein, 1995). To unravel these governance processes and to provide explanations for executive pay, by far most of the research on executive pay makes use of the perfect contracting thesis. Based on the assumption of divergence in interests between firm owners (principals) and firm management (agents), and given that the firm's goal is to maximize value for the owners, executive pay is seen as a "tool" to alleviate agency problems. Because managers have the delegated control over firm resources and because their wealth at risk is tightly linked to the firm by which they are employed, they are in the position to use firm resources in favor of their own interests. Firm owners on the other hand can spread their wealth at risk across multiple firms (Fama, 1980). To solve the problem of divergence of interests between firm owners and management, management is bonded to the firm by an explicit "optimal" contract (Jensen and Meckling, 1976). In order to make sure that agents uphold the contract and behave accordingly, and of central concern in the executive pay literature, it is important to formulate outcome based contracts. As market forces on the labor market for executives set the level of pay, it is a matter of how to pay executives that matters, rather than how much to pay them (Jensen and Murphy, 1990a).

This dominant conception of executive pay has triggered numerous empirical studies in search for a link between executive pay and corporate performance (Tosi *et al.*, 2000). After all, an observable positive pay-performance relationship would show that it is doable for shareholders to write efficient contracts and that managerial behavior can be influenced by incentives. In other words, a positive relationship would indicate that the delegated control executives have over firm resources is put to work to maximize shareholder value.

Unfortunately, after several decades of research, specialists in the area are still struggling to find positive pay-performance relationships as they are rarely observed in practice. Thus, a first problem with this line of research is that the overall weak relationship could indicate that pay-performance linkages are too weak to support arguments of incentive alignment between principals and agents and thus show evidence against the dominant approach (e.g. Jensen and Murphy, 1990b). The still dominant use of the perfect contracting in combination with debatable empirical tests of the theory have led us into a "blind alley" to explain the executive pay phenomenon (Gomez-Mejia, 1994).

A second problem with this line of research is that the focus on the perfect contracting thesis of agency theory has taken up so much of the field's research capacity in this area that it has rapidly exhausted other possibly fruitful research streams. Despite several previous attempts to use other theoretical frameworks (e.g. Finkelstein and Hambrick, 1988; Gomez-Mejia and Wiseman, 1997; see Balsam, 2002; Gomez-Mejia, 1994; Otten, 2007 for overviews of theoretical approaches), the dominant paradigm has been and still is the perfect contracting approach. Leading experts dare to stress, however, that we are reaching the explanatory limits of this paradigm (e.g. Bebchuk and Fried, 2004; Tosi *et al.*, 2000), whereas we have collectively left other, perhaps more promising, ways of approaching the problem of executive pay underexplored. As Bebchuk and Fried (2004) argue, scholars often come up with clever explanations for pay practices that appear to be inconsistent with the dominant paradigm. "Practices for which no explanation has been found have been considered 'anomalies' or 'puzzles' that will ultimately either be explained within the paradigm or disappear" (Bebchuk and Fried, 2004: 3).

Managerial discretion and executive pay setting practices: the individual level

At the heart of the arm's length contracting approach lies the assumption that the firm is considered to be a "nexus of contracts" (Alchian and Demsetz, 1972; Jensen and Meckling, 1976). Such a view considers that all decisions are made *ex-ante* and executed *ex-post*. Thus, the designer of the contract anticipates all possible future problems and conflicts *ex-ante* and therefore no problems exist *ex-post* (see van Oosterhout, 2007 and Zingales, 1998 for a discussion). Moreover, in the perfect contracting thesis, the governance objective function of the firm is to maximize the value for its owners. Negotiations and bargaining over executive pay is assumed to be set with this goal in mind. The underlying assumptions of rational maximizing behavior of the actors involved in this view would ultimately lead to a unique optimal contract and outcomes that are guaranteed to be achieved (March and Olsen, 1984). Managerial discretion is thereby ultimately ruled out as real possible behavior (Grabke-Rundell and Gomez-Mejia, 2002). Discretion (simply defined as the latitude of actions of executives and the individual's set of responses available which influence the context) is theoretically ruled out, because inefficient behavior (i.e. a boundedly rational behavior that has sub-optimal effects for shareholder value) is instantly sectioned by others in their own rational pursuit of maximizing their self-interests facilitated by pricing and market mechanisms. As Bebchuk and Fried (2003, 2004) rhetorically argue, why would an executive sign a contract based on the interests of the firm's owners if the contract is needed to overcome the interest misalignment in the first place?

Conversely, an incomplete contracting view on executive pay (see e.g. Baker *et al.*, 2002; Kidder and Buchholtz, 2002; Rosen, 1985) argues that a relational or implicit contract exists between an individual and another party. The contract is argued to be composed of the individual's beliefs about the nature of the exchange agreement and tends to rely on principles of generalized reciprocity. The contract is an individual's personal set of reciprocal expectations of his or her obligations and entitlements which do not necessarily have to be mutually agreed upon between the contractors (Kidder and Buchholtz, 2002). In this respect, Baker and colleagues (2002) argue that a contract is composed of informal agreements and unwritten codes of conduct that affect individuals' behavior. The contract is based on trust and the common beliefs of the parties regarding fairness and sense of justice. The job characteristics of executives and the nature of their positions are argued to create a relational psychological contract. Executive pay is in this respect seen as a symbol that reflects appreciation, accomplishment and dignity (Kidder and Buchholtz, 2002).

Adhering to the notion that written contracts can never be "perfect," and thus are at least partly based on and/or complemented by the notion of implicit agreements, has major consequences for the way we can explain executive pay. Namely, it emphasizes possible managerial discretion when executives negotiate their own pay. Executives, and each and any other individual such as shareholders, have their own set of beliefs, attitudes and perceptions about the incomplete explicit contractual relationship (cf. North, 2005). The differences between peoples' attitudes provide room for bargaining and the use of discretion.

Executives have their own individual notions and attitudes about the contract and thus face discretion when negotiating and signing the contract. Setting executive pay is therefore not the solution to the problem, but is in fact a representation of the agency problem itself (Bebchuk and Fried, 2003, 2004). An outcome based contract based on shareholders interests does not resolve this issue. Outcomes are unsure and can be influenced by unexpected events. Put differently, the *ex-ante* explicit contract cannot specify, predict and anticipate all possible future outcomes and resolve all disputes and bargaining processes about the distribution of quasi rents (Zingales, 1998). It is clear that market forces are not able to (immediately) section or influence all possible behaviors, especially not when bilateral interdependencies exist between the contractors and when investments are sunk (Roe, 2003; Shleifer and Vishny, 1997; Williamson, 1985, 1996; Zingales, 1998). Also, well known fraudulent cases indicate that executives are in a position to influence corporate decision making and firm outcomes with sub-optimal effects for shareholders (Bebchuk and Fried, 2004; Frey, 1997; Frey and Osterloh, 2005). In fact, the lack of evidence behind the link between pay and performance certainly does not support the prescription of agency theory. Ironically, it can be interpreted as evidence favoring one of its key assumptions: managers are likely to pursue private goals that deviate from and conflict with the objectives of the principal, which is a reflection of their discretion.

The actors involved in the pay setting process can perceive the importance of the different pay antecedents differently. They can attribute different weights to these antecedents when deciding on executive pay. The reflection of the importance of, for instance, firm size (or growth), industry, economic performance, executive human capital and firm specific corporate strategy can lead to specific weights to the antecedents and subsequently to different pay levels and structures across firms. Many of these antecedents have been subject of empirical studies (see for extensive overviews Murphy, 1999 and Gomez-Mejia and Wiseman, 1997). However, the numerous empirical studies on determinants of executive pay have resulted in many conflicting results and subsequently debates around theoretical implications and interpretations of these mixed results are common features in the executive pay literature. Possible causes of the mixed results and different interpretations could be the use of different estimation techniques, different datasets, differences in the degrees to which the whole or parts of the pay mix are taken into account, or different definitions of the variables used (Agarwal, 1981; Ciscel and Carroll, 1980; Finkelstein and Boyd, 1998; Gomez-Mejia, 1994; Murphy, 1999; Rosen, 1990; Schmidt and Fowler, 1990). Putting discussions around different datasets and other research methodologies aside, the different results of studies may also (partly) be attributed to a more conceptual issue. The different results could be explained by the variance in possible systematic unobserved specific factors. An explanation could be that differences in pay across comparable executives employed by comparable firms is due to the specific discretionary positions those individuals have when decisions on pay for specific executives are made. These individuals, although possibly constrained by market forces and other corporate governance mechanisms, could use their discretion in the pay setting process. Thus, the individuals' specific discretionary conditions could explain why under certain conditions given pay practices lead to different outcomes.

Corporate purpose and board of directors: the organizational level

Recognizing that managerial discretion influences compensation and that executives do not have discretion to use firm resources for personal gains only (opportunism) but also have the delegated control over resources that can be used in line with organizational goals (Cyert and March, 1963/1992; Gomez-Mejia et al., 2005; Murphy, 2002; Roe, 2003), a key question arises: What is the purpose of the corporation and its final goals?

This is not a trivial question. The firm's governance objective function plays a crucial role in shaping corporate governance arrangements. Organizational goals shape the mechanisms needed to provide checks and balances to constrain managerial discretion. Under the agency perspective the sole corporate purpose is to maximize the value for shareholders. However, as Jensen (2001) argues, maximizing shareholder value is not the same as maximizing long term firm value. To be able to sustain the firm's value in the long run, not only the interests of shareholders, but the interests of all stakeholders should be taken into account (Jensen, 2001). The involvement of many stakeholders that have some bearing on the long term firm value, and the choices management can make about how to use firm resources to achieve organizational and/or personal goals indicate that firm level characteristics, such as its constituencies and corporate purposes they establish, can have an effect on compensation mechanisms.

When admitting that managerial discretion plays an important role in the ongoing affairs of the firm, we also have to admit that discretion plays a role in the firm process of setting executive pay (cf. Bratton, 2005; Gibbons and Murphy, 1990; Jensen and Murphy, 2004). Subsequently, when we admit that executives have discretion, we also have to admit that other actors, such as the members of the board of directors, have discretion themselves. In the arm's length contracting view, boards of directors are assumed to be representatives of the shareholders and will act only on their behalf. However, as Bebchuk and Fried (2003, 2004, 2006) and others have argued there are no a priori reasons to believe that directors will automatically fully serve the interests of shareholders. Directors may collude for instance with managers in order to get reelected themselves. The nominal right to reelect directors may rest with shareholders, but in practice many of the director slates offered at annual meetings are the ones proposed by management (Bebchuk and Fried, 2006). Furthermore, directors may approve favorable pay packages for executives in the hope of receiving higher pay themselves (Brick *et al.*, 2006). In contrast to the assumption in most accounts of executive pay, and in most research on corporate governance in general, the altruistic role of the board of directors can be questioned. Their altruistic assumed role and position vis-à-vis shareholders is likely to be more comparable to the position of the executives they have to monitor.

Given that managerial discretion is often assumed to be used to pursue perverse goals, much of the literature on corporate governance is aimed at investigating governance arrangements that constrain managerial discretion. Such an instrumental approach has revealed many determinants of executive pay. Studies have for example examined the role of institutional shareholders (e.g. David *et al.*, 1998; Hartzell and Starks, 2003), and the market of corporate control (e.g. Bliss and Rosen, 2001; Datta *et al.*, 2001; Schmidt and Fowler, 1990). Most research however reserves a special place for the role of the board of directors as an important instrument to constrain managerial discretion (e.g. Bebchuk and Fried, 2004; Conyon and He, 2004; Hallock, 1997; Kerr and Bettis, 1987). Indeed, the monitoring function, often termed the "control" role, is perhaps the most common focus of work on governance, boards of directors and executive pay. The board of directors is addressed in most, if not all, studies and is either used as a control variable or is regarded as the most important determinant factor of executive pay.

Empirical studies typically investigate or control for the effects of board size, board structures (e.g. CEO/Chairman duality) and board compositions (board committees, number of outsiders or independent board members). The empirical results of these studies are however mixed. Ranging from no relationship to positive and negative relationships, with pay and board structure variables such as the proportion of executives to non-executives, proportion of inside to outside directors on the board and the composition of remuneration committees (Carpenter and Sanders, 2002; Conyon and Peck, 1998; Core et al., 1999; David et al., 1998; Sanders and Carpenter, 1998; Daily et al., 1998). The often contradictory empirical results cause problems for how these different findings can be interpreted. It could provide evidence that the board of directors take their jobs as gatekeepers seriously and thus play a role as guardians of shareholder interests. On the other hand, and in contrast to the dominant paradigm, it could provide evidence that boards of directors do not act on shareholders' interests only and take other interests into consideration as well.

In practice, the role of the board as a determinant factor in setting executive pay is clear. The board, through its committees, serves to hire and fire executives and determine the firm's pay policy (Conyon and He, 2004; Gibbons and Murphy, 1990). Although in some jurisdictions the ultimate decisions about these issues might be made by shareholders at the shareholders meetings (e.g. in the USA), this is certainly not the case in all jurisdictions (e.g. Germany, The Netherlands, Portugal). Either way, the board of directors is seen as a major determinant in pay setting practices.

Unaware of the number and capabilities of the executives on the market, and thus unaware of the "efficient" market price of executive services, boards of directors take information from other actors inside (e.g. the human resource department) and outside the firm (Gibbons and Murphy, 1990). This information is not only used to set pay and develop pay policy, it is also used to justify pay policies to a wider audience. Boards thereby often use consultants, headhunters and tax advisors, and benchmark their pay policy against others. Parties within and outside the firm help the board of directors with timely information about current pay policies against the background of current institutional order. One must be careful however to consider these seemingly impartial third parties, and the board of directors themselves, as "truth telling" institutional readers. A recent study by Conyon and colleagues (2006) using a dataset of over 200 publicly traded UK firms shows for instance that the board's choice for a specific pay consultant influences pay policy. One of the findings of this study is that the choice for a bigger consultant firm with a larger client portfolio results in higher pay. Also, the role of the media in ventilating possible public outcry over excessive executive pay may not be so impartial, as the media appear to some degree to sensationalize seemingly excessive pay (Core et al., 2005). Firm specific circumstances do also play a major role when boards of directors justify their firm's specific pay policy. Wade et al. (1997) have for instance shown that firms that pay out relative high fixed salaries emphasize the role of consultants in the pay setting process. Also, when accounting returns are high, market returns are downplayed in accounts of a firm's pay policy.

Boards of directors and others involved in the pay setting process thus have discretion in making decisions on executive pay and when they justify their pay policy to others. Each individual can perceive the constraining factors of pay antecedents differently. Subsequently, comparable firms may pay comparable executives differently. It then becomes an empirical question how and which combinations of mechanisms influence discretion effectively in the pay setting process, and subsequently how they may influence the level and structure of pay.

The view of considering pay setting practices as subject to influential forces at the individual and firm level lead us to also consider these pay practices to be embedded in more broadly defined socially constructed corporate governance arrangements. Extending such a view could further provide additional insights into the possible systematic variance in pay practices across national contexts.

Executive pay practices and national contexts: the institutional level

Of utmost importance but most often neglected in the executive pay literature is the "social embeddedness" (Granovetter, 1985; Uzzi, 1997) of these pay setting practices. Individuals are constrained in their capacity to make fully rational and optimal decisions based on market prices only, because of the cost and unavailability of appropriate information and because of their own cognitive limitations (Cyert and March, 1963/1992; DiMaggio and Powell, 1983; March and Olsen, 1984, Meyer and Rowan, 1977; North, 2005). Decision making is a social process because individuals also draw on norms, trust, culture, advice, history and authority when they make decisions (Cyert and March, 1963/1992; March and Olsen, 1984; North, 2005; Scott, 2001). Individuals have their own expectations, interpretations, comprehensions, notions, beliefs or attitudes of their environment and of appropriate means to make decisions (Jepperson, 1991; North, 2005). Decisions can be seen to be made against a background of perceived institutional norms, values and beliefs (Jepperson, 1991; Meyer and Rowan, 1977; North, 2005).

In this sense corporate governance can be seen as a problem of social action (Becht, Bolton and Roëll, 2002; Davis and Thompson, 1994; Guillén, 2000). "[S]ocial action is embedded in social structures that influence whether, when and how collective action is accomplished by interest groups" (Davis and Thompson, 1994: 141). An institutional view on executive pay would consider that corporate governance arrangements, including pay setting practices, are developed and contested by societal needs, wants and acceptance of these arrangements (cf. Aguilera and Jackson, 2003; Perkins and Hendry, 2005). Moreover, an institutional approach brings pricing and market mechanisms "under the jurisdiction of institutional meanings and controls" (Meyer and Rowan, 1977: 351). Institutions, seen as rule enforcing mechanisms (Elster, 1989), "simultaneously empower and control" (Jepperson, 1991: 146). Thus, institutions socialize individuals in order to interpret environmental cues "appropriately," sanction them positively if they follow suit, and punish them if they go against the grain of the prevailing institutional order. In other words, institutions not only make actors aware of the consequences of their decisions, but also equip them with selected means to make appropriate decisions.

A growing body of literature investigates the role of institutions in corporate governance and investigates the systematic variance in corporate governance arrangements across national contexts (e.g. La Porta *et al.*, 1997; Pagano and Volpin, 2005; Roe, 2003). The executive pay literature is however very scarce in the number of studies that analyze pay levels and structures across institutional settings. Although incorporating institutions in accounts of executive pay may cause explanations to lean on idiosyncratic explanations across different societies (Gomez-Mejia *et al.*, 2005), more knowledge about institutional implications could provide much-needed additional insights into how corporate governance arrangements and pay setting practices operate and vary across countries. It could provide insights into how these institutional differences systematically influence pay levels and structures (cf. Aguilera and Jackson, 2003; Conyon and Murphy, 2000; Tosi and Greckhamer, 2004).

To be able to generalize the implications of given pay practices for the level and structure of pay, more comparative studies are needed. This need becomes especially apparent when considering that most empirical research uses pay data from US based firms. Generalizations of the conclusions of these studies thus imply that the US example is most often considered to be the worldwide standard. However, well known variances between countries of pay levels and makeup indicate that the US case seems to be more of an outlier than the worldwide standard. Table 9.1 reports the levels and structures of average CEO pay in 2003 from 11 countries. The pay data that is reported is cash bonuses, fixed salary, the total of the two (total cash) and the cash bonus as a percentage of total cash. Shares and options are not reported because of a lack of available data. Information regimes differ enormously across countries, especially in regard of information about the use of options. This already provides clear indications of possible institutional influences.

As can be seen in the table, both the level and structure of pay differs across countries. The level of pay in the US is the highest. In the Scandinavian countries pay levels are overall lower and have lower cash bonuses as a percentage of total cash. Other studies have found comparable indications of these differences. More importantly, differences in pay levels and structures across and within countries seem to remain over time and still exist when controlling for firm and executive characteristics such as firm size and executive age (see e.g. Abowd and Bognanno, 1995; Conyon and Murphy, 2000; Kaplan, 1994; Murphy, 1999; Zhou, 1999). This evidence leads us to conclude that explanations based on assumptions of rational actors and of efficient market forces and on a global market for executives, clearly fall short as a comprehensive explanation for the still remaining large differences between and within countries. Inexorably, other factors are at play when decisions on pay are made (e.g. Finkelstein and Hambrick, 1989; Conyon and Murphy, 2000).

Table 9.1 CEO pay levels and structures

Country	Total cash	Salary	Cash Bonus	Cash bonus/Total cash
Denmark	650,712	584,112	93,327	14%
Finland	658,390	562,540	137,185	20%
France	1,832,493	991,100	950,396	46%
Germany	2,267,376	815,668	1,587,663	57%
Italy	1,369,791	970,578	857,586	43%
Spain	992,191	553,930	1,231,900	50%
Sweden	846,845	611,984	247,908	25%
Switzerland	1,638,072	1,409,954	618,269	20%
The Netherlands	1,109,904	700,285	409,618	30%
UK	1,981,526	1,053,113	960,428	41%
US	4,764,400	1,216,925	3,547,476	63%

Note: The number of observations can differ for the different pay components. Because of this the amounts do not have to add up to the totals as reported in the table and the percentage reported is not necessarily the same as the divisions of the amounts reported. The amounts are in US dollars from 2003, purchasing power parity-adjusted (2000 US dollars).

Source: Data from Otten (2007).

Because cross-country studies are a rarity, especially compared to the large number of studies based on US data, we know very little about the influences from national conditions on executive pay. The studies that do make international comparisons mostly only hint at the influence from specific national conditions, but do empirically take them into account (see for instance Conyon and Murphy, 2000). A notable exception is the study by Tosi and Greckhamer (2004) that shows that national cultures systematically influence executive pay. Especially the higher degrees to which differences in power and status are accepted in a culture seem to lead to higher pay. Apparently, in cultures where differences in social status and positions of power are more socially accepted it is also more acceptable for executives to have higher pay levels and possibly more discretion to influence their pay.

Discussion and conclusion

A global approach to executive pay adheres to the notion that not only executives but all those involved in the pay setting process take information from their social environment. This information, used to negotiate pay and develop pay policy, is however not "value free." Each individual can have their own interpretation, notion or attitude about what constitutes appropriate information and means when making decisions. Although constrained by relevant corporate governance arrangements and current pay practices, individuals have considerable discretion in the pay setting process. Environmental changes and or changes within the firm could lead to changes in current arrangements or could lead to the introduction of new ones.

Important to note is that purely economic explanations tend to consider institutions as exogenous (see for instance Jensen and Meckling, 1976's assumption that the legal environment in which the contract is made up is considered to be exogenous). Institutions are seen as playing a background role in shaping corporate governance and executive pay practices (see for example Lubatkin et al., 2005). The problem of considering institutions as exogenous is that behavior, although constrained by institutions, can also change institutions (see Nobel laureate North, 2005). Considering the existence and development of pay practices as static in a given environment, ultimately considers the actors involved to be "ontological actors, frozen in space and time and isolated from social and cultural context" (Aguilera and Jackson, 2003: 449). It is however a two-way street, in which regularities at the system- or macro-level are being produced and reinforced by variety and diversity at the actor- or micro-level (Hodgson 1988). Systematic jolts to the system could induce new or amendments to current regulation. For instance corporate fraud or the public outcry over high levels of stock option rewards could increase disclosure regulations of pay components, new taxes or amendments to accounting standards and regulations. The introduction of new practices or changes to current pay practices require however constant judgments of societal needs, wants and acceptance of these arrangements (Aguilera and Jackson, 2003; Perkins and Hendry, 2005).

Considering the social construction of pay setting practices has large implications about how we can understand the wide variety of executive pay practices in an international context. This notion is however not completely new in the executive pay literature. The social embeddedness of pay practices can also be found in ideas such as figurehead theory (Ungson and Steers, 1984), implicit contracting (Baker et al., 2002; Kidder and

Buchholtz, 2002; Rosen, 1985) and other theories based on social comparisons (see e.g. O'Reilly *et al.*, 1988; Simon, 1957). In these approaches executive pay is seen as socially constructed. The social status and socially constructed position of executives are considered to be the main drivers of pay. Differences in pay between comparable executives employed by comparable firms could be understood as a reflection of the socially constructed specific position of a given executive.

What is however new, and is in contrast to the dominant perfect contracting approach, is that such a view specifically considers the discretion individuals have in the pay setting process. Thereby organizational goals and the institutional conditions under which decisions are made are considered. Instead of considering that these decision making processes are aimed at maximizing shareholder value such a view implies that many more actors than only shareholders and managers are involved in governing the firm. Even Michael Jensen, one of the founding fathers of the contracting view on executive pay, has recently rejected this premise by arguing that the firm's governance objective should be to maximize long term firm value and not (short term) shareholder value. He argues that firms cannot maximize their long term value if they do not adhere to the interests of all stakeholders (Jensen, 2001). This "enlightened stakeholder theory" as Jensen (2001) calls it, argues that the decision to make tradeoffs between the interests of various stakeholders must be based on whether long term firm value is maximized or not. In other words, not only shareholders and management are involved in the governance processes of an organization, but also other types of stakeholders. Although this change in the firm's objective function may lead to different framing of preferred solutions to corporate governance and pay design, theorizing about these solutions is not necessarily beyond the scope of the perfect contracting approach. One of the core strengths of the theory is the generalizability of its analytical instruments to other types of agency problems.

Yet, the untenability of its assumption of fully rational self-interest maximizing actors, exogenous institutions and complete explicit contracts are the fundamental problems of the approach. Actors are simply incapable of making fully rational decisions as they are hampered by different notions and perceptions of appropriate means to make "explicit and timely calculations of optimality" (Cyert and March, 1963/1992: 214). This problem is considerably expanded if we broaden, as Jensen also suggests, the objective function of the corporation. An implication of the view that the modern corporation is a relatively diffuse, multi-stakeholder entity with a correspondingly broad objective function is that it will always be surrounded by an imperfect or ambiguous information regime. Individuals have different expectations about the incomplete explicit contract and different ideas about the implicit contractual relationships. The social actors that have a stake in the firm will therefore always have some discretion to create, deviate or circumvent governance mechanisms, or to bend rules, norms or values in their own favor. Corporate governance and debates about executive pay thus not only pertain to problems of conflicting interests between shareholders and managers. They also pertain to conflicts of opinions, expectations, notions and perceptions of appropriate means and actions to alleviate and settle the discussions.

Understanding executive pay cannot go without understanding the conditions in which decisions on executive pay are made. Executive pay practices are part of broader developed corporate governance arrangements. Facilitated and constrained by relevant institutions these arrangements are constantly developed and contested in society. Not only differences at firm level but also possible differences between countries are relevant to provide more insights into how given governance arrangements and pay practices function and how their functioning can be truly generalized across institutional contexts.

National culture is just one example of an institutional context that plays a role in shaping pay practices and discretion in the pay setting process. Investigating the influence from other institutions, such as legal, political and economic institutions, may provide additional insights into the pay setting process. These insights could lead to generalizations of the effects of the many different corporate governance mechanisms that can be found around the globe. Possibly socially or politically induced legal constraints on board structures serve as a good example. In Germany large listed firms are obligated by law to have employee representatives on the board: a feature not found in jurisdictions such as in the USA and the United Kingdom. Thereby, for instance in France and in Sweden, some firms do have representation of employees on the board and other firms do not. Allowing employees on the board could serve as a constraint on managerial discretion. Having employees on the board could systematically influence corporate governance arrangements and their outcomes, resulting in specific pay setting practices, and subsequently in different pay levels and structures. Another example is the phenomenon of CEO duality, the combination of both the function of Chairman of the board and Chief Executive Officer represented by a single person, and one/two tier board structures. Empirical tests with US data for instance typically find that CEO duality has a positive relationship with pay. Pay levels are higher when the board is chaired by a single person who is also the CEO (e.g. Boyd, 1994; Main and Johnston, 1993). In contrast, empirical studies with UK data indicate that this relationship is much weaker and doesn't seem to be a major influence on executive pay (Conyon and Peck, 1998). Institutional differences could explain why CEO duality has systematic different effects on pay in the two countries. Institutional differences could also provide additional insights into how the effects of different board structures can be generalized. In some jurisdictions, for example in Germany and The Netherlands, CEO duality is not even possible because of a two tier board structure – a board structure in which the executive board and the non-executive board are two separate organizational entities – as opposed to for instance the USA and the United Kingdom with a one tier board structure in which both executives and non-executive directors are present. A third type of board structure is typical in the Swedish governance model and is a sort of hybrid structure. Typical for this model is that the only executive on the board of directors is the CEO and this person is not the chairman of this first tier. Together with the other executives, the CEO forms a second tier, a sort of one-and-a-half tiered board structure as a result, with possible different effects on executive pay as opposed to other models.

An aspect obliquely mentioned in this chapter refers to the interaction between and across levels. Answers to the question: How do national contexts influence the functions of the boards of directors?, are certainly important. In this sense, Hillman and Haynes (2006) provide some insights. The authors argue that the importance of board monitoring to firm performance will be negatively related to the degree of in-group collectivism and the degree of product market competition in a country. The opposite would be true for the importance of board resource provision to firm performance. They offer three country level examples. Argentina, which has a relatively low product market competition and scores quite high on in-group collectivist cultural values (House *et al.*, 2004), is expected to place the importance of board monitoring relatively low, with board resource provision importance relatively higher. On the other hand, a country such as Germany with relatively high product market competition, but moderately low in-group collectivism is expected to exhibit board monitoring relatively more important than board resource provision. Finally, in situations such as the USA with high product market competition and moderate degree of in-group collectivism values, both board monitoring and resource provision will be moderately important. Understanding this rationale and the implications for executive pay clearly calls for further research in the area.

Arguably, systematic analyses of country specific factors could provide additional insights into generalizing the effects of corporate governance arrangements in the pay setting process. Important to note is that some governance mechanisms may not exist in some countries or firms but do, or do not as yet, exist in others. The combination of firm level governance arrangements together with country level conditions could provide more conclusive explanations for the variance of executive pay, both within and between countries. More empirical studies are however needed to investigate which combinations of arrangements constrain not only executives but also other parties when they make discretionary decisions in the pay setting process and how they shape pay setting practices and subsequently pay levels and structures.

References

Abowd, J.M. and Bognanno, M.L. 1995. International Differences in Executive and Managerial Compensation. In R.B. Freeman and L.F. Katz (eds), *Differences and Changes in Wage Structures*: 67–103. Chicago, IL: University of Chicago Press.

Agarwal, N.C. 1981. Determinants of Executive Compensation. *Industrial Relations*, 20(1): 36–45.

Aguilera, R.V. and Jackson, G. 2003. The Cross-National Diversity of Corporate Governance: Dimensions and Determinants. *Academy of Management Review*, 28(3): 447–65.

Alchian, A.A. and Demsetz, H. 1972. Production, Information Costs, and Economic Organization. *American Economic Review*, 62(5): 777–95.

Baker, G., Gibbons, R. and Murphy, K.J. 2002. Relational Contracts and the Theory of the Firm. *Quarterly Journal of Economics*, 117(1): 39–84.

Balsam, S. 2002. *An Introduction to Executive Compensation*. San Diego, CA: Academic Press.

Barkema, H.G. and Gomez-Mejia, L.R. 1998. Managerial Compensation and Firm Performance: A General Research Framework. *Academy of Management Journal*, 41(2): 135–45.

Bebchuk, L.A. and Fried, J.A. 2003. Executive Compensation as an Agency Problem. *Journal of Economic Perspectives*, 17(3): 71–92.

—— 2004. *Pay Without Performance: The Unfulfilled Promise of Executive Compensation*. Cambridge, MA: Harvard University Press.

—— 2006. Pay Without Performance: Overview of the Issues. *Journal of Applied Corporate Finance*, 17(4): 8–23.

Becht, M., Bolton, P. and Roëll, A. 2002. Corporate Governance and Control. ECGI Working Paper 02/2002.

Bliss, R.T. and Rosen, R.J. 2001. CEO Compensation and Bank Mergers. *Journal of Financial Economics*, 61(1): 107–38.

Boyd, B.K. 1994. Board Control and CEO Compensation. *Strategic Management Journal*, 15(5): 335–44.

Bratton, W.W. 2005. The Academic Tournament over Executive Compensation. *California Law Review*, 93(5): 1557–84.

Brick, I.E., Palmon, O. and Wald, J.K. 2006. CEO Compensation, Director Compensation, and Firm Performance: Evidence of Cronyism? *Journal of Corporate Finance*, 12(3): 403–23.

Carpenter, M.A. and Sanders, W.M.G. 2002. Top Management Team Compensation: The Missing Link between CEO Pay and Firm Performance? *Strategic Management Journal*, 23(4): 367–75.

Ciscel, D.H. and Carroll, T.M. 1980. The Determinants of Executive Salaries: An Econometric Survey. *The Review of Economics and Statistics*, 62(1): 7–13.

Conyon, M.J. and He, L. 2004. Compensation Committees and CEO Compensation Incentives in US Entrepreneurial Firms. *Journal of Management Accounting Research*, 16(1): 35–56.

Conyon, M.J. and Murphy, K.J. 2000. The Prince and the Pauper? CEO Pay in the United States and United Kingdom. *Economic Journal*, 110(467): F640–F671.

Conyon, M.J. and Peck, S.L. 1998. Board Control, Remuneration Committees, and Top Management Compensation. *Academy of Management Journal*, 41(2): 146–57.

Conyon, M.J., Peck S.I. and Sadler, G.V. 2006. Compensation Consultants and Executive Pay. Working paper, The Wharton School.

Core, J.E., Guay, W.R. and Larcker, D.F. 2005. The Power of the Pen and Executive Compensation. Working paper, The Wharton School.

Core, J.E., Holthausen, R.W. and Larcker, D.F. 1999. Corporate Governance, Chief Executive Officer Compensation, and Firm Performance. *Journal of Financial Economics*, 51(3): 371–406.

Cyert, R.M. and March, J.G. 1963/1992. *A Behavioral Theory of the Firm* (2nd edition). Oxford, UK: Blackwell Publishers.

Daily, C.M., Johnson, J.L., Ellstrand, A.E. and Dalton, D.R. 1998. Compensation Committee Composition as a Determinant of CEO Compensation. *Academy of Management Journal*, 41(2): 209–20.

Datta, S., Iskandar-Datta, M. and Raman, K. 2001. Executive Compensation and Corporate Acquisition Decisions. *The Journal of Finance*, 56(6): 2299–336.

David, P., Kochhar, R. and Levitas, E. 1998. The Effect of Institutional Investors on the Level and Mix of CEO Compensation. *Academy of Management Journal*, 41(2): 200–8.

Davis, G.F. and Thompson, T.A. 1994. A Social Movement Perspective on Corporate Control. *Administrative Science Quarterly*, 39(1): 141–73.

DiMaggio, P.J. and Powell, W.W. 1983. The Iron Cage Revisited: Institutional Isomorphism and Collective Rationality in Organizational Fields. *American Sociological Review*, 48(2): 147–60.

Eisenhardt, K. 1989. Agency Theory: An Assessment and a Review. *Academy of Management Review*, 14(1): 57–74.

Elster, J. 1989. *Nuts and Bolts for the Social Sciences*. Cambridge, UK: Cambridge University Press.

Fama, E.F. 1980. Agency Problems and the Theory of the Firm. *Journal of Political Economy*, 88(2): 288–307.

Fama, E.F. and Jensen, M.C. 1983. Separation of Ownership and Control. *Journal of Law and Economics*, 26: 301–25.

Finkelstein, S. and Boyd, B.K. 1998. How Much does the CEO Matter? The Role of Managerial Discretion in the Setting of CEO Compensation. *Academy of Management Journal*, 41(2): 179–99.

Finkelstein, S. and Hambrick, D.C. 1988. Chief Executive Compensation: A Synthesis and Reconciliation. *Strategic Management Journal*, 9(6): 543–58.

—— 1989. Chief Executive Compensation: A Study of the Intersection of Markets and Political Processes. *Strategic Management Journal*, 10(2): 121–34.

Frey, B.S. 1997. On the Relationship Between Intrinsic and Extrinsic Work Motivation. *International Journal of Industrial Organization*, 15(4): 427–39.

Frey, B.S. and Osterloh, M. 2005. Yes, Managers Should Be Paid Like Bureaucrats. *Journal of Management Inquiry*, 14(1): 96–111.

Gibbons, R. and Murphy, K.J. 1990. Relative Performance Evaluation for Chief Executive Officers. *Industrial & Labor Relations Review*, 43(3): S30–S51.

Gomez-Mejia, L.R. 1994. Executive Compensation: A Reassessment and a Future Research Agenda. *Research in Personnel and Human Resources Management*, 12: 161–222.

Gomez-Mejia, L.R. and Wiseman, R.M. 1997. Reframing Executive Compensations: An Assessment and Outlook. *Journal of Management*, 23(3): 291–374.

—— 2007. Does Agency Theory Have Universal Relevance? A Reply to Lubatkin, Lane, Collin, and Very. *Journal of Organizational Behaviour*, 28: 81–88.

Gomez-Mejia, L.R., Wiseman, R.M. and Dykes, B.J. 2005. Agency Problems in Diverse Contexts: A Global Perspective. *Journal of Management Studies*, 42(7): 1507–17.

Grabke-Rundell, A. and Gomez-Mejia, L.R. 2002. Power as Determinant of Executive Compensation. *Human Resource Management Review*, 12(1): 3–23.

Granovetter, M. 1985. Economic Action and Social Structure: The Problem of Embeddedness. *American Journal of Sociology*, 91(3): 481–510.

Guillén, M.F. 2000. Corporate Governance and Globalization: Is there Convergence across Countries? *Advances in Comparative International Management*, 13: 175–204.

Hallock, K.F. 1997. Reciprocally Interlocking Boards of Directors and Executive Compensation. *Journal of Financial and Quantitative Analysis*, 32(3): 331–44.

Hambrick, D.C. and Finkelstein, S. 1995. The Effects of Ownership Structure on Conditions at the Top: The Case of CEO Pay Raises. *Strategic Management Journal*, 16(3): 175–93.

Hartzell, J.C. and Starks, L.T. 2003. Institutional Investors and Executive Compensation. *The Journal of Finance*, 58(6): 2351–74.

Hillman, A.J. and Haynes, K. 2006. Institutional Environments, Board Functions and Firm Performance. *Arizona State University working papers*, 1–39.

Hodgson, G.M. 1988. *Economics and Institutions: A Manifesto for a Modern Institutional Economics*. Cambridge, UK: Polity Press.

House, R., Hanges, P., Javidan, M., Dofman, P. and Gupta, V. 2004. *Culture, Leadership and Organizations: The GLOBE Study of 62 Societies*. Thousand Oaks, CA: Sage.

Jensen, M.C. 2001. Value Maximisation, Stakeholder Theory, and the Corporate Objective Function. *European Financial Management*, 7(3): 297–317.

Jensen, M.C. and Meckling, W.H. 1976. The Theory of the Firm: Managerial Behavior, Agency Costs and Ownership Structure. *Journal of Financial Economics*, 3(4): 305–60.

Jensen, M.C. and Murphy, K.J. 1990a. CEO Incentives: It's Not How Much You Pay, But How. *Journal of Applied Corporate Finance*, 3(3): 36–49.

—— 1990b. Performance Pay and Top-Management Incentives. *Journal of Political Economy*, 98(2): 225–64.

—— 2004. Remuneration: Where We've Been, How We Got to Here, What Are the Problems, and How to Fix Them. ECGI Working Paper 44/2004.

Jepperson, R.L. 1991. Institutions, Institutional Effects, and Institutionalism. In W.W. Powell and P.J. DiMaggio (eds), *The New Institutionalism in Organizational Analysis*: 143–63. Chicago, IL: The University of Chicago Press.

Kaplan, S.N. 1994. Top Executive Rewards and Firm Performance: A Comparison of Japan and the United States. *Journal of Political Economy*, 102(3): 510–46.

Kerr, J. and Bettis, R.A. 1987. Boards of Directors, Top Management Compensation, and Shareholder Returns. *The Academy of Management Journal*, 30(4): 645–64.

Kidder, D.L. and Buchholtz, A.K. 2002. Can Excess Bring Success? CEO Compensation and the Psychological Contract. *Human Resource Management Review*, 12(4): 599–617.

La Porta, R., Lopez-de-Silanes, F., Shleifer, A. and Vishny, R. 1997. Legal Determinants of External Finance. *Journal of Finance*, 52(3): 1131–50.

Lubatkin, M.H., Lane, P.J., Collin, S.O. and Very, P. 2005. Origins of Corporate Governance in the USA, Sweden and France. *Organization Studies*, 26(6): 867–88.

Main, B.G.M. and Johnston, J. 1993. Remuneration Committees and Corporate Governance. *Accounting and Business Research*, 23(91A): 351–62.

March, J.G. and Olsen, J.P. 1984. The New Institutionalism: Organizational Factors in Political Life. *American Political Science Review*, 78(3): 734–49.

Meyer, J. and Rowan, B. 1977. Institutionalized Organizations: Formal Structure as Myth and Ceremony. *American Journal of Sociology*, 83(2): 340–63.

Murphy, K.J. 1999. Executive Compensation. In O. Ashenfelter and D. Card (eds), *Handbook of Labor Economics* (5th edition), vol. 3: 2485–563. Amsterdam, The Netherlands: Elsevier Science.

—— 2002. Explaining Executive Compensation: Managerial Power versus the Perceived Cost of Stock Options. *University of Chicago Law Review*, 69(3): 847–69.

North, D.C. 2005. *Understanding the Process of Economic Change*. Princeton, NJ: Princeton University Press.

O'Reilly, C.A., Main, B.G. and Crystal, G.S. 1988. CEO Compensation as Tournament and Social Comparison: A Tale of Two Theories. *Administrative Science Quarterly*, 33(2): 257–74.

Otten, J.A. 2007. *Origins of Executive Pay and Corporate Governance Reform Codes. An Institutional Approach to Corporate Governance.* PhD thesis, Utrecht School of Economics, Utrecht University.

Pagano, M. and Volpin, P.F. 2005. The Political Economy of Corporate Governance. *American Economic Review*, 95(4): 1005–30.

Perkins, S.J. and Hendry, C. 2005. Ordering Top Pay: Interpreting the Signals. *Journal of Management Studies*, 42(7): 1443–68.

Roe, M.J. 2003. *Political Determinants of Corporate Governance: Political Context, Corporate Impact.* Oxford, UK: Oxford University Press.

Rosen, S. 1985. Implicit Contracts: A Survey. NBER Working Paper W1635.

—— 1990. Contracts and the Market for Executives. NBER Working Paper W3542.

Sanders, W.M.G. and Carpenter, M.A. 1998. Internationalization and Firm Governance: The Roles of CEO Compensation, Top Team Composition, and Board Structure. *Academy of Management Journal*, 41(2): 158–78.

Schmidt, D.R. and Fowler, K.L. 1990. Postacquisition Financial Performance and Executive Compensation. *Strategic Management Journal*, 11(7): 559–69.

Scott, W.R. 2001. *Institutions and Organizations* (2nd edition). Thousand Oaks, CA: Sage.

Shleifer, A. and Vishny, R.W. 1997. A Survey of Corporate Governance. *Journal of Finance*, 52(2): 737–83.

Simon, H.A. 1957. The Compensation of Executives. *Sociometry*, 20(1): 32–5.

Taussig, F.W. and Baker, W.S. 1925. American Corporations and Their Executives: A Statistical Inquiry. *Quarterly Journal of Economics*, 40(1): 1–51.

Tosi, H.L. and Greckhamer, T. 2004. Culture and CEO Compensation. *Organization Science*, 15(6): 657–70.

Tosi, H.L., Werner, S., Katz, J.P. and Gomez-Mejia, L.R. 2000. How Much does Performance Matter? A Meta-analysis of CEO Pay Studies. *Journal of Management*, 26(2): 301–39.

Ungson, G.R. and Steers, R.M. 1984. Motivation and Politics in Executive Compensation. *Academy of Management Review*, 9(2): 313–23.

Uzzi, B. 1997. Social Structure and Competition in Interfirm Networks: The Paradox of Embeddedness. *Administrative Science Quarterly*, 42(1): 35–67.

van Oosterhout, J. 2007. Authority and Democracy in Corporate Governance? *Journal of Business Ethics*, 71: 359–70.

Wade, J.B., Porac, J.F. and Pollock, T.G. 1997. Worth, Words, and the Justification of Executive Pay. *Journal of Organizational Behavior*, 18(1): 641–64.

Werner, S. and Ward, S. 2004. Recent Compensation Research: An Eclectic Review. *Human Resource Management Review*, 14: 201–27.

Williamson, O.E. 1985. *The Economic Institutions of Capitalism: Firms, Markets, Relational Contracting.* New York: Free Press.

—— 1996. *The Mechanisms of Governance.* Oxford, UK: Oxford University Press.

Zhou, X. 1999. Executive Compensation and Managerial Incentives: A Comparison between Canada and the United States. *Journal of Corporate Finance*, 5(3): 277–301.

Zingales, L. 1998. Corporate Governance. In P. Newman (ed.), *The New Palgrave Dictionary of Economics and the Law*, New York: Palgrave MacMillan.

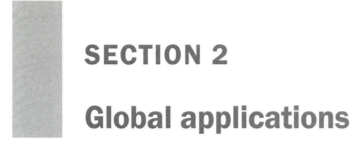

SECTION 2

Global applications

The global convergence of compensation practices

10

Charles H. Fay

Economists, international business specialists and a variety of organizational scholars have been concerned with the question of global convergence of management practices and employee outcomes for more than a decade. Arguments have been made that convergence of management practice is inevitable, and that employee outcomes, even wages, will tend to converge as well. Other scholars argue that the barriers to convergence such as national culture are so fundamental and so large that convergence is unlikely, certainly in the foreseeable future. Some note that practices vary so much within countries that it is unreasonable to expect convergence across countries.

This chapter focuses on the little we know about the global convergence of management practices relative to compensation programs. After considering in more detail the arguments advanced for convergence and non-convergence in general, a discussion of these arguments relative to compensation practice will be provided. Evidence of convergence of compensation practices will be discussed as well.

While not a major focus of this chapter, some mention will be made of convergence of employee outcomes relevant to compensation. Organization scholars have not generally argued that reward levels across countries are converging, but there is some evidence that reward levels for senior executives may be doing so.

The convergence argument

I am grouping the arguments for convergence into two broad categories: those that operate within the organization and those that operate on the organization from specific countries in which they operate or permeate global development across countries. The rationale is that organizations have some control over internal forces, but little control over forces operating outside the organization.

Internal arguments for convergence

Organizational strategies for production (Dickmann, 2003), marketing, information technology (Quintanilla and Ferner, 2003; Zivnuska et al., 2001), finance and other organization functions set the stage for integration around specific sets of policies and practices (Dickmann, 2003). When production and other functions are integrated globally, it seems only natural that the management practices supporting these functions be integrated globally as well. Integrated management practices make global transfer of managers less complicated (Geppert and Williams, 2006).

Organizational structures, and particularly those chosen by the multinational corporation, create a strong force for convergence (Andrews and Chompusri, 2005). The rationalization of the organization includes management practices, and the use of similar management practices (to the extent possible) across the organization provides ease of administration, increases efficiency of operations and enhances control of overseas operations by headquarters (Andrews and Chompusri, 2005; Dickmann, 2003). Most MNCs have unified practices in their home operations and the "administrative heritage of the firm" alone should forward the assumption that any new operations will adopt those practices as well (Dickmann, 2003).

The use of expatriates, especially in country startups, supports the export of home country practices and can make those practices a "given" in overseas units (Gomez and Sanchez, 2005). The use of "inpats" (foreign nationals brought into the home country headquarters temporarily or long term) immerses these employees into organizational culture and practices; their understanding of management practices in the organizational context makes it more likely that they will accept these practices on return to their home country, and they may even convince others of the usefulness of them.

There are a number of related attitudes that make convergence more likely. It is common in most large corporations today to benchmark practices, and benchmarking's underlying philosophy is that there is "one best way" to do things. Many managers still believe in the notion of "one best way" espoused by F.W. Taylor, and benchmarking is the way to seek out the best way (McGaughey and De Cieri, 1999; Rowley and Benson, 2002). It should not be surprising that most managers in the headquarters of an MNC are likely to think the way things are done in headquarters is the superior approach to management practice (Quintanilla and Ferner, 2003). In some cases, this may even take on moral overtones: a given practice may be seen as ethical (Dickmann, 2003).

Finally, the idea of convergence may be a self-fulfilling prophecy. To the extent that managers believe convergence is inevitable (Pudelko, 2005), they are likely to act as if that is the case and promote similar management practices throughout their own organization.

External arguments for convergence

The external arguments for convergence are all related to globalization. The most important of these is the globalization of the economy. With worldwide markets for global brands, whether products or services, economic competition pressures organizations into similar practices regardless of where they are (Rowley and Benson, 2002). Industry models of production efficiency are likely to require similar management practices for the most effective support (Geppert and Williams, 2006). Free trade advocates may tend to see convergence as inevitable, while others want to make sure employee protection requirements are built into trade agreements. Both approaches foster management practice convergence. Regional economic integration fosters regional management practice integration as an intermediate step; as regions become more closely integrated global convergence will occur (Rowley and Benson, 2002).

Other forms of globalization supporting convergence of management practices include the increase in global travel (Rowley and Benson, 2002), communications and management education (Woldu *et al.*, 2006). As individuals travel more, national differences tend to have less importance. Global brands promote the blurring of differences as well. Global communications promote convergence in two ways. The globalization of media promotes similar lifestyles in participating areas. Today management education programs (both degree and non-degree) are ranked internationally, and management gurus and books attract worldwide attention. Global management conferences attract global presenters and attendees. Technology (Zivnuska *et al.*, 2001), from the Web to aircraft to videoconferencing, makes all this possible.

The non-convergence argument

There are two sets of arguments against convergence of management practice. The first of these is a rejection of the Taylorist "one best way" in favor of contingency approaches to management practice (Rowley and Benson, 2002; McGaughey and De Cieri, 1999). Under contingency theory the best practice will be a function of the strategy and structure of the organization given its own unique set of internal and external environments. Equally successful organizations may have widely divergent practices that work because of differences in strategy, structure and environments. If there is no "one best way" then there is no reason to expect convergence to a single set of management practices; at best there might be convergence towards clusters of similar practices by MNCs that share similar strategies and internal/external environments. The most probable clusters under this view would be industry-based, so that global retailers might converge about one set of practices, while heavy equipment manufacturers might converge about another. Even then, to the extent that different members of the same industry have different strategies (e.g. cost leadership vs differentiation) one might expect different practices would evolve.

The other set of arguments focuses on national differences. The existence of national cultural differences is most frequently mentioned as the reason practices are not likely to converge across different units of the same MNC; these differences are so great that the Anglo-American (or German, or Japanese or other) model of management practices simply will not be acceptable in many cultures (Andrews and Chompusri, 2005; Dickmann, 2003; Rowley and Benson, 2002). Cultural differences account for differences in legal systems that may prohibit certain management practices, result in varied work norms, result in different internal channels of influence, create different authority structures and control over power sources, and result in different work and management values. There are cross-country differences in labor institutions (Freeman, 2007), national business systems, institutional approaches and political-economic frameworks. Countries are at different stages of economic, and industrial development, and at different stages in the absorption of technology. Countries have unique histories (such as South Africa and apartheid) that create unique legal and societal forces towards certain management practices (Horwitz *et al.*, 2006). Most countries, whether developing or developed, have a natural resistance to foreign influences, including the influence of management practices (Robertson *et al.*, 2001).

The convergence/non-convergence argument is not one of black versus white. Many economists speak of heterogeneous convergence (e.g. Levy, 2007; Gualerzi, 2007), which refers to different rates of convergence across economies, with some convergence occurring fairly rapidly and some occurring slowly, if at all. A Marxist interpretation sees the convergence/divergence forces synthesizing in crossvergence (Andrews and Chompusri, 2005), a process in which Western forces for convergence meet local forces for non-convergence, resulting in some combination of the two that meets at least part of the needs of both forces. A non-Marxist approach argues for similar ends: under transvergence (Gupta and Wang, 2004) practice undergoes a transformative reinterpretation in line with the indigenous cultural perspective.

Many economists (e.g. Herrmann, 2005; Petit, 2006) see regional convergence occurring, either as a midway point towards global convergence or as an end point, although others (e.g. Venables, 2003) argue that regionalization can lead to divergence within the region.

Bloom and Milkovich (1999: 293) note the flaws in any international compensation systems convergence argument based on a "national" model and suggest that under a "SHRM perspective, rather than meeting external factors first, effective international compensation systems might be those that match internal contingences (e.g. fit the organization's goals and culture) first and then respond to external forces within the constraints of strategic alignment." Two important points are made in their argument: first, that there is not a uniform set of compensation practices in any country and second, that organizational culture and strategy may be more important in developing an effective rewards program than any geographic/national culture characteristics.

On the other hand, convergence may be overstated because US MNCs avoid countries that are too different and those countries don't make it into comparisons (Bognanno *et al.*, 2005). Similarly, an organization may introduce a low-threat version of a rewards practice shaped by local attitudes and competencies but shift it over time to MNC practice (Lunnan *et al.*, 2005).

Both the convergence and non-convergence arguments have intuitive appeal. At the present time neither set of arguments is entirely persuasive. The idea that there is one best way in any area of management practice seems to fly in the face of the strategy literature. At the same time, the role of national culture in maintaining national differences in attitudes and behaviors appears to have been overstated by at least some of its proponents (Gerhart and Fang, 2005). The little case study and empirical literature that exists suggests that MNCs are attempting to create global practices, but not always with success. Even when a management practice appears constant across units of the MNC, implementation differences may make the practice the same in name only. It is probably safe to say that management practices are converging to the extent possible within the individual MNC; as to whether there will be global convergence across countries and across MNCs, the jury is still out.

Compensation and convergence

The convergence/non-convergence argument is of great interest to compensation professionals and scholars alike. Many global remuneration professionals will note life would certainly be much easier if remuneration policies and practices were constant across countries for their organization.

When dealing with compensation convergence issues it is important to differentiate compensation outcomes (wage, salary levels) from compensation policies and practices. Even fairly similar practices (e.g. market pricing of jobs, performance-based pay) may result in very different levels of wages and incentive payouts. Much of the economic literature on compensation focuses on explanations of wage differentials, even within a single city (e.g. Dunlop, 1957). It is unlikely that wage levels for any job would be similar across countries, since most jobs are priced either locally, regionally or nationally. Even within the United States, compensation levels differ so much that the US Government has 32 cities classified as "local pay areas" and varies the General Schedule rates for those areas.

While geographic factors account for part of observed wage differentials, some of these explain wage differentials within a single country (e.g. urban/suburban/rural location) and there are many sources of wage differentials other than geographic factors, including industry factors (e.g. profitability, capital/labor ratio), organizational characteristics (e.g. size, degree of unionization), job differences (e.g. any factor in a job evaluation scheme, criticality of job to strategy) and individual differences (e.g. incumbent performance, seniority).

There has been less focus in the literature on differences in pay policies and practices, though differences have certainly been observed. In terms of the discussion on global convergence of rewards policies and practices, the first issue is whether there is an attempt by organizations operating across countries to achieve convergence within their organization.

A recent survey (WorldatWork, 2006) provides some insight into attempts by multinational corporations to manage compensation globally. Survey respondents covered 275 MNCs: 82 percent are headquartered in North America, 13 percent in Europe, 2 percent in Japan and the rest in other countries. Respondents varied widely in breadth of operations: 2 percent operate in two countries; 29 percent in three to ten countries, 26 percent in eleven to twenty-four countries, 25 percent in twenty-five to forty-nine countries, and 18 percent in fifty or more countries.

Respondents were requested to provide three key global human resource program objectives. The most frequent was to improve attraction and retention of key talent (48 percent), followed by developing and maintaining a globally consistent HR strategy, and ensuring a consistent link between rewards and results (39 percent). Other rewards related goals included improving governance of compensation policies, implementation and administration (21 percent), ensuring a consistent link between rewards and behavior (15 percent), maintaining internal equity (13 percent), improving governance of benefits policies implementation and administration (11 percent) and complying with Sarbanes-Oxley (4 percent) (WorldatWork, 2006).

Based on this survey there does appear to be a conscious attempt by at least some global organizations to have consistent compensation policies and practices across the countries in which they maintain operations. This attempt is supported by the globalization of rewards consulting firms. Every major (and some minor) rewards consulting firm based in the USA is now represented in every developed country and in some less-developed countries where significant numbers of MNCs have operations. Initial business may be from units of MNCs, but as host country businesses become clients, getting exposure to and support in implementing rewards, their practices become more similar to those in North America and Europe.

Even when dealing with rewards practices, the convergence argument may hold at the very general level but not at the more specific level. Many organizations worldwide argue that they are committed to "pay for performance" rewards practices, but this covers a wide range of specific practices, from the merit pay system where there is little differentiation of high and low performers to incentive payouts that are entirely at risk, such as one-off bonuses. There may appear to be convergence at the surface level with no real convergence at the specific practice level.

Even if convergence occurs at the specific practice level, practices which on their face are similar can result in very different outcomes for employees: two divisions of an organization in different companies may both use job evaluation to create internal value hierarchies of jobs in their respective divisions, but one job evaluation system may result in a job hierarchy that reflects a traditional bureaucratic culture with many layers while the other system reflects a more participative, de-layered organization. Thus, similarity of practice is no guarantee of convergence in other than name.

There is not a lot of evidence of convergence of compensation policies and practices in the scholarly literature. Ding and colleagues (2006) find much the same kind of influences on managerial pay in China that has been described in the American literature: levels of compensation are affected by ownership, firm age, location and industrial sector, while differentials across managers within firms are affected by ownership, firm size, firm age, location and industrial sector. As ownership patterns have changed, divergence between state-owned enterprises and other organizations has increased. Increasing divergence within a country does not argue well for increasing convergence of that country with others.

However, the authors find that some Chinese organizations (publicly traded, non-state owned) increasingly have more pay at risk, increasingly base compensation on the skills, knowledge and abilities of incumbents, increasingly base a larger component of pay on performance, and increasingly include intrinsic rewards in the rewards system as a whole, thus becoming more like Western organizations. Some have even introduced options, although this is considered an experiment (2006: 710). Similarly, Gamble (2003) concludes China is moving towards performance-based rewards with greater differentials and away from egalitarian pay and perquisites. Finally, Shibata (2002) notes Japanese firms have moved towards US practices in wage determination and performance appraisal for some employees (especially managers) but less so for unionized workers. He predicts that Japan will continue to move towards US rewards systems, but companies are likely to adapt to Japanese culture.

There have been a few studies that look at the impact of national culture on compensation systems. Black (2001) found wage dispersions were negatively correlated with the degree of centralization of collective bargaining, that higher masculinity scores (on Hofstede's scale) were associated with larger wage differentials between men and women while lower power distances were associated with lower wage differentials. Similarly, Chiang (2005) found reward preferences of bank employees in Canada, Hong Kong, the United Kingdom and Finland varied as predicted by Hofstede's model. Neither of these studies speaks directly to compensation policies or practices. Black's study (2001) speaks to wage outcomes at the national level rather than practices or policies. Chiang's study (2005) speaks to preferences about pay; it is not clear that such preferences would actually restrict practices by an organization.

Bloom and colleagues (2003) discuss an emerging model of international compensation systems in which a global organization might take one of three approaches towards building rewards systems in the countries in which they operate. The organization might be an "adapter" (or localizer) and simply match the typical systems in the host country, an "exporter" and build reward systems based on the system in the home country, or a "globalizer" (or integrator) and build reward systems using the best ideas and practice from any and all locations.

They also note three separate possible reactions to local host contexts: conformance, avoidance or resistance. In conformance mode, an organization would simply conform to local practice. In avoidance mode, contextual factors might be ignored, buffers might be set up or a smaller pool of applicants amenable to the desired practice might be accepted. In resistance mode, the organization tries to maneuver within the local context, perhaps seeking permission from different state employees until a favorable interpretation of the requirements is given. Choice of reaction mode is argued by Bloom and colleagues (2003) to be a function of variation in local practice: conformance is more likely when local practice variation is low and resistance is more likely when local practice variation is high (p.1360).

The WorldatWork survey (2006) provides insight into what multinational companies are actually doing in terms of global rewards systems in noting which rewards practices are managed globally, which are managed regionally and which are managed locally. This information is shown in Table 10.1.

Rewards practices related to non-executive/non-sales employees vary considerably in locus of control. Nearly half of the MNCs surveyed manage performance appraisal globally, but only 23 percent manage base pay globally and only 42 percent manage short-term incentives globally. One possible explanation is that because performance management is increasingly being driven by the corporate business plan it makes sense

Table 10.1 Management level of global rewards programs

	Managed globally (%)	*Managed regionally (%)*	*Managed locally (%)*
Performance management	48	22	30
Base pay (non-executive)	23	34	44
Short-term incentives (non-executive)	42	32	26
Long-term incentives (non-executive)	79	9	12
Sales compensation	24	38	37
Executive compensation	92	5	3
Perquisites	10	30	59

Source: Adapted from WorldatWork (2006: 6).

to organizations to insure conformity so that all units work towards the same outcomes, regardless of location.

Base pay may be managed locally more frequently than globally because a sensitivity to local regulations and local labor markets is required. Short-term incentives for non-executives may be managed globally more successfully than can base pay because (for non-executives) incentives are relatively small compared to base pay and to the extent that incentives are tied to performance (individual and organizational), control to insure conformity is desirable. Long-term incentives for non-executives are likely to be so heavily managed from headquarters because (1) long-term incentives are largely/exclusively stock vehicles (either options, actual shares or phantom stock) and thus control is necessary, and (2) non-executive long-term incentives are an extension of executive long-term incentive programs, which are centralized.

Sales compensation is likely to be managed regionally or locally because most sales management is also regional or local. Sales compensation is in many companies run by marketing and sales units rather than by compensation units in human resources departments, so it could be expected that sales compensation would be managed at the same level that sales management occurs.

Executive compensation presents an interesting contrast. Executive compensation itself is largely managed from headquarters. This may be in part because executives are more likely to transfer across countries than are other employees, making global conformity of executive pay policies and practices critical. Similarly, executive compensation and compensation systems are typically approved by the Board of Directors; having regional and local management would be unwieldy and inefficient. On the other hand, perquisites are mostly managed locally and regionally. This is likely to be the case for two reasons. Perquisites are markers of organizational status and this hierarchy varies considerably across different countries, as do the costs and status level of different perquisites. Perquisites also are frequently taxed at a lower rate than cash payments (or not taxed at all) and companies use them to make total rewards across countries more comparable. While perquisites in the USA are no longer very important parts of the total rewards package, they are very important in many countries and it is logical that they be managed at the local level.

The literature on executive pay suggests that policies and practices are converging, as suggested by the WorldatWork (2006) data. Earlier studies argued that differences in executive pay systems were a function of differences in country culture; and that Europeans (for example) have very different understandings of and expectations for pay from those in the USA (Pennings, 1993). In a later study, Cheffins (2003) notes the existence of a "global compensation imperative" brought on by more diffuse share ownership (with the corresponding increase in power of the CEO), cross-border hiring, transnational mergers and acquisitions and the growth of multinational enterprises. While cross-country differences in corporate law, taxes, labor law, "soft" law (regulations of professional organizations and stock exchanges, for example) and culture have slowed the rate of convergence, convergence is occurring.

Sanders and Tuschke (2007) assess the introduction of stock options in Germany, where they initially violated normative, regulatory and cultural-cognitive standards of legitimacy. Among their findings is that the use of options in one respected environment may confer legitimacy to other environments. The wide use of options in respected American MNCs made their adoption in Germany more palatable. Similarly, they found that MNC leaders with contacts in organizations where the practice is legitimate are more likely to adopt. Success with a prior adoption of a contested practice makes adoption of another more likely. Adoption of a practice by another organization in the same country makes adoption more likely, though same industry adoption made it less likely. This study suggests how pay practices promoted by an MNC that were initially seen as non-legitimate can be diffused throughout a country. It also suggests why executive pay practices are more likely to converge than are pay practices for non-executives.

Point and Tyson (2006) document some degree of convergence across France, Germany, Switzerland and the United Kingdom with respect to the transparency of reporting director pay. Published materials by organizations have even adopted some of the same language justifying pay levels and practices, to the point that the language is becoming clichéd.

It is not only executive rewards policies and practices that may be converging. One possible segment where rewards levels might begin to converge is as CEO (and other senior executive) rewards are more frequently being priced in global markets, and even that is the exception rather than the rule. Towers Perrin (Worldwide Total Remuneration, 2001–2 to 2005–6) publishes data on four jobs in twenty-five countries. The coefficient of variation of CEO total remuneration dropped (from .60 to .50) over the period covered while the coefficient of variation of total remuneration for Director of Human Resources, Accountant and Manufacturing Employee either remained the same or grew slightly.

Towers Perrin (2007) provide evidence that some executive rewards levels may be retreating from global convergence towards regional convergence. Based on 61 US MNCs, the report notes that these companies used to export long-term incentive awards identical to those in the US, but with required options expensing and cost consciousness increasing, this is no longer the case. Instead companies are grouping countries into regions or tiers by clustering countries with similar competitive values. The median long-term incentive award for Europe is now 80 percent of US award size; Asia and the rest of the world get only 60 percent of US award size.

Summary

There is not enough evidence in the convergence argument with respect to rewards systems policies and practices to come down firmly on either side. Contingency and strategic HRM arguments argue against rewards policies and practices being uniform within any given country, and particularly within the USA. It is difficult to argue for convergence to a national model when there is no single national model. At the same time survey data suggest that a substantial minority of MNCs are managing various rewards systems from corporate headquarters, suggesting that some degree of compensation convergence is taking place across global boundaries, if only within individual organizations. Research focusing on within-organization rewards policies and practices convergence across global boundaries is needed to confirm this. Such research should look for convergence of specific policies and practices such as establishment of job/ person value, market benchmarking, individual wage increases, short-term and long-term incentive schemes, and special target rewards systems for unionized, sales and executive employees.

References

Andrews, T.G. and Chompusri, N. 2005. Temporal Dynamics of Crossvergence: Institutionalizing MNC Integration Strategies in Post-Crisis ASEAN. *Asia Pacific Journal of Management*, 22(1): 5–22.

Black, B. 2001. National Culture and Industrial Relations and Pay Structure. *Labour*, 15(2): 257–77.

Bloom, M. and Milkovich, G.T. 1999. A SHRM Perspective on International Compensation and Rewards Systems. *Research in Personnel and Human Resource Management. Supplement IV*: 283–303.

Bloom, M., Milkovich, G.T. and Mitra, A. 2003. International Compensation: Learning From How Managers Respond to Variations in Local Host Contexts. *International Journal of Human Resource Management*, 14(8), 1350–67.

Bognanno, M.F., Keane, M.P.O. and Yang, D. 2005. The Influence of Wages and Industrial Relations Environments on the Production Location Decisions of US Multinational Corporations. *Industrial and Labor Relations Review*, 58(2): 171–200.

Cheffins, B.R. 2003. Will Executive Pay Globalize Along American Lines? *Corporate Governance*, 11(1): 6–24.

Chiang, F. 2005. A Critical Examination of Hofstede's Thesis and its Application to International Reward Management. *International Journal of Human Resource Management*, 16(9): 1545–63.

Dickmann, M. 2003. Implementing German HRM Abroad: Desired, Feasible, Successful? *International Journal of Human Resource Management*, 14(2): 265–83.

Ding, D.Z., Akhtar, S. and Ge, G.L. 2006. Organizational Differences in Managerial Compensation and Benefits in Chinese Firms. *International Journal of Human Resource Management*, 17(4): 693–715.

Dunlop, J. 1957. The Task of Contemporary Wage Theory. In G.W. Taylor and F.C. Pierson (eds), *New Concepts in Wage Determination*: 117–39. New York: McGraw-Hill.

Freeman, R.B. 2007. Labor Market Institutions Around the World. Working Paper 13242. Cambridge, MA: National Bureau of Economic Research.

Gamble, J. 2003. Transferring Human Resource Practices from the United Kingdom to China: The Limits and Potential for Convergence. *International Journal of Human Resource Management Research*, 14(3): 369–87.

Geppert, M. and Williams, K. 2006. Global, National and Local Practices in Multinational Corporations: Towards a Sociopolitical framework. *International Journal of Human Resource Management*, 17(1): 49–69.

Gerhart, B. and Fang, M. 2005. National Culture and Human Resource Management: Assumptions and Evidence. *International Journal of Human Resource Management*, 16(6): 971–86.

Gomez, C. and Sanchez, J.L. 2005. Human Resource Control in MNCs: A Study of the Factors Influencing the Use of Formal and Informal Control Mechanisms. *International Journal of Human Resource Management*, 16(10): 1847–61.

Gualerzi, D. 2007. Globalization Reconsidered: Foreign Direct Investment and Global Governance. *International Journal of Political Economy*, 36(1): 3–29.

Gupta, V. and Wang, J. 2004. The Transvergence Proposition Under Globalization: Looking Beyond Convergence, Divergence and Crossvergence. *The Multinational Business Review*, 12(2): 37–57.

Herrmann, A. 2005. Converging Divergence: How Competitive Advantages Condition Institutional Change under EMU. *Journal of Common Market Studies*, 43(2): 287–310.

Horwitz, F.M., Heng, C.T., Quazi, H.A., Nonkwelo, C., Roditi, D. and van Eck, P. 2006. Human Resource Strategies for Managing Knowledge Workers: An Afro-Asian Comparative Analysis. *International Journal of Human Resource Management*, 17(5): 775–811.

Levy, D. 2007. Heterogeneous Convergence. *Emory University School of Law: Law & Economics Research Paper Series, Research Paper No. 07–2*.

Lunnan, R., Lervik, J.E.B., Traavik, L.E.M., Nilsen, S. M., Amdam, R.P. and Hennestad, B.W. 2005. Global Transfer of Management Practices Across Nations and MNC Subcultures. *Academy of Management Executive*, 18(20): 77–80.

McGaughey, S.L. and De Cieri, H. 1999. Reassessment of Convergence and Divergence Dynamics: Implications for International HRM. *International Journal of Human Resource Management Research*, 10(2): 235–50.

Pennings, J.M. 1993. Executive Reward Systems: A Cross-National Comparison. *Journal of Management Studies*, 30(2): 261–80.

Petit, P. 2006. Globalisation and Regional Integration: A Comparative Analysis of Europe and East Asia. *Competition and Change*, 10(2): 113–40.

Point, S. and Tyson, S. 2006. Top Pay Transparency in Europe: Codes, Convergence and Clichés. *International Journal of Human Resource Management*, 17(5): 812–30.

Pudelko, M. 2005. Cross-national Learning from Best Practice and the Convergence–Divergence Debate in HRM. *International Journal of Human Resource Management*, 14(3): 363–8.

Quintanilla, J. and Ferner, A. 2003. Multinationals and Human Resource Management: Between Global Convergence and National Identity. *International Journal of Human Resource Management*, 16(11): 363–8.

Robertson, C.J., Al-Khatib, J.A., Al-Habib, M. and Lanoue, D. 2001. Beliefs about Work in the Middle East and the Convergence Versus Divergence of Values. *Journal of World Business*, 36(3): 223–44.

Rowley, C. and Benson, J. 2002. Convergence and Divergence in Asian Human Resource Management. *California Management Review*, 44(2): 90–109.

Sanders, W.G. and Tuschke, A. 2007. The Adoption of Institutionally Contested Practices: The Emergence of Stock Option Pay in Germany. *Academy of Management Journal*, 50(1): 33–56.

Shibata, H. 2002. Wage and Performance Appraisal Systems in Flux: A Japan–United States Comparison. *Industrial Relations*, 41(4): 629–52.

Towers Perrin (2002, 2004, 2006) *Worldwide Total Remuneration*. New York.

—— (2007) *US Multinationals Show Significant Changes in Participation in Long-Term Incentive Programs, Towers Perrin Survey Finds*. Stamford, CT. (Press Release)

Venables, A.J. 2003. Winners and Losers From Regional Integration Agreements. *The Economic Journal*, 113(490): 747–61.

Woldu, H.G., Budhwar, P.S. and Parkes, C. 2006. A Cross-National Comparison of Cultural Value Orientations of Indian, Polish, Russian and American Employees. *International Journal of Human Resource Management Research*, 17(6): 1076–94.

WorldatWork 2006. *Effectively Managing Global Compensation and Benefits: September 2006*. Scottsdale, AZ.

Zivnuska, S., Ketchen, D.J. and Snow, C.C. 2001. Implications of the Converging Economy for Human Resource Management. *Research in Personnel and Human Resource Management*, 20: 371–405.

Compensation and national culture

Barry Gerhart

The study of compensation includes work on its measurement, determinants and consequences. Contextual factors may act not only as determinants, but also as contingency factors in influencing a firm's choice of compensation strategy, as well as the consequences of that choice for the firm's effectiveness (Gerhart and Rynes, 2003; Gomez-Mejia and Balkin, 1992; Milkovich, 1988). Key aspects of the context include external factors such as regulatory, institutional (e.g. labor unions) and market factors, as well as internal factors such as organization characteristics (e.g. strategy) and employee characteristics. In this chapter, I focus on the role of one aspect of context, national culture, and its relevance to compensation.

As markets have become more global (see, e.g. Werner, 2002), firms have increasingly found it necessary to understand how the contextual environment for management (including compensation) decisions differs from country to country. Such contextual differences might either constrain the use of certain management (including compensation) practices or suggest caution in their use because they are expected to be less effective in certain country contexts than in others (of course, the use and effectiveness of management practices could also be enhanced in some countries).

As such, there has been a call for greater awareness of national context differences, and this need is sometimes seen as especially acute among US academics. According to Hofstede (1993: 82): "not only practices but also the validity of theories may stop at national borders," something that "it has taken much longer for the US academic community to accept" and "I wonder whether even today everybody would agree with this statement." Similarly, Boyacigiller and Adler (1991: 263) state that: "Parochialism is based on ignorance of others' ways. . . . Americans have developed theories without being sufficiently aware of non-US contexts, models, research, and values" and that without this awareness, it will be difficult to "avoid relegating the American academic management literature to the curiosity of a mid-twentieth century fossil."

Which aspect of local (or national) context is seen as most important in limiting the use and validity of theories and practices? According to Hofstede (1983), an important candidate is national culture, something he believed that both academics and managers had largely overlooked:

> Both management practitioners and management theorists over the past 80 years have been blind to the extent to which activities like "management" and "organizing" are culturally dependent . . . and if we see what effective organizations in different cultures have done, we recognize that their leaders did adapt foreign management ideas to local cultures.

(88)

Among the management practices that can be affected by local context, of course, are human resource (HR) management practices, including those dealing with compensation. Indeed, according to Evans and colleagues (2002: 162): "Of all the management domains, HR management is generally considered to be the most sensitive of all to local context." While recognizing that there are other dimensions to local context that matter, the potential importance of national culture seems to receive considerable attention in most or all textbooks in HR as a factor to consider in designing HR strategies in different countries. Likewise, Dowling and Welch (2004), in their book, *International Human Resource Management*, state that "Activities such as hiring, promoting, rewarding and dismissal will be determined by the practices of the host country and often are based on a value system peculiar to that country's culture" (14).

As with management and HR practices generally, it has been argued that compensation and reward practices differ in their use and effectiveness across cultures. For example, according to Early and Erez (1997: 75):

> The type of reward schemes that emerge in each country . . . accords with the prevailing cultural characteristics. Attempts to transfer a reward system from one culture to another can result in a mismatch, and dissonant systems are likely to be ineffective and rejected.

Similarly, Schuler and Rogovsky (1998: 161) argue that "in order for MNCs [multinational corporations] to be globally competitive, it is crucial that they . . . adjust their compensation practices to the cultural specifics of a particular host country," but that, in fact, they have observed an "astonishingly small number of strategies and policies that are used by MNCs to adjust to national culture, particularly in the area of compensation" (162).

In this chapter, my goal is to describe research on the relationship between compensation decisions and national culture, as well as the implications of any such relationship. Is it, for example, a major concern that MNCs do not adjust their compensation strategies more often? How strong are national culture differences and must organizations adjust to them? I begin by briefly reviewing how national culture has most typically been defined and measured. I then provide a critical review of evidence on the relationship between compensation and national culture and what it means in practical terms for international firms.

Definition and measurement of national culture

The most influential work on national culture was conducted by Geert Hofstede and his colleagues. Hofstede's (1980) landmark multi-country study, *Culture's Consequences*, used survey data collected from IBM employees worldwide to develop four national culture dimensions: uncertainty avoidance, masculinity/femininity, power distance and individualism. (Later, Hofstede and Bond, 1988 added a fifth dimension, long-term orientation.) Hofstede described his approach to studying culture as relying on the concept of values. He defined values as a "broad tendency to prefer certain states of affairs over others" (19). He further stated that values could be an attribute of individuals as well as of collectivities (e.g. countries) and that "culture presupposes a collectivity" (19).

Hofstede (1980, 2001) constructed measures of national culture and quantified between-country mean differences on these measures. He recognized that culture varies not only between, but also within countries. However, the focus of his book is on the importance of between-country differences, and information on within-country variance was not provided. Subsequent research in the management field has made extensive use of Hofstede's country scores in studying the effect of national culture. (For reviews of international management research and the role of Hofstede's work, see Kirkman *et al.*, 2006; Tsui *et al.*, 2007.) As we saw earlier, following his 1980 study, Hofstede's writings emphasized that national culture differences have important implications for management theory and practice. Hofstede's five national culture dimensions and their definitions are shown in Table 11.1.

More recently, the Global Leader and Organizational Behavior Effectiveness (GLOBE) research program (House *et al.*, 2004) has constructed another set of national culture scores. This research uses a sample of 17,730 middle managers from 951 organizations in three industries (food processing, financial services, telecommunication services) in 62 countries. The GLOBE study represents a very impressive collaboration between 170 scholars from the 62 countries and sought to build on the seminal work of Hofstede (1980) and others. In contrast to Hofstede (1980), where the focus was on values, the GLOBE data explicitly ask questions regarding values ("what should be?") and practices ("what is?") of their sample for all culture dimensions. Another difference from Hofstede is that GLOBE uses society as the level of analysis in its items whereas Hofstede used the individual level of analysis. Thus, for example, to measure national culture, GLOBE asks respondents to describe the values of the society/country they live in, whereas Hofstede asked respondents to describe their own personal values. Table 11.1 also summarizes the GLOBE national culture dimensions and GLOBE's hypotheses regarding how they relate (conceptually) to Hofstede's dimensions.

National culture and compensation: hypotheses and evidence

As noted above, it has been argued that HR strategy, including compensation strategy, must be adjusted to fit with different national cultures (Early and Erez, 1997; Schuler and Rogovsky, 1998). Most attention has been paid to the pay for performance (PFP) decision in this work. PFP practices can vary on a number of dimensions, including (Gerhart and Rynes, 2003): the strength of the pay-performance relationship; the relative importance of individual versus collective (group, organization level) performance in determining performance-based payouts; and the degree to which PFP is combined with other HRM practices such as participation in decision-making. See Chapter 12 for an in-depth discussion of PFP programs for global employees.

Table 11.1 National culture dimensions, Hofstede and GLOBE

GLOBE culture dimensions	Hofstede culture dimensions
Power distance. The degree to which members of a collective expect power to be distributed equally.	Power distance. The extent to which the less powerful members of organizations and institutions accept and expect that power is distributed unequally. The basic problem involved is the degree of human inequality that underlies the functioning of each particular society.
Uncertainty avoidance. The extent to which a society, organization or group relies on social norms, rules and procedures to alleviate unpredictability of future events.	Uncertainty avoidance. The extent to which a culture programs its members to feel either uncomfortable or comfortable in unstructured situations. Unstructured situations are unknown, surprising, different from usual. The basic problem involved is the degree to which a society tries to control the uncontrollable.
Humane orientation. The degree to which a collective encourages and rewards individuals for being fair, altruistic, generous, caring and kind to others.	
Collectivism I (Institutional Collectivism). The degree to which organizational and societal institutional practices encourage and reward collective distribution of resources and collective action.	Individualism. On the one side versus its opposite, collectivism, is the degree to which individuals are supposed to look after themselves or remain integrated into groups, usually around the family. Positioning itself between these poles is a very basic problem all societies face.
Collectivism II (In-Group Collectivism). The degree to which individuals express pride, loyalty and cohesiveness in their organizations or families.	
Assertiveness. The degree to which individuals are assertive, confrontational and aggressive in their relationships with others.	Masculinity. Versus its opposite, femininity, refers to the distribution of emotional roles between the genders, which is another fundamental problem for any society to which a range of solutions are found; it opposes "tough" masculine to "tender" feminine societies.
Gender egalitarianism. The degree to which a collective minimizes gender inequality.	
Future orientation. The extent to which individuals engage in future-oriented behaviors such as delaying gratification, planning and investing in the future.	Long-term versus short-term orientation.[a] Refers to the extent to which a culture programs its members to accept delayed gratification of their material, social, and emotional needs.
Performance orientation. The degree to which a collective encourages and rewards group members for performance improvement and excellence.	

Note

[a] House *et al.* did not make a hypothesis regarding convergence between this national culture dimension from their framework and the national culture dimension from Hofstede's framework. It is my hypothesis.

Source: Table 3.1 and Table 8.7, House *et al.*, 2004; Hofstede (2001: xix–xx).

Several dimensions of national culture clearly deal with related areas. For example, individualism–collectivism would seem to relate to the issue of whether individual or collective performance measures would be better received. Stronger pay-performance relationships often use so-called variable pay plans (e.g. commissions, profit-sharing) that may come with lower base pay, but higher upside earnings potential. Variable pay plans of this sort carry greater downside earnings risk as well for employees. Thus, to the degree that employees in a country are high on the national culture dimension of uncertainty avoidance, less aggressive pay-performance plans might be expected. These and related ideas in the form of hypotheses have been provided by Gomez-Mejia and Welbourne (1991) and Schuler and Rogovsky (1998) and are summarized in Table 11.2. This work, in turn, is informed by work on reward allocation rules, which is reviewed below.

Reward allocation rules

While there is little evidence on national culture and compensation in work organizations, there is a large literature on the related topic of how the use of different reward allocation rules or principles (see Deutsch, 1975) is explained by national culture. According to Fischer and Smith (2003: 252), "the typical reward allocation experiment" uses a scenario that describes "two or more individuals working on a task with different performance inputs." Subjects are "asked to divide a reward between the individuals described." As noted above, participants from countries having different national cultures are expected to differ in the weight given to performance in allocating the reward among individuals in the scenario.

Reward allocation rules (and the hypothesized importance of national culture) have been described as follows (Early and Erez, 1997: 73):

> Reward systems across cultures are created under the guiding influence of three different allocation principles . . . *equity* (each according to contribution) . . . *equality* (to each equally), and . . . *need* (to each according to need). These principles are the result of preferences for individualism or collectivism, for egalitarianism or for higher power differential.

Another way of describing the equity rule is to say that it uses performance as the criterion in making reward allocations across employees. According to Early and Erez (1997: 73), national culture influences the degree to which the equity rule is used:

> The equity principle is commonly used in individualistic cultures . . . for instance, the United States, Canada, and Britain . . . In these countries, individual accomplishment and recognition are emphasized over group harmony and teamwork.

Finally, Early and Erez state that the equity principle is not used in a country such as China: "Reward principles are quite different in other cultures, of course. As an example, managers in China use the equality principle more often in allocating rewards" (74).

To the degree that national culture differences matter in compensation, one would expect that comparing two countries such as China and the United States would provide a good test because of their different national culture profiles. As shown below, with the exception of the masculinity–femininity dimension, there are substantial differences

Table 11.2 Hypothesized relationships between national culture and compensation practices

Power distance	Compensation systems are likely to be more hierarchical (greater pay and benefits differentials between job levels) in high power distance countries. Compensation systems that rely on employee participation (e.g. gainsharing) are more likely in low power distance countries (Gomez-Mejia and Welbourne, 1991).
	Broad-based employee stock option and ownership plans are more likely in low power distance countries (Schuler and Rogovsky, 1998).
Individualism	Performance-based pay (especially for individual performance), extrinsic rewards, external equity and short-term orientation are more likely in individualistic countries. In less individualistic countries, personal need, seniority, intrinsic rewards and internal equity are more likely important (Gomez-Mejia and Welbourne, 1991).
	Performance-based pay (especially for individual performance) is more likely in individualistic countries. Broad-based employee stock option and ownership plans is more likely in low power distance countries (Schuler and Rogovsky, 1998).
Uncertainty avoidance	Variable pay/incentives, external equity and decentralized pay-setting are more likely in low uncertainty avoidance countries. Fixed pay (e.g. base salary), centralized pay-setting and internal equity play a greater role in high uncertainty avoidance countries (Gomez-Mejia and Welbourne, 1991).
	Performance-based pay (especially for individual performance) more likely in low uncertainty avoidance countries. Also, compensation based on acquisition of skills and abilities is more likely in low uncertainty avoidance countries whereas compensation based on seniority more likely in countries higher on uncertainty avoidance (Schuler and Rogovsky, 1998).
Masculinity	Differential pay policies that allow inequality in pay, promotions and so forth based on gender, as well as paternalistic benefits intended to be geared primarily toward women (e.g. day care, paid maternity leave) are more likely in countries lower on masculinity (Gomez-Mejia and Welbourne, 1991).
	Maternity leave, flexible benefits, workplace child-care and career-break schemes are more likely in low masculinity countries. Performance-based pay (especially for individual performance) is more likely in individualistic countries (Schuler and Rogovsky, 1998).

across the board between them using Hofstede's (1980) country scores, with differences on the power distance, individualism–collectivism and long-term orientation dimensions being particularly notable.

Table 11.3 Hofstede's national culture means for China and the United States

	China (Hong Kong)	United States
Power distance	80	40
Individualism	20	91
Masculinity	66	62
Uncertainty avoidance	30	46
Long-term orientation	118	29

Consistent with Early and Erez's (1997) later conclusion, early work (e.g. Bond *et al.*, 1982) hypothesized that Chinese respondents would be more likely than US respondents to use the equality rule because the Chinese culture, consistent with Hofstede (1980), was seen as more collectivist, while the US culture was seen as more individualistic. Bond and colleagues argued that "collectivism entails the need to preserve group harmony and will consequently result in a more egalitarian assignment of rewards and punishments for a given task input to a group product" (1982: 187). Their empirical results supported the hypothesis that Chinese (specifically, Hong Kong) respondents would be more likely than US respondents to use the equality rule.

However, the Bond and colleagues (1982) empirical results, as well as the broader literature, fail to provide evidence of a practically significant relationship between individualism–collectivism and reward allocation. Although any use of terms such as small, medium and large to describe effect sizes is arbitrary, given that the importance of effect sizes depends on the specific application, it can nevertheless be useful to make use of the conventions suggested by Cohen (1992) for the correlation, r (and its square, which yields an index of variance explained), which are as follows:

Table 11.4 Cohen's effect size benchmarks

Effect size estimator	Effect size descriptor		
	Small	Medium	Large
r	0.10	0.30	0.50
r^2	0.01	0.09	0.25

Keeping Cohen's conventions in mind, let us first examine studies that compare Chinese and US respondents. Here, the effect size found by Bond and colleagues for country (their measure of national culture) was r = 0.18. (See Fischer and Smith, 2003, Appendix.) Squaring this yields a variance explained of r^2 = 0.03. This is a "small" effect size using Cohen's conventions. In more recent research, not even this small effect for country is found as it appears that Chinese respondents use the equity rule as much as or even more than US respondents and/or have as positive or more positive attitudes toward the use of performance in performance and reward management (e.g. Wang and Bozionelos, 2007; Chen, 1995; Chen *et al.*, 1998; He *et al.*, 2004; Zhou and Martocchio, 2001).

Typically, in these recent comparisons of US and Chinese respondents, researchers describe the lack of support for the hypothesized lesser use of the equity rule among those from the (collectivist) Chinese as surprising, counterintuitive and so forth. Given the increasingly consistent lack of support for the hypothesis, it is perhaps time to recognize that the data simply do not support it and that conventional wisdom may be incorrect.

Second, looking at the broader literature (i.e. adding studies using comparisons other than Chinese and US respondents) on reward allocation, support for the relationship between country differences in collectivism and use of the equity rule is again very limited. A meta-analysis by Fischer and Smith (2003) examined the use of the equity (performance) rule versus the equality rule as a function of the national culture dimension of collectivism. Data were used from 14 different countries (k = 21 samples, N = 4,165 respondents). Their effect size was calculated such that "a positive sign indicates that the participants from the more collectivistic cultural sample preferred equality to equity, whereas individuals from the more individualistic culture preferred equity to equality" (254).

Fischer and Smith (2003) report that "Most studies showed a small but positive effect" (255). Specifically, mean r = 0.065. Squaring that to obtain a variance explained estimate yields a mean r^2 = 0.0042. With a variance explained of less than 1 percent, their meta-analysis indicates that country is a very small factor in determining whether respondents use the equity/performance rule in reward allocation.

However, Fischer and Smith (2003) identify three studies as outliers, one of which compared employees from the People's Republic of China with a sample from the US (Chen, 1995). When these three studies are excluded, mean r = 0.160 (N = 3,543, 18 studies) and mean r^2 = 0.0256. Although the variance explained here is somewhat larger, it is still a "small" effect size under Cohen's conventions. Additionally, it comes at the cost of eliminating about 15 percent of the total sample size. Moreover, it can be argued that an "outlier" study such as that of Chen (1995) should receive more weight (rather than being excluded), given that it has a relatively large sample size (thus, making its effect size more precise) and uses working adults (rather than student samples), one of only three such studies included in the meta-analysis. Also, as we saw earlier in the discussion of studies comparing Chinese and US respondents, the Chen (1995) study does not, in fact, appear to be an outlier in that line of research.

To further illustrate the small effect sizes that are often found in this line of research, let us examine two studies comparing Chinese and US respondents, both of which were conducted after publication of the Fischer and Smith (2003) meta-analysis. Both studies are very helpful in that their reporting of results is sufficiently complete and clear to allow the following examination. The first example is a study by Zhou and Martocchio (2001). They examined the impact of individual performance, co-worker relationship, manager relationship and needs on bonus amount allocated to individuals. They also examined the impact of country (China or United States) and the interactions of country with the other independent variables. They found that individual performance explained 64.2 percent of the variance in bonus allocation decisions. In contrast, the four interactions (i.e. the degree to which respondents from China and the USA used these factors differently in their decisions), while statistically significant, explained together an additional 1.1 percent of the variance in bonus allocations. Thus, the effect size for country was not only small, but was also dominated by the effect size for performance.

In addition, Zhou and Martocchio used their model to generate predicted bonus allocations (in standard score units) at high and low levels of performance and at high and low levels of need separately by country. These appear below:

Table 11.5 Predicted bonus allocations (in standard score units), performance, and need: respondents from the United States and China

	Excellent performance	Poor performance	High need	Low need
China	0.80	−0.80	0.06	−0.06
United States	0.98	−0.71	0.04	−0.04

Thus, while, as noted above, the interactions are statistically significant (with Chinese respondents using performance less strongly and need more strongly than their US counterparts), these differences in predicted means are small and seem unlikely to have practical significance in a workplace setting. This is consistent with the small amount of variance explained by these interactions. Again, as noted, it is the similarity between Chinese and US respondents in their use of performance that is perhaps more notable than any differences.

The second example comes from a study by Giacobbe-Miller and colleagues (2003) that compares reward allocations of 66 US, 87 Russian and 113 Chinese managers. They observe that "China and the United States represent cultural opposites in the dimensions of individualism/collectivism and power distance" (392). As such, the standard hypothesis as we have seen is that Chinese managers would be expected to make greater use than US managers of need (versus performance). On the other hand, the authors state that "Russia shares cultural characteristics with both the US and China," meaning that Russia is not expected to differ as much from either country.

Keeping in mind that making inferences regarding countries based on samples of this modest size (and representativeness) is not advisable, it is interesting nevertheless to examine the results of their bonus allocation scenario which manipulated worker need (low, average, high) and productivity (low, average, high) in a 3×3 design. They conclude that US and Russian managers are similar in their reward allocations but that "China is significantly higher on equality and significantly lower on the amounts awarded to . . . productivity" (400). Again, it is true that the differences are statistically significant. But, what about practical significance?

Controlling for need, the regression coefficients for average and high need (low need is the reference category) and the ratio of these coefficients across the three countries are as follows (in local currencies):

Table 11.6 Bonus allocations and need: regression coefficients for respondents from China, Russia, and the United States

Need	China	Russia	United States
Average	31	67	14
High	70	168	35
High/average ratio	2.3	2.5	2.5

Controlling for productivity, the regression coefficients for average and high productivity (again, low productivity is the reference category) and the ratio of these coefficients across the three countries are as follows:

Table 11.7 Bonus allocations and productivity: regression coefficients for respondents from China, Russia, and the United States

Productivity	China	Russia	United States
Average	338	366	445
High	766	913	1,016
High/average ratio	2.3	2.5	2.3

These results suggest two important observations. First, across all three countries, changes in productivity result in much larger absolute changes in bonus allocations than do changes in need. In the case of China, a high need worker is allocated compensation that is higher by 39 (70 – 31) yuan compared to an average need worker. In contrast, a high productivity worker is allocated 438 (766 – 338) more yuan than an average productivity worker. In other words, the change in productivity results in an approximately eleven times larger increase in pay than does a similar change in need. A second observation is that the high/average ratio is very similar across countries for both need and productivity. In other words, the percentage differential awarded for a particular increase in need or productivity is almost the same across the three countries. Thus, this study, while finding some statistically significant differences between countries, seems more importantly to be another example of similarities being much more notable than differences across these countries in reward allocation.

Compensation practice differences by country

In the studies described above, the design typically uses a scenario methodology. Another type of evidence, which is more scarce, deals with actual compensation practice in organizations and how that relates to national culture differences. In one of the few such studies, Schuler and Rogovsky (1998) make use of three international surveys of organizations' compensation practices. The three datasets use n = 12, n = 11 and n = 12 countries respectively. Although it is not clear what the level of analysis is in their study, it appears to be the country. Thus, the sample size for the analyses range from n = 11 to n = 12. Schuler and Rogovsky report their "results suggest that national culture provides an important explanation for the variance in the utilization of different compensation practices in different countries" (1998: 172). Specifically, "MNCs operating in countries with high levels of Uncertainty Avoidance may be advised to offer more certainty in compensation systems" and "as MNCs strive for greater productivity through the use of individual incentive compensation, a country's culture must be taken into account. More specifically . . . individual incentive compensation practices have a better fit in countries with higher levels of Individualism" (172). Thus, their results appear consistent with their hypotheses (see Table 11.2 of this chapter) and with the overarching hypothesis that compensation and national culture are related.

One issue with interpreting Schuler and Rogovsky's (1998) results is that they used the Kendall correlation coefficient, which does not lend itself to expression in variance explained terms. Thus, it is difficult to know just how practically important the relationship between country and compensation practice was in their data. A second issue, which they raise, is that their approach did "not allow us to control for other important macro-level, social, legal, economic, political, and historical variables" (173).

Thus, it is not possible to know how much of the overall country differences are due to differences in national culture, per se.

Another study of compensation practices examined differences and similarities in the extent to which various practices were used for managerial employees across 10 different countries (Lowe *et al.*, 2002). Lowe and colleagues report a number of findings that do not support the conventional hypothesis that performance plays less of a role in more collectivist countries. For example, they found that incentive pay was used more, not less, in countries such as China, Korea and Taiwan than in the United States. Thus, the Lowe *et al.* (2002) and Schuler and Rogovsky (1998) studies provide conflicting results on the importance of national culture in compensation practice.

Summary

While some studies support the hypothesized relationship between national culture and the use of the equity/performance rule in pay-setting, these relationships are, as we have seen, generally small in practical terms (and sometimes even in the opposite direction of that hypothesized). Studies of actual compensation practice are rare and provide no consensus view.

Another important point is that while the core hypothesis in these literatures deals with the effect of national culture on compensation, in most cases, what is actually estimated is instead the effect of country, which not only includes any national culture effect, but also other characteristics of countries. Thus, using a country effect as a proxy for a more direct estimate of a national culture effect is likely to result in an overestimate of the national culture effect.

Finally, and perhaps most important, even if empirical evidence did show a consistent and practically significant effect, the fact that national culture is related to the *use* of equity/performance in compensation tells us nothing regarding either (1) the degree to which the use of the equity/performance as a basis for compensation is *constrained* in countries having different national cultures, or (2) whether the *effectiveness* of using equity/performance as a basis for compensation is different in countries having different national cultures. Thus, little has changed since Gomez-Mejia and Welbourne stated in 1991 that "the amount of empirical research on the interaction between compensation strategies and national culture, and their combined effect on firm performance, is practically nil" (41). Without such research, it is difficult to say just how much of a factor national culture is in the success or failure of different compensation strategies and whether strategies at odds with the norm in a country are generally ill-advised.

National culture effects: caveats and cautions

Two issues raised above were the use of country dummy variables to measure national culture and the inference that a relationship between national culture and compensation implied the existence of a constraint. I consider both practices/assumptions further below.

Effect sizes and confusion of country with national culture

Reviews of nation/national culture differences in the broader management literature have begun to emphasize the need to do a better job of reporting useful effect size estimates (e.g. variance explained) and have observed that when these are reported, they often seem to be "small" (e.g. Kirkman *et al.*, 2006; Leung *et al.*, 2005). One major potential problem is that the country level scores provided by Hofstede (1980) and used widely in management (and reward allocation) research may only poorly describe collections of individuals from those countries. In this vein, Gerhart and Fang (2005) re-analyzed data from Hofstede (1980) to compute variance explained effect sizes for country differences in individuals' cultural values. They found that country accounted for no more than 4 percent of the variance in individual employees' cultural values. In other words, the great majority (96 percent) of variance in employees' cultural values occurred within, not between countries. The fact that within-country differences are much larger than between-country differences may go a long way toward explaining the weak effect sizes for national culture found generally and specifically in the reward allocation and compensation literatures as well (see above).

Another problem is the tendency for academic studies to say they are studying national culture, but rather than using national culture scores as the independent variable, they use country (e.g. dummy variables for countries) as the independent variable. (See the review by Schaeffer and Riordan, 2003.) Typically, any effect of country is interpreted as a national culture effect. However, this is not warranted because countries differ in many respects besides national culture (Dowling and Welch, 2004). Thus, even when small effect sizes are observed for country, these may actually be biased upward as estimates of national culture effects.

National culture as a constraint

National culture may act as a constraint on certain compensation practices. However, when looking at competitive advantage and the preferences of the workforce, the constraint may not be as daunting as frequently thought.

Compensation practices as a competitive advantage

Even if national culture is related to the use or prevalence of compensation practices in different countries, it does not necessarily follow that current practice is optimal. The strategy literature distinguishes between competitive parity and competitive advantage. According to a strategy framework like the resource-based view (RBV) of the firm (Barney, 1991), a firm that does everything like its competitors cannot gain a competitive edge over them. It is only by finding ways to create value in unique (and difficult to imitate) ways that competitive advantage can be achieved. In other words, adapting HR and compensation practices to the local context, if that is the norm, will not contribute to competitive advantage.

Being strategic also implies alignment. In this vein, Bloom *et al.* (2003: 1351) contrast the "strategic alignment model," which focuses on matching compensation systems in a consistent fashion across countries to the organizational context (defined in terms of global strategic orientation, management systems and organizational culture), with the "national culture model," which emphasizes matching (i.e. adapting) to each local host context, "most importantly to the local culture."

Bloom *et al.* (2003: 1358) report that "Managers across the firms we explored consistently expressed a strong preference for aligning the design of compensation systems with the [multinational's] organizational context rather than conforming to local host contexts." The reason appeared to be the "assumption that conformance would, at best, create competitive parity and that only through strategic alignment can competitive advantage be obtained" (1359). This is consistent with the RBV of the firm.

Although national culture and other country-related contextual factors can certainly make it difficult to use certain management, including compensation, practices, some authors have cautioned that national culture is sometimes used as an excuse:

> Among local managers, culture is often used as an alibi for not introducing change, protecting local fiefdoms against head office interference. Because culture is "impenetrable" it is difficult to argue against such explanations. When the local manager in Thailand tells the head office that "confronting poor performers is not possible here for face saving reasons," there is some truth in it, but it is also an exaggeration. It is often a question of adapting the approach, rather than the objective.
>
> (Evans *et al.*, 2002: 168)

Similarly, among the several caveats and cautions raised by Gomez-Mejia and Welbourne (1991: 40) in the study of compensation and national culture is that

> It is important to resist the temptation to blame cultural differences too quickly for failures of compensation plans overseas. We have found that, quite often, these failures are traced to poor management practices and not to any inherent values in the work force that block the success of these compensation programs.

Given the different contextual environments faced in different countries, multinational firms must decide on a balance (see, e.g. Dowling and Welch, 2004) between localization (tailoring management practices to each country) and standardization (using the same management practices in each country). A similar balancing act is required in the design of global compensation strategies (Bloom *et al.*, 2003). Dowling and colleagues (2008: 5), for example, argue that "considering the complexity of global pay patterns, we suggest that research should involve some combination of universalist and contextualist ideas."

The Bloom *et al.* (2003) paper sought to answer why managers would, in some local contexts, for at least some practices, choose to conform to the local context. Their answer is that within some local contexts, there is little variation in contextual factors (e.g. culture, laws, institutions, market characteristics), whereas in other local contexts there is considerable variation. Their basic hypothesis is that greater "variation provides organizations with greater latitude in how they can respond in their compensation system design decisions" (1360). In contrast, using institutional theory (DiMaggio and Powell, 1983), they note that contextual factors to which multiple organizations and/or stakeholders must conform impose strong pressures, which can take on "a deterministic, rule-like status or contagion of legitimacy (Oliver, 1991) such that non-conformance is difficult, costly, and consequently, unlikely" (1360).

Evans and colleagues (2002: 163) state that in considering how locally responsive to be, "The real question concerns *what to respect*, *what to ignore*, and *what to reinvent* when adapting work practices to another [country] environment." As an example of how firms may reinvent, Bloom *et al.* (2003) describe a US-based financial services firm that sought to use its US-based business practices worldwide. On the compensation front, the focus was on "individual, preferably equity-based, incentives" (1355). They note that "where stock was unavailable because of legal constraints the firm sought to use phantom stock or stock appreciation rights to simulate, as closely as possible, the incentive plan used at its New York headquarters" (1355).

Workforce preferences and fit

Bloom and Milkovich (1999) made the important observation that even if the mean national culture in a country does conflict with an organization's compensation strategy, the organization does not have to hire employees that are typical of that country. Rather, the organization only needs to be able to find enough employees that fit with the organization's compensation practices and management practices more generally. This should be possible to the degree that there is significant variation in cultural values (using, for example, Hofstede's approach to measuring culture) between people within countries. As Gerhart and Fang (2005) have shown, the variance in cultural values within countries far exceeds the variance in cultural values between countries. Thus, finding a workforce that fits country-atypical compensation practices through selective hiring and retention should be possible in many cases. Clearly, this will depend to a degree on just how different the distributions of cultural values are between any two countries. Where cultural distance (e.g. Kogut and Singh, 1988) is high, it is possible that greater localization of compensation practices will be necessary. Even with such (mean) differences, however, to the degree that significant variance exists within a country, an organization may find sufficient flexibility to differentiate itself from the country mean.

Conclusion

While there are clearly important differences across countries in the context of human resource decisions, including those dealing with compensation and rewards, my review suggests that the importance of national culture differences, as typically measured, may be less important than commonly believed. Indeed, empirical research shows that effect sizes are generally small at best in this literature and sometimes countries differ in ways opposite to conventional predictions. Further, the practical significance of even statistically significant hypothesized effects may be overestimated for two reasons. First, country effects may be mistakenly interpreted as national culture effects. Second, it may be mistakenly assumed that any observed relationship between national culture and compensation necessarily constrains firms to a significant degree in their choice of compensation practices and strategies.

References

Barney, J.B. 1991. Firm resources and sustained competitive advantage. *Journal of Management*, 17: 99–120.

Bloom, M. and Milkovich, G.T. (1999). A SHRM perspective on international compensation and reward systems. *Research in personnel and human resource management, supplement 4*: 283–303. Greenwich, CT: JAI Press.

Bloom, M., Milkovich, G.T. and Mitra, A. 2003. International compensation: Learning from how managers respond to variations in local host contexts. *International Journal of Human Resource Management*, 14: 1350–67.

Bond, M.H., Leung, K. and Wan, K.C. 1982. How does cultural collectivism operate? The impact of task and maintenance contributions on reward allocation. *Journal of Cross-Cultural Psychology*, 13: 186–200.

Boyacigiller, N. and Adler, N.J. 1991. The parochial dinosaur: The organizational sciences in a global context. *Academy of Management Review*, 16(2): 262–91.

Chen, C. 1995. New trends in rewards allocation preferences: A Sino-US comparison. *Academy of Management Journal*, 38: 408–28.

Chen, C.C., Meindl, J.R. and Hui, H. 1998. Deciding on equity or parity: a test of situational, cultural, and individual factors. *Journal of Organizational Behavior*, 19: 115–29.

Cohen, J. 1992. A power primer. *Psychological Bulletin*, 112: 155–9.

Deutsch, M. 1975. Equity, equality, and need: What determines which value will be used as the basis of distributive justice? *Journal of Social Issues*, 31: 137–50.

DiMaggio, P.J. and Powell, W.W. 1983. The iron cage revisited: Institutional isomorphism and collective rationality in organizational fields. *American Sociology Review*, 48: 147–60.

Dowling, P.J. and Welch, D.E. 2004. *International human resource management: Managing people in a multinational context* (4th edition). London: Thomson Learning.

Dowling, P., Engle, A.D. Sr., Festing, M. and Mueller, B. 2008. Complexity in global pay: A meta-framework. Unpublished manuscript.

Early, P.C. and Erez, M. 1997. *The transplanted executive: Why you need to understand how workers in other countries see the world differently*. New York: Oxford University Press.

Evans, P., Pucik, V. and Barsoux, J. 2002. *The global challenge: Frameworks for international human resource management*. Boston, MA: McGraw-Hill.

Fischer, R. and Smith, P. 2003. Reward allocation and culture: a meta-analysis. *Journal of Cross-Cultural Psychology*, 34: 251–68.

Gerhart, B. and Fang, M. 2005. National culture and human resource management: Assumptions and Evidence. *International Journal of Human Resource Management*, 16: 975–90.

Gerhart, B. and Rynes, S.L. 2003. *Compensation: Theory, evidence, and strategic implications*. Beverly Hills, CA: Sage.

Giacobbe-Miller, J.K., Miller, D.J., Zhang, W. and Victorov, V.I. 2003. Country and organization-level adaptation to foreign workplace ideologies: A comparative study of distributive justice values in China, Russia and the United States. *Journal of International Business Studies*, 34: 389–406.

Gomez-Mejia, L.R. and Balkin, D.B. 1992. *Compensation, organizational strategy, and firm performance*. Cincinnati, OH: South-Western Publishing.

Gomez-Mejia, L.R. and Welbourne, T. 1991. Compensation strategies in a global context. *Human Resource Planning*, 14(1): 29–41.

He, W., Chen, C.C. and Zhang, L. 2004. Rewards-allocation preferences of Chinese employees in the new millennium: The effects of ownership reform, collectivism, and goal priority. *Organization Science*, 15: 221–31.

Hofstede, G. 1980. *Culture's consequences: International differences in work-related values*. Beverly Hills, CA: Sage.

—— 1983. The cultural relativity of organizational practices and theories. *Journal of International Business Studies*, 14: 75–89.

—— 1993. Cultural constraints in management theories. *Academy of Management Executive*, 7: 81–94.

—— 2001. *Culture's consequences: Comparing values, behaviors, institutions, and organizations across nations* (2nd edition). Thousand Oaks, CA: Sage.

Hofstede, G. and Bond, M.H. 1988. Confucius and economic growth: New trends in culture's consequences. *Organizational Dynamics*, 16(4): 4–21.

House, R.J., Hanges, P.J., Javidan, M. Dorfman, P.W. and Gupta, V. 2004. *Culture, leadership, and organizations*. Thousand Oaks, CA: Sage.

Kirkman, B.L., Lowe, K.B. and Gibson, C.B. 2006. A quarter century of Culture's Consequences: A review of empirical research incorporating Hofstede's cultural values framework. *Journal of International Business Studies*, 37: 285–320.

Kogut, B. and Singh, H. 1988. The effect of national culture on the choice of entry mode. *Journal of International Business Studies*, 19: 411–32.

Leung, K., Bhagat, R.S., Buchan, N.R., Erez, M. and Gibson, C.B. 2005. Culture and international business: Recent advances and their implications for future research. *Journal of International Business Studies*, 36: 357–78.

Lowe, K.B., Milliman, J., De Cieri, H. and Dowling, P.J. 2002. International compensation practices: A ten-country comparative analysis. *Human Resource Management*, 41: 45–66.

Milkovich, G.T. 1988. A strategic perspective on compensation management. *Research in Personnel and Human Resources Management*, 6: 263–88.

Oliver, C. 1991. Strategic responses to institutional processes. *Academy of Management Review*, 16: 145–79.

Schaeffer, B.S. and Riordan, C.M. 2003. A review of cross-cultural methodologies for organizational research: A best-practices approach. *Organizational Research Methods*, 6: 169–215.

Schuler, R.S. and Rogovsky, N. 1998. Understanding compensation practice variations across firms: The impact of national culture. *Journal of International Business Studies*, 29: 159–77.

Tsui, A.S., Nifadkar, S.S. and Ou, A.Y. 2007. Cross-national, cross-cultural organizational behavior research: Advances, gaps, and recommendations. *Journal of Management*, 33: 426–78.

Wang, L. and Bozionelos, N. 2007. An investigation on the attitudes of Chinese workers towards individually-based performance related reward systems. *International Journal of Human Resource Management*, 18: 284–302.

Werner, S. 2002. Recent developments in international management research: A review of 20 top management journals. *Journal of Management*, 28: 277–305.

Zhou, J. and Martocchio, J.J. 2001. Chinese and American managers' compensation award decisions: A comparative policy-capturing study. *Personnel Psychology*, 54: 115–45.

Pay for performance for global employees

12

Aino Salimäki and Robert L. Heneman

Three overarching themes characterize the debate over international compensation systems in Europe, the USA and Japan (Sparrow, 2004). First, there is a shift from job- to person-based human resources systems, a trend that breaks the historically comparative patterns of wage structure. Second, there is a process of transferring social costs and risks away from organizations and the state to the individual. Third, there are significant threats to the psychological contract and a fragmentation and individualization of the reward–effort bargain.

All these trends have implications for pay for performance practices. The first trend presents a shift from looking at the job as a basis for compensation to focusing on desired skills, knowledge and competencies of individual employees as well as knowledge transfer between people. This also implies individualized pay negotiations, and greater dispersion between pay levels in the organization. The second trend is associated with the shift from institutional isomorphism to competitive isomorphism in the global economy. Competitive isomorphism arises from market forces and institutional isomorphism arises from competition for political and organizational legitimacy (DiMaggio and Powell, 1983). The trend generates more coherent pay structures in multinational corporations, but at the same time increases the degree of income insecurity and thus the value attached to immediate financial rewards for employees. The third trend further emphasizes the importance for an employee to acquire knowledge that is transferable in the wider labor market. The decentralization of the collective bargaining structure (with an increase in company-level bargaining) has lent a strong impetus to the introduction and spread of pay for performance pay schemes, especially in Europe. As a result of all these trends, pay for performance practices are not only becoming more and more prevalent, but also desired among employees.

Pay for performance practices

Pay for performance plans reward certain sets of behaviors or the results of those behaviors on an individual or collective level via a diverse set of technical solutions.

See Table 12.1 for a categorization of the types of pay for performance plans. Pay for performance plans seek to motivate increased effort, focus on the job, or co-operation to achieve common goals by granting pay increases or rewards based on previous performance. Pay for performance plans also aim at attracting and retaining a highly performing and skilled work force. Pay for performance can be a fixed part of salary based on the appraisal of superiors in the form of merit pay increases, skill-based increases or promotion. It can also vary based on measures of productivity, efficiency or performance of the individual or collective, and be paid in the form of cash awards, such as bonuses, or in the form of ownership such as shares, share options or stock. Pay for performance can be contrasted with flat-rate percentage increases to all employees based on market conditions (e.g. cost of living adjustments), or pay increases based on seniority (e.g. years of service, rank, status) of the employee.

Pay for performance can be based on performance on multiple levels of an organization, ranging from individual to team, department or plant to the national company, or even the internationally operating company. Variable collective pay for performance plans aim at motivating group work, knowledge sharing or achievement of common goals. Whereas merit pay on the individual level creates dispersion to base pay in the organization, collective incentives allow for yearly fluctuation of labor costs. Downward variation in pay for performance is possible, especially in shares or share options, or sales commissions.

Performance-based pay increases that become a fixed part of base pay are often criticized because they may promote an entitlement culture and because they fail to differentiate between high and low performers (Heneman and Gresham, 1998). This is because even though the supervisors would want to differentiate between employees, they need to consider the broader effects of rewards on, for example, group harmony. A policy capturing study shows that especially Russian, but also US managers, made significant base allocations – not based on productivity – to everyone (Giacobbe-Miller et al., 1998). This resulted in less money available for distribution based on productivity, relations or need. The managers most often cited group relations and cohesiveness as the reason for equal allocations. According to the study it seemed that both productivity and group harmony are important objectives for managers (particularly Russians in this case) resulting in allocations based on both equity and equality principles.

Table 12.1 Pay for performance plans have many names and forms

	Individual	Collective
Fixed	Merit pay Skill-, or competency-based pay Promotion	
Variable	Payment by results Piece-rate pay Commissions Bonuses Individual incentives	Performance-related pay Financial participation Gain-, goal- and profit sharing Ownership Group incentives

The main challenges with pay for performance systems are related to:

(1) *effectiveness* of the external reward to motivate the right behaviors and results;
(2) *acceptance* of the plan by different parties.

An effective reward system focuses employee efforts on the right kinds of tasks, and also motivates effective accomplishment of results. The costs of the practice are not higher than the benefits. Thus, the main challenge is to determine the right reward criteria, to be able to measure them in a valid and reliable manner, as well as to manage the pay budget in a balanced fashion. Obviously if the criteria make employees focus on unrelated tasks, the plan will not be effective. Pay for performance can have unintentional consequences, such as adverse effects on work climate in the case of strong individual incentives, and free riding of some group members in the case of strong group incentives. An effective compensation system should be aligned with business strategy, structure, desired culture or other human resource systems. However, note also that it makes a poor candidate for leading organizational change (Ledford and Heneman, 2000).

There are several stakeholders that need to be considered when planning a compensation practice. Even the best plan for pay for performance can fail miserably because of low acceptance of the employees, organizational politics or lack of consideration of institutional factors. Employees generally are accepting of the distribution of rewards according to their performance. For example, according to a study on pay criteria preferences, performance was rated the most preferred criterion in Hong Kong and Australian employee samples, and the second most preferred criterion in Indonesian and Malaysian samples (after responsibility) (Mamman *et al.*, 1996). Another study reveals a high degree of agreement between bank employees from Canada, Hong Kong, the United Kingdom and Finland on what criteria should be used to determine rewards (Chiang and Birtch, 2005). Performance was ranked the most important criterion in all samples, closely followed by human capital (e.g. skills, experience and education) and job inputs (e.g. responsibility, workload, effort).

In practice, the employees might not trust the management of the system to be fair – and they also expect to be able to maximize their own rewards. The research has also found that employees vary in the amount of risk they are willing to accept in their pay. The willingness to accept uncertainty in pay varies as a function of career stage and personality (e.g. employee risk preference) (Pappas and Flaherty, 2005). Thus, fair and effective administration of pay for performance can be very challenging. Also since employee needs, values and preferences are heterogeneous, the motivational effectiveness of a reward relies on whether it is valued and meaningful to the recipient.

If considering a shift to pay for performance from a global perspective, consequences must be weighed in terms of:

● the capacity of managers in different employment systems to *co-ordinate a pay for performance system competently and credibly*, where input and output factors are likely to interact in complex ways;
● the willingness of employee groups socialized within different traditions to put forward *more effort motivated by a compensation system that introduces a level of risk associated with their extrinsic reward*;
● whether the implementation of the system would be *aligned with the business strategy, structure, desired culture or other human resource systems*: for example, whether the

emphasis is placed on individuals isolated from the collective context (determining mix of individual and collective rewards).

Global perspective on compensation practices

The prevailing conceptualization of strategy in the international business context has been the global integration–local responsiveness framework. While the global nature of a business may call for increased standardization, diverse cultural environments may, simultaneously and paradoxically, call for differentiation. One study demonstrated that when a subsidiary is highly dependent on the parent to provide crucial resources, it is common for the multinational company to exert control through formal coordination mechanisms and globally integrated international human resource management (IHRM) strategies (Hannon *et al.*, 1995). In turn, the dependence on local resources is related to locally responsive IHRM strategies, compensation policies as a part of them. Also, the influence of host institutions on IHRM strategy depends on the level of the parent's ownership. When the multinational's ownership stake is large, global integration is prevalent despite the level of the host institution dependence.

Human resource management consists of practices which differ in their relative resemblance to local practices and parent practices (Rosenzweig and Nohria, 1994). Those human resource management practices that involve executives (i.e. executive bonuses) or speak to the internal decision-making of the firm (i.e. participation in decision-making) tend to resemble the parent's practices more, relatively speaking. Thus, the research shows that executive compensation tends to resemble the parent's practices but at the same time the employee practices might not, depending on the context.

The two prevalent international human resource management models use a similar set of contextual factors; however, they adopt different views of how these factors influence the design of international compensation systems (Bloom *et al.*, 2003). *The strategic alignment model* assumes that managerial responses determine whether organizations can exploit and manipulate their environments successfully. The compensation design is viewed as purposeful, driven primarily by organizational considerations and amenable to managerial control. *The national cultural view* assumes that external cultural forces operating through institutional arrangements, such as trade union federations, employee considerations and government agencies, transcend any single organization's control. International compensation system design is viewed as reactive, driven primarily by external considerations and largely beyond managers' influence. Thus, the attainment of the goals for pay for performance practices can be approached from two directions (see Figure 12.1).

In order to consider whether the particular pay for performance practice will be globally effective, the company needs to address the following questions:

● Is universal application of a global (headquarters-designed) approach to compensation system management to be pursued as *a necessary reflection of corporate organization strategy*?
● To what degree is there *a need to adapt universal reward management norms* to accommodate different regulatory political factors, institutions and stakeholders, the

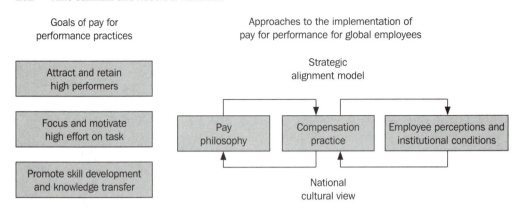

Figure 12.1 Implementation of pay for performance from strategic alignment and national cultural perspective

industry competitive environment and local market conditions as well as pre-existent employee values encountered in the multiplicity of operating environments around the world?

In practice, the results of the global compensation practices survey from 228 global companies demonstrate that there is not a single, dominant approach to managing global compensation; companies are evenly split between centralized (*globally integrated*) and decentralized (*locally responsive*) approaches to their global compensation structure (49 percent centralized vs 51 percent decentralized) (WorldatWork and Watson Wyatt Worldwide, 2004). However, both groups expect to see a growing trend toward greater centralization in the near term. The primary objectives for having a centralized compensation structure are to have a consistent link between rewards and results, and to have a consistent position with regard to market and internal equity. The majority of survey respondents have a uniform approach to short- and long-term incentives and bonuses for executives and management (executives 82–83 percent, management 52–65 percent), while less than half have a uniform global approach for professional employees (35–44 percent).

In terms of applying a pay for performance program internationally, over two-thirds of the 63 international managers who responded to a reward and recognition survey in 2005 aimed at applying a pay for performance *philosophy* internationally (always 67.7 percent, sometimes 27.4 percent, never 4.8 percent) (Perskins, 2006). However, less than half applied the philosophy *in practice* (always 38.7 percent, sometimes 54.8 percent, never 6.5 percent). Only about a fourth of those surveyed believed that rewards are always linked to performance appraisal *in employee perception* (always 24.2 percent, sometimes 72.6 percent, never 3.2 percent). Almost three-quarters of respondents said the pay for performance solution is associated with basic pay (73.8 percent), and five out of six (85.2 percent) of respondents said the link is to variable bonus payments. Over a third (34.4 percent) of respondents reported that performance appraisal is linked with noncash recognition. This shows the popularity of the idea of rewarding for performance (both in fixed and variable form) in global companies, but also shows how hard it is to apply the philosophy in practice, and how hard it is to make employees believe that the system really rewards the relevant behaviors and/or results of those behaviors in practice.

As research shows, in some locations managers might feel compelled to conform to local conditions while in other locations they may be able to focus on strategic alignment (Bloom *et al.*, 2003). Thus, although managers would claim to respond strategically, they often encounter constraints imposed by the local host environment.

Expatriate considerations

Subsidiary staffing is a primary strategic means for multinational corporations (MNCs) to 1) *share knowledge* between the parent and subsidiary, and 2) *coordinate* activities and exercise *control* over their foreign subsidiaries (Gaur *et al.*, 2007). When making subsidiary staffing decisions, the MNC can choose between parent country nationals (here called expatriates), host country nationals and third country nationals. The MNCs are likely to rely on expatriates the greater the institutional distance of the host country from the home country (Gaur *et al.*, 2007). The larger the difference between parent and host country formal regulations and informal norms, the higher the proportion of parent country nationals.

There are demonstrated advantages from employing expatriates on organizational performance through improved control and coordination, especially when the company ages (Gaur *et al.*, 2007). However, it has also been demonstrated that too high of a proportion of parent country nationals can reduce subsidiary legitimacy and reduce subsidiary performance, particularly in subsidiaries situated in institutionally distant environments.

The goals for an expatriate compensation system are often presented as follows: to *attract personnel* in areas where the multinational has its greatest needs and opportunities, to facilitate the transfer of international employees in the most *cost-effective* manner, to *facilitate re-entry* into the home country at the end of foreign assignment, and to contribute to *organizational strategy* (Suutari and Tornikoski, 2001). However, these objectives might vary in importance, and implementation of them might contradict each other (Bonache, 2006).

The first approach to expatriate compensation is a *host-country approach* that aims at fitting the expatriate into the assignment location salary structure (Bonache, 2006). This approach reduces costs, and helps to create a sense of equity between expatriates and local employees. However, this method is limited in motivating international mobility. This approach is usually adopted when the expatriate has become replaceable by a local hire but wants to remain abroad for personal reasons.

The second is the *global approach* that intends to pay on an international scale (Bonache, 2006). This approach might be most relevant in the case of expatriates who are expected to move to more than one foreign country, thereby losing direct connection with their home country or their host country compensation policy. Costs and difficulties of re-entry are often mentioned as the main shortfalls of this system.

The third, and currently most prevalent, is the *home-country approach* that provides expatriates with equivalent purchasing power abroad to help them maintain a home country life style (Bonache, 2006). This approach might have a side-effect of placing the host county nationals in a disadvantageous position relative to the expatriate (Toh and Denisi, 2003). Host country nationals who become aware of this position are likely to perceive inequity and engage in withdrawal behaviors, which in turn are likely to reduce the effectiveness of expatriates.

In expatriate compensation decisions, the company faces the potential conflict of maintaining some form of internal equity while providing sufficient incentive to attract and motivate employees for overseas assignments. The situational factors need to be considered and balanced on an individual basis.

Institutional context

Local institutions influence the prevalence of pay for performance in different countries. For example, France, Japan and Brazil made greater use of organization-level pay for performance than the USA, Canada, the United Kingdom, Germany and Australia, for a variety of reasons (Brown and Heywood, 2002). The French government provides generous tax benefits to both firms and workers as part of a largely mandated plan of profit sharing. The plan originated not as a way to create performance incentives or build commitment, but as a way to encourage savings. In comparison, the Japanese government provides no tax breaks. However, in Japan, employee stock ownership plans and profit sharing are popular tools to build employee commitment to the long-run success of firms. The Brazilian provisions were initiated with the intention to promote social equity and reduce income inequality.

Even though pay for performance is often associated with decentralization of the decision-making, it also depends on the sociopolitical context. For example in Brazil, profit and gain sharing plans were made mandatory subjects of bargaining, requiring employee representation in scheme design and implementation. Despite the substantial financial participation in France, profit sharing has not been integrated with worker participation in decision-making (Brown and Heywood, 2002). However, a study found that generally firms with profit sharing report a large decrease in union influence compared to firms without profit sharing (D'Art and Turner, 2003).

The local isomorphism helps to explain the prevalence of the pay for performance practices within boundaries of a country. First, the local laws and regulations compel isomorphism (coercive pressures). Second, local practices are perceived to be important in improving competitiveness (normative pressures). Third, adopting local practices is an attempt to fit in (mimetic pressures) (DiMaggio and Powell, 1983). These pressures emphasize the primacy of the motive of organizational legitimacy over the motive of organizational efficiency. When forced to choose, organizations will select options which preserve and enhance organizational legitimacy.

As an example, comparing the use of performance-based pay practices in the UK and France, two factors are argued to help explain why French firms make more use of incentive pay, particularly merit pay, than their British counterparts (Marsden *et al.*, 2007). As mentioned above, the French government provides tax incentives for profit sharing (coercive pressures). Also the network activities of industry employer organizations have boosted diffusion of merit pay (normative pressures). French employers are more active in industry local employer networks, and this has, in part, promoted the use of incentive pay (Marsden *et al.*, 2007). Both of these explanations stem, again, from the institutional context.

As a result, the prevalence of the practice does not necessarily imply that the practice would be effective. A study by D'Art and Turner (2003) demonstrates that even though there was a significant positive association between the use of profit sharing and organizational performance in European firms, the association did not hold consistently when the association was analyzed country-specifically. In particular, there was a significant association between profit sharing and financial performance only in Belgian and UK firms (but not in Sweden, Finland, Denmark, Norway, Germany, Ireland, Switzerland or The Netherlands).

Local cultural sensitivities

The national cultural view claims that since the effectiveness of a pay for performance system is greatly influenced by the way in which it is perceived by employees, a company should first identify pay and benefit practices that are desired by employees in the respective nations and cultures (Lowe *et al.*, 2002). Once employee needs and desires are appropriately identified, then the mechanics of selectively adopting existing programs to a variety of operations might be addressed and the need to develop new programs identified.

Lowe and colleagues (2002) asked primarily managers and engineers in ten different locations (Australia, Canada, China, Indonesia, Japan, Korea, Latin America, Mexico, Taiwan and the USA) about the *current state* of the practice for a variety of compensation practices. They also inquired about the extent the compensation practices *should be used* in these countries. The general trend was that while pay for performance is considered important, it was not desirable for variable pay to comprise a large proportion of an employee's total pay. The trend was more dispersed in the case of seniority. In the Chinese, Korean and Mexican samples seniority was viewed as a characteristic that would be increasingly valued in the future. In contrast, in the Australian, Canadian, Japanese and US samples seniority would be less of a determinant of pay than has historically been the case in these countries.

Financial rewards and incentives were found to be more important to the respondents in Hong Kong, Canada and the United Kingdom than in Finland in a study on bank employees (Chiang and Birtch, 2005). The authors conclude that the finding supports the notion that *masculine countries* value material rewards more than feminine countries. A study from diverse sets of companies from variety of countries demonstrates that pay for performance practices may have a better fit in countries with high levels of *individualism* than those with high levels of collectivism (Schuler and Rogovsky, 1998). Countries with high levels of *uncertainty avoidance* may be advised to offer more certainty in compensation systems, for example through seniority-based or skill-based compensation.

In addition to employee preferences, another important aspect of cultural dispositions is to recognize that when a company is pursuing a global pay for performance plan, it can be implemented differently in different countries because of allocators' national identity. This is shown in several studies that assess managers' pay allocations. One study that compared Singaporean, Indonesian and US managers demonstrated that Singaporeans and Indonesians were significantly more generous in their merit pay allocations than their US counterparts (Gully *et al.*, 2003). The result implies that allocator's national identity, over and above individual differences, and more importantly, independently of subordinate's actual performance, influences merit pay decisions. The effects of national identity on merit pay allocations were partly mediated by individual collectivism and goal orientations.

In a pay allocation role play, both Russian and US managers placed primary emphasis on individual performance as allocators, and secondary emphasis on co-worker relations and equality (Giacobbe-Miller *et al.*, 1998). In addition, Russian managers utilized need in their pay allocations – although the effect of need was quite modest. This difference was associated with collectivistic culture, and the loss of a safety net in Russia.

According to a policy capturing study on Chinese and American managers' compensation award decisions, Chinese managers put less emphasis on work performance and more emphasis on personal needs when making bonus decisions, and put more emphasis on relationship with co-workers and managers when making nonmonetary decisions (Zou and Martocchio, 2001). They conclude based on the results that Chinese are more relationship and needs oriented, whereas American managers are more performance oriented.

While pay for performance practices are generally accepted in principle by employees and managers, cultural sensitivities exist. Pay for performance as a financial incentive might be mostly appreciated by masculine cultures. Cultures high in individualism appreciate pay for performance where individual achievement is rewarded. Variable pay for performance practices might be a better fit with low uncertainty avoidance cultures. Managerial role plays show that implementation of a global pay for performance plan might be influenced by the national identity of the manager (in addition to individual differences). For example, managers from collective cultures are likely to partially emphasize personal needs and employee relationship in pay decisions.

Conclusions

Research that informs the global challenges of implementing a pay for performance practice currently focuses on institutional and cultural differences. Research that compares the effectiveness of pay for performance practices in different countries is virtually nonexistent. As D'Art and Turner (2003) discuss, future studies should assess variation in the profit sharing policies, such as cash- and share-based schemes, or whether the scheme functions as a substitute or additional benefit to base pay. Note also that organization-level studies typically assume causality and do not measure the influencing process directly. Instead, longitudinal studies with appropriate control groups would be desired.

As reviewed here, there is some literature that demonstrates the prevalence of cultural sensitivities of the employees in different countries. The setback with the studies that address country differences is that most of them assume cultural value differences but do not measure them directly. As Chiang and Birtch (2005) state it may be the nature of the job itself more than national culture that affects employee perception about what criteria should be used to determine rewards. They also argue that the situational factors such as massive layoffs, downsizing and increased use of technology might influence the desire for job security above the influence of culture. Also, as the study by Chen (1995) demonstrates, the current economical conditions have an impact on the preferences.

Consequently, political, economic, institutional and other forces rather than national culture explain a significant amount of variation in the expressed desires of employees from different countries (Bloom and Milkovich, 1999).

However, these studies inform us in a very important fashion: they coherently demonstrate that performance is the preferred criterion for distribution of rewards. From a strategic point of view, whether the system is effective is more dependent on the choice of criteria to attract the right kind of employees and motivate them to focus on the right tasks and share knowledge than to find out what the preferences of the work force pool are in that specific area. The possibility to coordinate compensation practices is partly dependent on institutional factors and cultural sensitivities, but the choice to do so is probably more dependent on the role of the subsidiary, such as method of founding, dependence of local inputs, the presence of expatriates and the extent of communication with the parent (Rosenzweig and Nohria, 1994).

References

Bloom, M. and Milkovich, G.T. 1999. A SHRM perspective on international compensation and reward systems. *Research in Personnel and Human Resources Management*, Supplement 4: 283–303.

Bloom, M., Milkovich, G.T. and Mitra, A. 2003. International compensation: Learning from how managers respond to variations in local host contexts. *International Journal of Human Resource Management*, 14: 1350–67.

Bonache, J. 2006. The compensation of expatriates: A review and future research agenda. In G. Stahl and I. Björkman (eds), *Handbook of research in international human resource management*: 158–75. Cheltenham: Edward Elgar.

Brown, M. and Heywood, J.S. 2002. Paying for performance: What has been learned? In M. Brown and J.S. Heywood (eds), *Paying for performance: An international comparison*. Armonk, NY: M.E. Sharpe.

Chen, C.C. 1995. New trends in rewards allocation preferences: A Sino-US comparison. *The Academy of Management Journal*, 38: 408–28.

Chiang, F.F.T. and Birtch, T.A. 2005. A taxonomy of reward preference: Examining country differences. *Journal of International Management*, 11(3): 357–75.

D'Art, D. and Turner, T. 2003. Profit sharing, firm performance and union influence in selected European countries. *Personnel Review*, 33: 335–50.

DiMaggio, P.J. and Powell, W.W. 1983. The iron cage revisited: Institutional isomorphism and collective rationality in organizational fields. *American Sociological Review*, 48: 147–60.

Gaur, A.S., Delios, A. and Singh, K. 2007. Institutional environments, staffing strategies, and subsidiary performance. *Journal of Management*, 33: 611–36.

Giacobbe-Miller, J.K., Miller, D.J. and Victorov, V.I. 1998. A comparison of Russian and US pay allocation decisions, distributive justice judgments, and productivity under different payment conditions. *Personnel Psychology*, 51: 137–63.

Gully, S.M., Phillips, J.M. and Tarique, I. 2003. Collectivism and goal orientation as mediators of the effect of national identity on merit pay decisions. *International Journal of Human Resource Management*, 14: 1368–90.

Hannon, J.M., Huang, I.-C. and Jaw, B.-S. 1995. International human resource strategy and its determinants: The case of subsidiaries in Taiwan. *Journal of International Business Studies*, 26: 531–54.

Heneman, R.L. and Gresham, M.T. 1998. Performance-based pay plans. In J.W. Smither (ed), *Performance appraisal: State-of-art methods for performance management*: 496–536, Society for Industrial Organizational Psychology Practice Series. San Francisco, CA: Jossey-Bass.

Ledford, G.E. and Heneman, R.L. 2000. Compensation: A troublesome lead system in organizational change. In M. Beer and N. Noria (eds), *Breaking the code of change*: 307–22. Cambridge, MA: Harvard Business School Press.

Lowe, K.B., Milliman, J., De Cieri, H. and Dowling, P.J. 2002. International compensation practices: A ten-country comparative analysis. *Human Resource Management*, 41: 45–66.

Mamman, A., Sulaiman, M. and Fadel, A. 1996. Attitudes to pay systems: An exploratory study within and across cultures. *The International Journal of Human Resource Management*, 7: 101–21.

Marsden, D., Belfield, R. and Benhamou, S. 2007. *Incentive pay systems and the management of human resources in France and Great Britain*. Centre for Economic Performance Discussion Paper no. 796.

Pappas, J.M. and Flaherty, K.E. 2005. The moderating role of individual-difference variables in compensation research. *Journal of Managerial Psychology*, 21: 19–35.

Perskins, S.T. 2006. *International reward and recognition. Research report*. The Chartered Institute of Personnel and Development (CIPD). London.

Rosenzweig, P.M. and Nohria, N. 1994. Influences on human resource management practices in multinational corporations. *Journal of International Business Studies*, second quarter: 229–51.

Schuler, R. and Rogovsky, N. 1998. Understanding compensation practice variations across firms: The impact of national culture. *Journal of International Business Studies*, 29: 159–77.

Sparrow, P. 2004. Intenational rewards systems: To converge or not to converge? In C. Brewster and H. Harris (eds), *International HRM: Contemporary issues in Europe*: 102–9. London: Routledge.

Suutari, V. and Tornikoski, C. 2001. The challenge of expatriate compensation: The sources of satisfaction and dissatisfaction among expatriates. *International Journal of Human Resource Management*, 12: 1–16.

Toh, S.M. and Denisi, A.S. 2003. Host country national reactions to expatriate pay policies: A model and implications. *Academy of Management Review*, 28: 606–21.

WorldatWork and Watson Wyatt Worldwide. 2004. Global compensation practices. A WorldatWork Survey Brief. Arizona.

Zou, J. and Martocchio, J.J. 2001. Chinese and American managers' compensation award decision: A comparative policy-capturing study. *Personnel Psychology*, 54: 115–45.

13

Global wages in industries with low entry barrier occupations

The case of quick service restaurants, call centers and hotels/motels

Jerry Newman and Richard Floersch

Andy Card, a recent White House Chief of Staff, made 85 cents an hour working at a McDonald's in South Carolina. Jerry Newman, the senior author here, made $5.50–$6.50 an hour doing essentially the same jobs working at McDonald's in New York and Michigan (Newman, 2007). It's not too difficult to explain the difference in wages in these two situations. After all, we're holding constant the type of job, the skill set of the crew members – ok, ok, I flatter myself – and the organization. Most of the almost four dollar difference can be explained by changes in minimum wage laws over the years, and labor market competition. What about a similar comparison, though, between Jerry Newman and a recent graduate of his who worked in a Korean McDonald's just prior to entering the SUNY Buffalo MBA program. We can still hold constant the type of job, skill set (again the truth is stretched) and organization. But why were my wages almost twice as high? Now the explanation becomes more complex. Differences in labor markets, legislation, macro-cultures, McDonald's strategic intent in Korea and Asia in general, individual expectations of crew members – all these factors and more may influence and explain wage differences. In fact, we chose Korea for this example to make the explanation more challenging. In general, compensation experts (Hansen, 2005) report that the Asian region is much more challenging to develop global compensation policies and practices (55 percent of multinationals classify this region as the toughest challenge). Western Europe (33 percent) and South America (24 percent) presented the next greatest challenges. In this chapter we look at compensation in global organizations where the majority of jobs have low barriers to entry (e.g. short training times to reach acceptable performance levels). Certainly this includes companies like McDonald's in the quick service industry. But we also will punctuate our discussion with examples from call centers located in global markets and the hospitality industry.

Factors affecting global compensation decisions

When we join firms as employees, explicit contracts exist. Often these contracts are written, sometimes oral. Usually they are quite explicit about starting base wages. To a

lesser extent the roadmap for getting increases in base wages and qualifying for short/
long term incentives also might be a part of this explicit contract.

An implicit contract also looms over this employment relationship: we expect both that
the explicit contract will be upheld and that other rewards, not explicitly mentioned in
any written and verbal discussion, will be unveiled over time. The details of these explicit
and implicit contracts are the core issues in compensation decision making. At a global
level three categories of variables influence compensation details of the contract. They
are environmental factors, organizational factors and employee characteristics. See Table
13.1 for a list of variables relevant to each category.

For US based compensation and reward decisions, these factors affecting the employment
contract are markedly easier. The Macro culture, the way the US as a nation affects
organization and individual views of what are appropriate behaviors and what rewards
should flow from these behaviors, is relatively constant. Similarly, government policies
and laws are similar, if not at the state level, certainly more so at the federal level. "All"
we have to contend with (and we use the word all advisedly) is differences across
organizations in labor markets, cost of living, level of unionization, strategies, structures,
cultures and the level and differential with which we reward individual characteristics.
When we start considering compensation on a global sphere, many of the constants no
longer are, well, constant. And the first decision, perhaps the most important, is whether
and how much we allow all these differences introduced in global marketplaces to affect
compensation and reward decision making. Should Multinational Enterprises (MNEs)
pay someone working in Bangkok the same as in Biloxi? Our immediate reaction is, of
course, to say no. But should the principles guiding decision making across countries be
left to local authorities, thus probably increasing the strength of the resounding NO, or
should consistency be introduced in the form of centralized decision making based on
common principles applied across diverse marketplaces? Recent surveys suggest MNEs
are moving more towards a centralized process. More than half of decentralized
organizations (59 percent) are opting for centralized structures in the near future.
Almost half of all companies currently have centralized structures, and roughly a fourth
(23 percent) of these intends to increase the level of centralization. McDonald's illustrates

Table 13.1 Categories of variables influencing compensation decision making

Environmental factors
        Economic: labor markets and cost of living
        Capital markets: funding and ownership
        Government and legislation: minimum wages and taxes
        Macro culture
        Third parties: unions and employer federations

Organizational factors
        Organization culture
        Organization structure
        Strategy

Employee characteristics
        Attitudes and expectations
        Skill/knowledge
        Tenure

a balance between global decision making and localized flavor in the pay process. Although reward philosophies are formulated at corporate headquarters, McDonald's still debates over ways to recognize country differences. Much of the localization, in a pattern repeated often across MNEs, evidences in variable pay goals and payouts. Headquarters provides a list of metrics important to corporate success, and country managers identify those which matter most at a local level (Marquez, 2006). For example, a new rice item introduced in Korea might be the impetus for creating goals around McDonald's country sales of that new product.

Companies always wrestle with external and internal equity issues. The question distills down to: How much should the market influence compensation decisions relative to organizationally generated compensable factors? Evidence of increased centralization suggests a greater concern about internal equity. In particular, MNEs want to create a results–reward link that fosters a level playing field across countries. Goals might not be the same, but the effort and ability required to achieve them, so far as possible, should be similar. Centralization increases the chances of universal standards.

The quick service restaurant (QSR) industry: the case of McDonald's

McDonald's overall global compensation goal is to have a total compensation package positioned at the 55th–60th percentile. In general this is actualized by having a base pay that strives to be competitive (pay the median rate) and be a leader in short and long term incentives and benefits. Somewhat more stress is placed on short term incentive leadership (60th–65th percentile) than long term incentives or benefits (55th–60th percentile). These overall policy decisions reflect a company, any company, trying to balance internal and external fairness concerns. Competitive base wages require that local and regional labor markets have a central role in a somewhat decentralized decision process. Thus, base wages for a General Manager or Regional Manager in Korea might be decidedly different from those of their counterparts in Central Europe. This decentralization is even more evident in the benefits determination process. Local customs sometimes dictate interesting variability across countries. For example, sabbaticals are relatively rare in the United States, being reserved for the likes of pampered university professors and scientific/engineering personnel, in general. Europe, though, has a very different attitude about the work–leisure balance. QSR store managers in the United Kingdom, The Netherlands, Germany and Switzerland get significant sabbatical leaves after some length of service (e.g. 8 weeks after 10 years in the United Kingdom). No such option is available, though, in bordering countries (e.g. France, Sweden, Italy and Poland). Why? McDonald's would say that local markets for store managers don't require these benefits for a competitive package. Efforts to provide a component of centralization (and thus introduce an element of internal equity) leads McDonald's to focus heavily on the TIP program (Targeted Incentive Plan) – its global short term incentive program. Country managers look at performance objectives of all managers reporting to them and make an effort to reconcile goal difficulty to that of other countries. The bars may differ dramatically across countries, but the height of the bars is supposed to be comparable. Granted, achieving an equitable level across countries is a formidable job, but it is an exercise that McDonald's feels is essential in a fair pay system.

Crew member compensation

McDonald's strives to be competitive at this level. Decisions about base wages and employee benefits are driven by two decentralized forces: local labor markets and local laws. The global comparison group for determining market rates tends to be MNEs with familiar names: Yum! Brands (e.g. Taco Bell, KFC), Starbucks, Wendy's, Burger King, Pepsi Co and Coca Cola. Wages and benefits are driven by these and other competitors for entry level workers. Across countries the competition for labor yields some interesting benefits and perks that reflect unique local expectations. For example, most European countries don't provide hospital insurance (as distinct from health insurance). The one exception, Germany, mandates coverage by law. Other examples include sick pay, premium pay, transportation costs and vacation time.

Sick pay

The number of days and level of compensation for each day varies widely by country custom and social security requirements. Most of the policies tend to be more liberal than in the United States, reflecting again a more liberal work/leisure tradeoff. For example, Austria has a policy of ten paid sick days in the course of a year, while Belgium's restaurants only give sick pay for two days before Social Security kicks in. Social Security pays roughly half of the sick costs at that point. In contrast, France, Finland and Germany have more liberal sick day policies with length of coverage being as much as a month to two years. In France, the employer covers 40 percent of the cost for the first month, then 20 percent in the second month. Social Security augments these monthly figures by adding 50 percent more. In Finland and Germany, McDonald's pays the total cost with coverage ending at a maximum of six weeks (less in Finland).

Premium pay

Most European countries have no premium pay for Saturdays and Sundays. The exceptions are Finland (double time on Sunday) and Belgium (12 Euros per day extra for Sunday). Almost all countries, though, require a premium for working the graveyard shift (post midnight) averaging just under one Euro per hour of extra pay. Overtime pay is roughly one and a half times base wages, but it generally doesn't kick in until workers have worked some hour total exceeding 40 hours per week, roughly approximating US rules.

Transportation costs

In the US crew members ride cars, buses, skate boards, bikes and roller blades to get to work. No restaurants cover the cost of these modes of transport. While this is also true in some European countries, places such as Belgium (70 percent of bus or train tickets), France (50 percent of transportation costs in the greater Paris area) and Spain (up to 12 percent of wages) do have transportation allotments.

Vacation time

This is an area where local practices create a huge variance from US practices. It's rare for a European crew member to have less than a month of vacation time. Domestic policy for McDonald's usually allots one week of vacation after 1–2 years of service.

Managers and senior staff compensation

At the crew level wage issues are relatively straight forward: focus on external equity by paying the market level for base wages and concentrate other reward concerns on employee benefits. Therefore, decentralized decision making and external equity dominate the compensation process. Variable pay is negligible. At higher organization levels, though, internal equity becomes an issue. Short term incentives under the Target Incentive Plan (TIP) require managers to set individualized goals reflecting local market concerns. Country managers are charged with balancing internal equity concerns. Negotiations with individual managers focus on adjusting goal levels so that the relative level of goal difficulty is reasonably constant. For example, operating income is a universal factor in determining the size of short term incentives. But the level of operating income each manager must achieve for any given incentive payout depends in part on the operating income of their geographic region – an adjustment in recognition of internal equity issues. Long term incentives are linked primarily to stock options and restricted stock units and are awarded based upon subjective estimates of sustained employee performance and long term potential.

Conclusions about the quick service industry

In lower level jobs, where barriers to entry are relatively small, neither employee characteristics nor organizational factors (see Table 13.1) play much of a role in pay determination. The third group of factors affecting global compensation decisions, environmental determinants, is the major driver of wages and benefits. Notice our discussion of wages and benefits for crew members. Almost everything was driven by the market and the legal environment of the country. Employee performance or tenure weren't major factors in decisions. Organizational culture didn't affect pay of crew members. As we moved up to higher level jobs, external equity still mattered, but internal equity also began to affect decisions. No one neglects the market, but efforts to link pay to organizational and individual factors rise. We see similar patterns in the call center industry. Firms that rely on part-time workers who are relatively less trained link compensation to market forces. In contrast, call centers that hire more full-time employees tend to train longer and differentiate pay on important organizational and individual characteristics.

The call center industry

Both authors have worked in the quick service industry. The first author's recent experiences as an undercover crew member are well-documented elsewhere (Newman,

2007). Even though I was out of my element behind the counter at McDonald's, Burger King and elsewhere, I started to feel relatively competent by the end of the first week. Certainly, I was passably okay on the less complex tasks by the end of the second week. Not so for many workers in the call center industry. For an industry with a huge presence in the international community and across many countries, there are surprising similarities in training time (Holman *et al.*, 2007). It takes about three weeks to complete initial training of new employees, and a bit more than two more months to be judged proficient. Within this apparent consistency though, there is a huge dual labor market. One part of the market has a large full-time workforce with practices not unlike those in staff and managerial jobs in the quick service industry. The other segment relies more on part-time workers and has HR practices like those of crew members in fast food jobs.

The dual labor market in the call center industry

Bifurcation of call center labor markets arises because of product differentiation, country labor legislation and economic conditions. For example, South Korean call centers have contracts to answer customer calls for products that are technologically uncomplicated. Because there are few problem options it's easier to write scripts covering all contingencies. This cuts down on training time. Further, the call center industry in South Korea arose in the late 1990s when the Asian economic meltdown had all companies worried about taking on long term economic burdens. Much like crew member staffing patterns in the QSR industry, more than 60 percent of this workforce is part-time. About one-half of the call center labor force is part-time in Israel, The Netherlands and Spain. All of these countries also seek to minimize permanent labor costs. Why? Labor legislation in these countries makes it very difficult to fire permanent employees. The need to have flexible contracts, similar to the motivation in South Korea, makes the use of part-time workers efficient. Other countries, with less restrictive legislation, and more stable economic markets, hire full-time workers at a rate greater than the fast food industry. The perception is that this industry has higher barriers to entry in lower jobs – training times approach three months. Call centers in India (97 percent of employees) and South Africa (88 percent of employees) hire mostly full-time employees. They also focus on higher end technical contracts with correspondingly longer training times and, thus, have a greater incentive to keep employees on longer contracts. Base wages in these centers average about 10 percent higher than in lower end centers with higher concentration of part-time workers. This pattern mirrors that of fast food workers.

Variable pay

In contrast, it's harder to generalize about variable compensation in this industry. Unlike QSRs, which tend to have very low unionization rates, call centers tend to show inter-country differences in unionization. Countries with large part-time workforces (e.g. Israel and Spain) also have low unionization rates. In countries with high unionization of call centers, unions resist variable pay. Perhaps because of this, the level of variable pay tends to be similar across countries and across patterns of employment (part-time vs full-time), averaging 12–13 percent. Even given these factors, the reliance on variable pay is still higher in this industry than in QSR, probably because the sophistication of performance measurement in call centers permits a larger part of the total compensation pie to be allocated to variable pay.

Wage determination comparisons of call centers and QSRs

A number of factors related to wage determination differ in the two industries. They include the measurement of performance, employee characteristics and country labor legislation.

Performance measurement

Performance measurement in the call center industry is highly quantified. Call times are closely monitored (the goal is 20–30 minutes). Number of calls per day also are monitored. At their discretion, center supervisors can have calls monitored for quality. Having objective performance indicators on key factors makes it easier to link compensation to performance (Milkovich and Newman, 2008). In the entry jobs at call centers a significant part of compensation is incentive based. Fifteen percent of pay is incentive based, and for call centers with a selling function, this incentive is usually individually based. The portion of compensation that is variable is about the same at higher organization levels.

In contrast, fast food has little or no variable compensation at low levels. Given that performance metrics are easily developed, and readily available for key measures such as drive time (essentially the amount of time between an order being placed and order completion – a figure that is roughly one-tenth the average time budgeted for call center calls) it's somewhat surprising that lower level jobs don't have any variable component to their pay. Then again, the close proximity of customer and worker, and the implied expectation that food will be delivered fast, creates a very powerful motivation to work fast during rush periods. Variable compensation may not be needed to spur productivity! In addition, production in fast food is heavily team-based, unlike the individual nature of jobs in call centers. It's simply harder to design team-based variable pay that works (Milkovich and Newman, 2008). Both of these factors lessen the attractiveness of individual variable pay. At higher organization levels variable pay does surface in the fast food industry. Corporate and restaurant financial measures trigger a component of bonus. The short term incentive, TIP at McDonald's, also has an individual component, but this is based on a subjective evaluation influenced by broad performance dimensions with associated behaviors. An example from McDonald's is shown in Table 13.2.

The TIP program specifies that variable pay is a function of corporate performance, and/or team performance (teams units smaller than the corporation) and individual evaluations on factors such as the scaled item shown in Table 13.2. McDonald's uses a forced distribution ranking as a guide for this individualized component. Only 20 to 25 percent of employees can be ranked in the top performance category. Seventy percent are expected to fall into the satisfactory category, and 5 to 10 percent into the bottom group. This "rank and yank" variant and the team performance measure are the decentralized components of the variable pay. Using corporate financial results as the first-order driver gives a centralized component (although, local anomalies sometimes are used to justify lowering of the corporate target).

Table 13.2 Example of performance factor at McDonald's

Factor 1: Sets clear objectives with results accountability.
Establishes high standards of performance with clear objectives for self and the employees he/she manages. Holds self and others accountable for achieving results. Clearly differentiates between levels of performance, and differentiates compensation and other forms of recognition accordingly.

Behavioral requirements:

- Ensures that he/she, and all his/her direct reports, has clear annual performance objectives, specified in writing.

- Completes his/her own mid-year and year-end performance updates on time, and if managing people, ensures all mid-year and year-end reviews are conducted on time.

- Seeks feedback and uses it to enhance his/her performance.

- If managing people, does not inflate ratings of either performance or readiness for advancement.

- If managing people, takes appropriate action to recognize outstanding accomplishments, and aligns rewards accordingly.

- If managing people, takes timely and decisive action to improve or remove low performers, ensuring that these individuals get appropriate feedback and coaching and have a written plan for improvement.

Employee characteristics

Motivating workers is a major goal of compensation. In part this depends upon understanding what matters to workers. The carrot dangling at the end of the stick is more enticing to a vegetarian. Research indicates this factor plays an important role in country differences in the use of variable pay. Workers in the USA, Taiwan, Mexico and Latin America show strong preferences for larger variable pay components in their compensation package. Workers in countries such as Australia and Japan want larger base components (Lowe *et al.*, 2002). While some of these differences can be explained by collective (group oriented) vs individualistic orientations of countries, part of the variance is still unexplained.

Country labor legislation

The legal environment has a clear impact on the use of profit sharing and long term incentives such as equity awards. While LTIs are usually linked to higher level jobs in the QSR industry and not to call centers, country perceptions of ownership override these differences (Pendleton *et al.*, 2003). For example, in Germany it's rare to have stock options as part of any contract, no matter what level the job is. Experts argue that this underutilization can be explained by the labyrinth quality of German law and the formalized German workplace. It's simply too hard to do anything creative in this kind of environment. Conversely, Great Britain has a legal environment and country culture that are much more receptive to variations of employee ownership and profit sharing. Consequently, profit sharing is much more prevalent there. These country differences shape the nature and level of variable payouts.

The hospitality industry

Pay for low skill jobs in the global hospitality (hotel/motel) industry is heavily influenced by legislation and collective bargaining arrangements. For example, the industry is heavily unionized in Australia, and to increase flexibility in this restrictive environment (e.g. overtime for full-time workers on nights and weekends can be very high), management hires a higher proportion of part-time labor but at a higher negotiated wage (Taylor and Davies, 2004). In contrast, in nearby (relatively speaking!) Singapore, unionization is lower, legislation doesn't award weekend and night work with multiples of base salary, and there is a higher use of full-time workers. In a nod to internal equity issues for this more permanent staff, workers in low skill jobs here receive a premium for seniority.

Hospitality workers in other countries tend to have base wage packages closely linked to the minimum wage. Much as in the USA, debate centers on whether increases in the minimum wage result in lowered hiring. Studies in the United Kingdom and New Zealand suggest worker shortages keep wages somewhat above, but inevitably linked to, the level of the minimum wage.

One possible glimpse of the future comes from emerging markets. The hospitality industry, much like the QSR industry, is plagued by labor shortages in lower end jobs. Slovakia attacks its chronic shortages in this industry by paying wages that are slightly below market, but linking the remainder of compensation to performance. Bonuses in most Slovak hotels are given every quarter to both managerial and staff employees and amount to about 8 percent of salary. In a similar bid to stabilize employment in lower end jobs, McDonald's is looking closely at wage packages for entry crew jobs. Much like Slovakia, there is a greater emphasis on differentiating pay of workers and rewarding performance and seniority. McDonald's is an early leader in recognizing that crew member jobs have a strong interpersonal skill component, particularly in interactions with customers. This skill is relatively rare and needs to be rewarded with compensation packages that aren't pegged to the minimum wage. The Slovak hotel industry makes similar arguments, claiming that many lower end hotel employees have significant interactions with customers, and the skills needed to promote these interactions need to be nurtured – hence the reliance on bonuses that are a significant part of compensation.

Conclusions

All three of these industries – QSR, call center and hospitality – have wage structures that, at least for lower skilled jobs, have been linked historically to minimum wage levels. This means base wages are heavily influenced by external equity. The market heavily influences base wages. But there are also growing signs that customer interaction skills imbedded in these jobs need to be rewarded. Market leaders such as McDonald's, emerging market leaders such as Slovakia and call centers with greater reliance on permanent employees (e.g. India) are all experimenting with different wage models. Greater emphasis on internal equity, with more performance-based rewards and unique benefits configurations, may well be the outcome. At higher job levels all three industries show concerns about internal equity. Variable pay is the lever that balances internal equity concerns. Broad goals are set in centralized locales as a nod to internal equity.

Then specific targets are set to reflect localized conditions. The result is a total package reflecting both internal and external equity concerns.

References

Hansen, F. 2005. Currents in Compensation and Benefits. *Compensation and Benefits Review*, 37(1):6–18.

Holman, D., Batt, R. and Holtgrewe, U. 2007. *The Global Call Center Report*. Institute of Work Psychology, University of Sheffield Working Paper.

Lowe, K., Milliman, J., DeCieri, H. and Dowling, P. 2002. International Compensation Practices: A ten-country comparative analysis. *Human Resource Management*, 41(1): 45–66.

Marquez, J. 2006. McDonald's Rewards Program Leaves Room for some Local Flavor. *Workforce Management*, 85(7): 26.

Milkovich, G. and Newman, J. 2008. *Compensation* (9th edition). New York: McGraw-Hill.

Newman, J. 2007. *My Secret Life on the McJob*. New York: McGraw-Hill.

Pendleton, A., Poutsma, E., van Ommeren, J. and Brewster, C. 2003. The Incidence and Determinants of Employee Share Ownership and Profit Sharing in Europe. In T. Kato and J. Pliskin (eds), *The Determinants of the Incidence and Effects of Participatory Organizations, Advances in the Economic Analysis of Participatory and Labor Market*, Volume 7: 141–72. Greenwich, CT: JAI Press.

Taylor, R. and Davies, D. 2004. Aspects of Training and Remuneration in the Accommodation Industry: A comparison between Australian and Singaporean providers. *Journal of European Industrial Training*, 28(6/7): 466.

14

Employee benefits around the world

Joseph J. Martocchio and Niti Pandey

In his latest bestseller *The World is Flat*, Thomas L. Friedman talks about how the current state of technology-driven globalization has resulted in a high level of interconnections between the economies of various parts of the world. This means US employers will be increasingly required to do business with entities in many other countries as erstwhile underdeveloped parts of the world experience tremendous economic, trade and standard-of-living growth. Additionally, the move from traditional manufacturing to knowledge-and service-based employment also means jobs as well as markets are more likely to be geographically dispersed. As the need increases for employers to interact globally, human resource management professionals will have increased opportunities to develop employment practices for US employees in foreign assignments, as well as deal with indigenous employees in the parent company's foreign offices. While most employers may choose to offer attractive benefits above and beyond the minimum required by the host nations, so as to attract the desired talent, it's important to first know the basic legal employment context and the minimum employment statutory employment standards of the country where they propose to do business. In this chapter, we provide a glimpse of the wide variety of employment practices around the world, we peruse basic benefits issues, including paid time-off, protection programs (for instance, retirement, healthcare) and stand-out benefits in particular regions. We start off each review with a brief treatment of that country's governmental structure, norms and historical events in order to help shed light on its version of employee benefits.

North America

This section offers a brief glimpse at employment relationships and employee benefits in Mexico and Canada. Both countries, along with the United States, are part of a trade bloc known as NAFTA – the North Atlantic Free Trade Agreement. As of January 1, 1994, NAFTA called for the elimination of duties and the phasing out of tariffs over a period of 14 years (Office of the US Trade Representative, 2007). Under NAFTA, trade restrictions were removed from industries such as motor vehicles and automotive parts, computers, textiles and agriculture. In addition, the treaty also delineated the removal of investment restrictions between the three countries. As a result of supplemental agreements signed in 1993, worker and environmental protection provisions were added.

The labor side of NAFTA is the North American Agreement on Labor Cooperation (NAALC), which was created to promote cooperation between trade unions and social organizations in order to champion improved labor conditions. While there has definitely been a convergence of labor standards in North America as a result of NAALC, there has been no convergence in employment, productivity or salary trends. Overall, NAFTA is reported as having been good for Mexico, which saw a fall in poverty rates and a rise in real income as a result of the trade agreement. This section presents a brief overview of the employment relationship in Canada and Mexico and some basic employee benefits required by law in these countries.

Canada

Canada is a constitutional monarchy that is also a parliamentary democracy and a federation consisting of ten provinces and three territories (Central Intelligence Agency, 2007). With a per capita gross domestic product (GDP) of $35,200 and a 17.59 million-strong labor force, the Canadian economy is very similar to the United States' market-based economy. GDP per capita generally indicates the standard of living within a country; the larger the per capita GDP, presumably the better is the standard of living. Table 14.1 lists per capita GDP for several countries, including the ones reviewed in this chapter. Clearly, the United States shows the largest per capita GDP and India reports the lowest amount. These differences are evident in the extent of government-sponsored benefits offered in those countries. While Canada has enjoyed a trade surplus and balanced budgets for many years, recent concern and debate has grown over the increasing cost of the publicly funded healthcare system.

Employment law researchers report that the basic rule of Canadian law holds that labor and employment law fall within the exclusive jurisdiction of the provinces. Thus, both individual and collective employment relationships are controlled at the province level, and federal legislation cannot override provincial laws, even when the industry or employer primarily conducts business overseas (except in the cases where the industries are expressly assigned to federal jurisdiction). The origins of the common law governing individual employment contracts are in the English Statute of Labourers of 1562, which established working hours and wages. This statute was eventually repealed in the early nineteenth century but became part of the English common law and later part of the common law governing all the provinces besides Quebec. Quebec, instead, operates under the Civil Code of Quebec (instituted in 1866), whose modernized version became effective January 1, 1994.

Paid time-off benefits

Canadian employment law holds that employees are entitled to between eight and nine annual paid holidays as well as two weeks paid vacation time, along with a sum of money as vacation pay (increasing to three weeks after six years of employment). The amount of

Table 14.1 Per capita expenditures by country

Country	Per capita GDP ($)	Labor force size (millions)
United States of America	43,500	151.4
Canada	35,200	17.59
Mexico	10,600	38.09
Brazil	8,600	96.34
Argentina	15,000	15.35
France	30,100	27.88
Germany	31,400	43.66
Spain	27,000	21.77
United Kingdom	31,400	31.1
The Netherlands	31,700	7.6
Italy	29,700	24.63
Poland	14,100	17.26
Sweden	31,600	4.59
Russia	12,100	73.88
People's Republic of China	7,600	798
Hong Kong	36,500	3.63
Japan	33,100	66.44
South Korea	24,200	23.77
India	3,700	509.3
Saudi Arabia	13,800	7.125
South Africa	13,000	16.09
Australia	32,900	10.66

Source: Central Intelligence Agency, 2007.

vacation pay is equal to 2 percent of the employee's pay for the preceding year per week of vacation. Slight variations exist from province to province. Maternity and paternity leave provisions are coordinated under the Federal Employment Insurance Act. Employees are eligible for a total of 17 weeks' benefits during pregnancy and after childbirth. Most recently, the Canadian government introduced compassionate care leave, which provides eight weeks of unpaid leave to care for a seriously ill family member. For the purposes of this leave, family members include spouse, common law partner, children and parents. No laws require the granting of time-off for military service.

Protection benefits

Protection benefits include pension and retirement benefits as well as health and disability benefits. Canada has two state pension plans, one for Quebec residents only and one for the rest of Canada. Both are funded by matching contributions from employers and employees and are fully portable upon employment changes, much like 401(k) plans in the United States. In addition to the public plans, many employers provide supplementary pension plans that are regulated by provincial or federal legislation, which establishes minimum funding standards, specifies the types of investments the plans may make, and deals with matters such as portability, benefit vesting and locking-in contributions. Employers frequently have different plans for executive, managerial and other employees.

Medical and basic hospital care in Canada are paid for by provincial medical insurance plans with compulsory coverage for all residents, and funding revenue derived from both general federal taxation and provincial taxes. While public health plans normally do not provide employed persons with prescription drugs except while they are hospitalized, additional benefits are provided by private supplementary insurance by employers, including dental and vision care. Employers also provide long- and short-term disability benefits for sickness or injury as part of a benefits package. Canada's per capita expenditure on health (the sum of Public Health Expenditure and Private Expenditure on Health) as of 2003 at international dollar rates was $2,989.

Mexico

Mexico is a federal republic and Mexican labor law is based on the Constitution of the United States of Mexico, adopted in January 1917. Mexico's labor force is about 38 million strong and its per capita GDP is $10,600 (Central Intelligence Agency, 2007). The free market economy is comprised of a mix of new and old industries as well as agriculture, which have become increasingly dominated by the private sector. The "Labor and Social Security" article of the constitution is still in effect. Employment relationships in Mexico fall under the Federal Labor Law, which was last revised in January of 1997 and clearly defines the terms *worker* and *employer* for the purpose of individual employment. Some of the employee benefits ensured under federal jurisdiction in Mexico are discussed in the following.

Paid time-off benefits

Mexican employment laws stipulate certain paid time-off benefits for all employees, as reported in publications on international employment laws. Workers are entitled to paid time-off during public holidays, and workers required to work during a mandatory holiday are entitled to double pay. Female employees are entitled to maternity leave – six weeks' leave prior to giving birth, and six weeks' leave after birth on full salary. Maternity leave can also be extended with half pay for as long as necessary and does not affect seniority rights. Employees are entitled to six vacation days after being employed for one year, and get two more days for each subsequent year, up to a maximum of 12 days. As of the fifth year, the worker is entitled to 14 days vacation, and for each additional group of five years, two more vacation days are added. Employers must pay workers a vacation premium equivalent to 25 percent of the salary earned during scheduled vacation days; vacations must be taken on the date indicated by the employer, within the six months following the end of the work year.

Protection benefits

Social security programs in Mexico are administered by the Mexican Social Security Institute, which protects employees in the matters of occupational accidents and illnesses, maternity, sicknesses, incapacitation, old age, retirement and survivor pensions, day care for children of insured workers, and social services. The system is financed by contributions from workers, employers and the government, with contributions based on salary levels (workers earning the minimum salary are exempt from making contributions), while employers bear the bulk of the contributions to the different insurance funds.

The benefits for employees are laid out as follows. Workers with at least 52 weeks' worth of payments into the system who withdraw are entitled to continue making voluntary payments. Should they return to salaried employment again, they may return to the system and maintain all benefits, which may be in cash or in kind. Cash benefits take the form of transfer payments in the early stages of illness or incapacitation, depending on the medical condition and its effects on work and pensions. In-kind benefits take the form of medical attention, including surgery and medicines, hospitalization services and so forth.

As of July 1, 1997, all workers must join the mandatory individual account system, slowly replacing the former social insurance system (Social Security Administration, 2007). At retirement, employees covered by the social insurance system before 1997 can choose to receive benefits from either the social insurance system or the mandatory individual account system.

Medical services are normally provided directly to patients (including old-age pensioners covered by the 1997 law) through the health facilities of the Mexican Social Security Institute. Benefits include general and specialist care, surgery, maternity care, hospitalization or care in a convalescent home, medicines, laboratory services, dental care and appliances, and are payable for 52 weeks and may be extended in some cases to 104 weeks. In addition, the wife of an insured man also receives postnatal benefits in kind, and medical services are provided for dependent children up to age 16 (age 25 if a student, no limit if disabled). Mexico's per capita expenditure on health (the sum of the Public Health Expenditure and the Private Expenditure on Health) as of 2003 at the international dollar rate was $582.

Europe

The European Union (EU) is a unique international organization that aims to become an economic superpower while retaining quintessential European practices, such as high levels of employment, social welfare protection and strong trade unions. While the EU has its own legal powers and performs executive, legislative and judicial functions like any other governing body, it has limited authority in the area of labor and employment laws. While the EU does not attempt to harmonize the employment laws of Member States, under the laws of all Member States, employers must provide employees with a written document about the terms of the employment contract. The concept of "employment at will" does not exist in the EU as in the United States. The EU makes use of Directives and Community Legislations to ensure some minimum standards are adopted by Member States. All Member States either have specific legislation or unfair dismissal or general civil code provisions that apply to termination of employment contracts. They all provide employers with a substantive basis for challenging employment dismissal and procedural mechanisms for adjudicating claims.

EU community labor law was designed with the aim of ensuring that the creation of a single market did not result in a lowering of labor standards or distortions in competition.

But it has also been increasingly called upon to play a key role in making it easier for the EU to adapt to evolving forms of work organization. On the basis of article 137 of the Treaty, the Community shall support and complement the activities of the Member States in the area of social policy. In particular, it defines minimum requirements at the EU level in the fields of working and employment conditions, and the information and consultation of workers. Improving living and working conditions in Member States depends on national legislation, but also to a large extent on agreements concluded by the social partners at all levels (country, sector and company). This section briefly presents some of the basic employee benefits practices in the EU Member States of France and the United Kingdom.

France

France, a democratic republic, is currently transitioning from the traditional model (in which government ownership and intervention were strongly featured) to greater reliance on market mechanisms (Central Intelligence Agency, 2007). France's per capita GDP is $30,100 and its labor force is 27.88 million strong. The government has recently given up stakes in such large companies as Air France, Renault and Thales, while still maintaining a strong presence in public transport and defense. The population, however, has resisted reforms targeted at labor market flexibility. Also, with the highest tax burden in Europe at nearly half the GDP, the French economy is slacking off.

A compendium on international labor and employment laws reports that with 35-hour-long workweeks and five weeks of paid vacation, French workers typically get better benefits than their US counterparts. Employment laws are incorporated in the French Labor Code (*Code du Travail*) and reflect the social-democratic ideology that has guided the employment relationship. Such features as mandatory profit sharing and greater employee participation in management as well as "just cause dismissal" (as opposed to "employment at will") make French employment relationships different from the United States.

Paid time-off benefits

French law grants every employee the right to a minimum of five weeks paid leave after one year of employment. Employees are paid during statutory holidays. The only mandatory public holiday in France is Labor Day (May 1) and employees who work on this day must be paid double time. Paid vacation cannot exceed 24 working days; a period of vacation is decided by the employer after consultation with employee representatives or based on mutual agreement; paid leave cannot be replaced by a cash payment. Employees between the ages of 18 and 21 receive an additional benefit of a 30-day annual leave regardless of the time they have served in a company. Maternity leave is provided to female employees at a minimum of 16 weeks, at least 10 weeks of which should be after a child is born. The employer has no legal obligation to pay an employee during maternity leave. Following a mother's return to work, the employer will grant the employee an interview to help place her in an equivalent activity. Companies must provide employees with at least 24 months of employment, half of which is with the current employer, to pursue training opportunities not included in the company's training program.

Protection benefits

Effective August 21, 2003, the government mandated that employees must work longer before they may receive full government pension. The increase from 40 to 41 years will take effect by 2012. Retirees will also be prohibited from receiving their pensions while working on a part-time basis because the pension amount is set at a generous level – 85 percent of annual earnings prior to retirement.

Social security benefits granted to employees contain three components: health insurance, unemployment insurance and retirement insurance. A base regime of social insurance applies equally to all employees with rules on reimbursement rates for medical expenses, rules on calculation of unemployment allowance or the right to a retirement allowance. Each is the same for all employees. Also, private employers can provide company benefits such as additional medical coverage and additional retirement benefits. In addition, French law provides for mandatory profit sharing for employers with more than 50 employees. Employers and employees may also enter into a variety of voluntary profit sharing programs. The use of either voluntary or mandatory schemes is encouraged by the government.

Organization of medical services for employees is the responsibility of the employer, who must bear the costs. Also, a doctor selected by the employer conducts medical examinations but has no power to prescribe treatment or sick leave. France's per capita expenditure on health (the sum of the Public Health Expenditure and the Private Expenditure on Health) as of 2003 at the international dollar rate was $2,902. Workers' medical benefits include general and specialist care, hospitalization, laboratory services, medicines, optical and dental care, maternity care, appliances and transportation (Social Security Administration, 2007). The insured normally pays for services and is reimbursed by the local sickness fund. A €1 flat-rate contribution is paid for each medical service up to an annual ceiling (pregnant women or women on maternity leave, hospitalized persons and persons with low income are exempt). After the deduction of the flat-rate contribution, the sickness insurance reimburses fully or in part the cost incurred by the insured. The amount reimbursed depends on the type of service: 100 percent of the medical service cost for certain severe illnesses, for work injury beneficiaries who are assessed as 66.6 percent or more disabled, and for pregnant women from the sixth month of pregnancy up to the twelfth day after childbirth, regardless of whether the costs are related to the pregnancy or not; 70 percent for medical services; 60 percent for paramedic services; 35 percent or 65 percent for pharmaceuticals; 60 percent or 70 percent for laboratory services; 65 percent for optical and appliance fees up to an annual ceiling; and 80 percent for hospitalization after the deduction of a flat-rate daily contribution of €15 (€16 in 2007) (1 USD = €0.744).

United Kingdom

The United Kingdom (UK) is a constitutional monarchy and one of the biggest economies in Europe (Central Intelligence Agency, 2007). With a labor force of 31.1 million and a per capita GDP of $31,400, the government has been scaling back on public ownership of businesses and social welfare programs. The employment relationship in the UK is governed by a variety of common law and statutory provisions. The most recent reforms instituted by the Labor government resulted in the Employment Relations Act of 1999. Employers are generally free to agree to the employment relationship with their employees at their discretion, with a few statutory restrictions.

Paid time-off benefits

Workers are entitled to four weeks paid annual leave, including statutory and public holidays. Employers are allowed to introduce an accrual system to help manage leave during the first year of employment. The employee is entitled to 28 weeks of statutory sick pay in any three-year period. The employer can recover the money paid as sick pay if the payment exceeds 13 percent of the employer's liability to pay National Insurance Contributions in the income tax month in question. The employer reserves the right to require the employee to undergo a medical examination to verify an illness.

Employers cannot permit women to work in the two weeks immediately following birth. Employees can get a leave of 26 weeks, which may not begin prior to 11 weeks before birth. Contractual benefits other than remuneration, such as health insurance, are preserved during maternity leave. The employee also has a right to statutory maternity pay. Employees with one year of service are entitled to take 13 weeks of unpaid leave with respect to childcare. Fathers can get paid paternity leave within eight weeks of the child's birth. An employee is entitled to take a reasonable amount of time-off during working hours to take care of dependents, a term which includes the spouse, children, parents or relatives living under the same roof. Parents of young children have the right to flexible work arrangements in relation to hours/times/place of work, though requests can be refused by disruption. Employees must have 26 weeks of qualifying service to be eligible for these benefits, and a sufficient relationship with child and responsibility for childcare. The cut-off is two weeks before the child's sixth birthday (or their eighteenth, if the child is disabled).

Protection benefits

All employees with the requisite National Insurance Contributions are entitled to the basic state pension. However, this is a small amount and employees must supplement it in one of four ways:

- State second pension: Pays a certain proportion of lifetime average earnings over a quite limited band.
- Company pension: Occupational plans such as defined contribution and defined benefit plans are available from individual employers.
- Personal pension: Established arrangements between employees and insurance companies; employer need not be directly involved although they may choose to contribute.
- Stakeholder pension: May be operated by insurers and other providers in much the same way as personal pensions or they may be established by employers and administered by trustees as occupational pension plans and are defined contribution arrangements with strict statutory limits.

Every employer is required to maintain liability insurance under an approved policy with an authorized insurer. This indemnifies the employer against claims for civil liability that may arise as a result of injury and/or disease.

The UK's per capita expenditure on health (the sum of the Public Health Expenditure and the Private Expenditure on Health) as of 2003 at the international dollar rate was $2,389. Employment relationship-based health benefits are as follows. Medical services are provided by public hospitals and by doctors and dentists under contract with, and paid directly by, the National Health Service. Benefits include general practitioner care, specialist services, hospitalization, maternity care, dental care, medicines, appliances, home nursing and family planning. Patients pay £6.40 for each prescription and 80 percent of the cost of any dental work, up to a maximum of £390. Those receiving means-tested benefits and their adult dependents, children younger than age 16 (age 19 if a student), pregnant women and nursing mothers are exempt from dental and prescription charges. Persons older than the state pension age and certain other groups are exempt from prescription charges. The National Health Service's Low Income Scheme exempts certain individuals with low income from prescription charges (1 USD equals approximately £0.50).

Asia

As of 2007, China is the largest economy in Asia, followed by India and Japan. Although the Japanese economy in the 1980s and 1990s used to be larger than that of the entire continent combined, since then the Chinese currency has grown and become the second largest, and is expected to surpass Japan. Asia has several trade blocs, such as the Asia-Pacific Economic Cooperation, the Asia-Europe Economic Meeting, the Association of Southeast Asian Nations and the South Asian Association for Regional Cooperation, to name a few. However, given the wide variation and diversity in the world's largest and most populous continent, there is no unifying economic body (like the EU or NAFTA) that represents all the countries of Asia. This section examines a representative sample of the relatively more developed/developing economies in Asia – China, India, Japan, South Korea, Hong Kong and Saudi Arabia. A bloc of countries that is not examined here, but that nonetheless deserves mention since considerable jobs are being outsourced there, are those in southeast Asia – Thailand, Vietnam, Singapore, Malaysia, Philippines, Cambodia and Laos. These economies are seeing a current influx of foreign investment, though they are not close to the countries discussed here in terms of annual growth rates.

The People's Republic of China

The People's Republic of China (PRC) is a communist state characterized by a fast-growing economy, which over the past couple of decades has shifted from a centrally planned system to a more market-oriented one (Central Intelligence Agency, 2007). With a massive labor force of 798 million and a per capita GDP of $7,600, the PRC has been experiencing continuously high annual GDP growth at around 10 percent. While the purchasing power parity of PRC has vaulted to the top in the world, the lower per capita GDP is an indication of income disparity within various strata of society. One of the key challenges for the government has been in sustaining adequate job growth for tens of millions of workers laid off from state-owned enterprises, finding work for migrants, as well as for new entrants to the workforce.

The PRC Labor Law was established in 1995, resulting in a break from the traditional "iron rice bowl" system of employment, with a shift from state-owned enterprises to private ones, a move which has given rise to new employment relationship issues. Under the older welfare system, the workforce was considered the property of the State and many benefits such as housing, medical and retirement schemes were payable directly by state-owned enterprises to the employees. With the introduction of the PRC Labor Law, the employment relationship is now defined by individual contracts.

Paid time-off benefits

The length of an employer-approved medical treatment period generally depends on the employee's age and length of service and can range from 3 to 24 months. During this period, the salary paid to the employee may not be less than 80 percent of the local minimum wage. Employees who have worked for one or more years are entitled to paid annual leave but no binding laws exist about this; national policy guidelines recommend 7 to 14 days. Employees who have worked for more than one year are entitled to "home leave" if they do not live in the same place as their spouse or parents. Employees earn normal wages during this period, and employers are obligated to pay all travel expenses for employees visiting their spouse and for unmarried employees visiting their parents. Women are entitled to no less than 90 days of maternity leave starting 15 days prior to birth.

Protection benefits

There has been a new law to decouple the employment relationship from the social insurance system, setting up a unified basic pension system (Social Security Administration, 2007). The system now has social insurance and mandatory individual accounts. (Provincial and city/county social insurance agencies and employers adapt central government guidelines to local conditions.) Coverage includes employees in urban enterprises, and urban institutions managed as enterprises, and the urban self-employed. In some provinces, coverage for the urban self-employed is voluntary. (Urban enterprises comprise all state-owned enterprises, regardless of their location.) Old-age provision in rural areas is based mainly on family support, as well as community and state financial support. Pilot schemes in the form of individual accounts, supported at the town and village level, and subject to preferential support by the state, operate in some rural areas. Employees of government and communist party organizations, as well as those in cultural, educational and scientific institutions (except for institutions financed off-budget), are covered under a government-funded, employer-administered system. Enterprise-based pension systems cover some employees (including the self-employed) in cities.

An employee contribution to mandatory individual accounts is 8 percent of their gross insured earnings. (The contribution rate is higher in some provinces.) The minimum earnings for employee contribution and benefit purposes are equal to 60 percent of the local average wage for the previous year. The maximum earnings for employee contribution and benefit purposes vary but may be as much as 300 percent of the local average wage of the previous year. Employer contributions to mandatory individual accounts are 3 percent of the insured payroll. The contribution is taken from the total contribution made to basic pension insurance. Central and local government subsidies are provided to city/council retirement pension pools as needed.

China has a unified medical insurance system with all employers and workers participating in the system; employers contribute 6 percent of the payroll, while employees contribute 2 percent of their salary. Health insurance is based on a Basic Medical Insurance Fund consisting of a Pooled Fund and Personal Accounts. Employees' contributions go directly to their Personal Accounts and 30 percent of employer contributions are paid into this account. Covered workers receive medical benefits at a chosen accredited hospital or clinic on a fee-for-service basis. The individual account is used to finance medical benefits only, up to a maximum equal to 10 percent of the local average annual wage. The social insurance fund reimburses the cost of the medical benefit from 10 percent up to 400 percent of the local average annual wage, according to the schedule. Medical treatment in high-grade hospitals results in lower percentage reimbursements, and vice versa. Reimbursement for payments beyond 400 percent of the local average annual wage must be covered by private insurance or public supplementary schemes. Contract workers receive the same benefits as permanent workers. The per capita expenditure on health (the sum of the Public Health Expenditure and the Private Expenditure on Health) as of 2003 at the international dollar rate was $278 (World Health Organization, 2007).

Japan

Japan is a constitutional monarchy with a parliamentary government, a labor force of 66.44 million, and a per capita GDP of $33,100 (Central Intelligence Agency, 2007). The Japanese economy is the second most technologically powerful in the world after the USA, and the third largest in terms of purchasing power parity after the USA and China. The Japanese economy is also characterized by government–industry cooperation, a strong work ethic, mastery of high technology and a comparatively small defense allocation (1 percent of GDP). A unique characteristic of the Japanese economy used to be *keiretsu* or the close-knit relations between manufacturers, suppliers and distributors representing a guarantee of lifetime employment for a substantial portion of the urban labor force – a system that has now been eroded considerably.

The employment relationship is based on the traditional notion of freedom of contract and some basic provisions for individual employment are contained in the Civil Code of 1896. However, the outdated Civil Code has been replaced and there are currently numerous recent laws enacted post-WWII that deal with labor standards, unions, minimum wages, childcare and family leave – just to name a few – as well as employee benefits laws. Employee benefits laws include various insurance schemes, participation in which is mandatory, with premiums borne either solely by the employer or by a combination of the employer and employee.

Paid time-off benefits

Annual paid leave is allowed for 10 days after six months of consecutive service, and one additional day for each additional full year, for a total service of three years and six months. Thereafter, workers are granted two additional days for each full year of service, up to a maximum of 20 days. Menstruation leave is available to females when they find attendance at work difficult, and employers are not required to pay employees during this period. Maternity leave is granted if requested within six weeks of giving birth. Post-birth leave of eight weeks is mandatory, although an employee may return to work after six weeks with the approval of a physician. Employer-specific contracts determine the rate of pay during maternity leave; if the employer does not pay anything, then employment insurance pays for 42 days before birth and 56 days after birth at the rate of 60 percent of standard wages. Employees must be granted childcare leave upon request for the duration of one year if the child is less than one year old. Family care leave for three months is allowed in order to care for family members. Employers are not required to pay wages; however, employment insurance provides up to 40 percent of regular wages. There is no military leave granted; employers must give time-off for civic duties such as voting in political elections.

Protection benefits

Japan has a social insurance system involving a flat-rate benefit for all residents under the national pension program and earnings-related benefits under the employees' pension insurance program or other employment-related program; residents aged 20 to 59; voluntary coverage for residents aged 60 to 64 (aged 65 to 69 in special cases); and for citizens residing abroad (aged 20 to 64). The national pension program is one in which the contribution is included in the insured person's contribution to the employees' pension insurance or other employment-related program. A proportionate amount is transferred to the national pension program. All other insured persons contribute 13,300 yen a month. Low-income spouses of workers insured under the employment-related program may apply for exemption from payment. Employees' pension insurance includes 6.79 percent of basic monthly earnings and salary bonuses before tax for most employees; miners and seamen contribute 7.48 percent of basic monthly earnings, including salary bonuses before tax, accorded for most employees. If the employer is contracted-out, the contribution is between 5.29 percent and 5.59 percent of monthly earnings, including salary bonuses before tax. The minimum monthly earnings for contribution and benefit purposes are 98,000 yen. The maximum monthly earnings for contribution and benefit purposes are 620,000 yen. The minimum and maximum earnings levels are adjusted on an ad hoc basis in line with any increases in the national average wage. The government covers one-third of the cost of benefits, plus 100 percent of administrative costs (1 USD = 119.04 yen).

Japan's per capita expenditure on health (the sum of the Public Health Expenditure and the Private Expenditure on Health) as of 2003 at the international dollar rate was $2,244. The National Health Insurance program covers medical care and treatment that is usually provided by clinics, hospitals and pharmacists under contract with, and paid by, the insurance carrier (some carriers provide services directly through their own clinics and hospitals) (Social Security Administration, 2007). Benefits include medical treatment, surgery, hospitalization, nursing care, dental care, maternity care (only for a difficult childbirth) and medicines. There is no limit to duration. The cost sharing amount depends on the person's age: under age 3, 20 percent of the cost; ages 3 to 69, 30 percent of the cost; ages 70 or older, 10 to 20 percent based on income. Japan's national program is available to all individuals unless they are covered by an employer health plan. Employees' health insurance benefits are similar to those provided under the country's national health insurance program.

Conclusion

This chapter provided a brief overview of employee benefits practices in North America and in other parts of the world. Understanding the minimum standards for employee benefits around the world requires a consideration of the role of government in employment affairs. Also, understanding necessitates consideration of the economic conditions that contribute to the shape of employment practices.

References

Central Intelligence Agency, 2007. World Factbook. Online. Available: www.cia.gov/cia/publications/factbook (accessed September 17, 2007).

Office of the US Trade Representative, 2007. North American Free Trade Agreement. Online. Available: www.ustr.gov/Trade_Agreements/Regional/NAFTA/Section_Index.html (accessed September 25, 2007).

Social Security Administration, 2007. Social Security Programs Throughout the World. Online. Available: www.ssa.gov/policy/docs/progdesc/ssptw (accessed October 18, 2007).

World Health Organization, 2007. Countries. Online. Available: www.who.int/countries (accessed October 3, 2007).

Explaining high US CEO pay in a global context

An institutional perspective

David B. Balkin

Chief Executive Officers (CEOs) in US firms are the world's highest paid top executives. There is substantial evidence to back this claim up. A 1997 study of CEO pay in 23 countries in mid-sized firms with $250 million annual revenues revealed that CEOs in the USA were paid nearly double the amount of pay received by CEOs in all other developed countries (Murphy, 1999). In the USA, CEOs received total annual pay of $901,000 compared to $524,000 for France, $490,000 for the United Kingdom, $424,000 for Germany and $398,000 for Japan. In 2003, a global pay survey of companies with annual revenues of $500 million conducted by Towers Perrin, a human resource consulting firm, showed that the CEOs in the USA earned $2,250,000 in total annual pay compared to $954,000 in Germany, $830,000 in the United Kingdom and $735,000 in France (Bordet, 2003). In yet another global pay survey, this one conducted in 2005 by Mercer Human Resource Consulting of the largest public firms in several countries, the median annual pay for CEOs in the USA was $6.8 million compared to that of global counterparts with $4.3 million in the United Kingdom, $3.0 million in France and $470,000 in Japan (Fabrikant, 2006). All the firms in the Mercer study reported over $1 billion revenues in 2005. In all these studies CEOs in the USA fared better in the pay arena than their global counterparts after controlling for the size of the organization. Further, a meta-analysis of CEO compensation research by Henry Tosi and his colleagues (2000) indicated that company size was by far the most potent determinant of CEO pay.

Why do CEOs in the USA receive so much more compensation compared to their counterparts in other advanced developed countries such as Germany, Japan, the United Kingdom and France (the countries that will be compared to the USA based on per capita GNP and number of large, multinational corporations)? This chapter argues that institutional factors that influence CEO pay within the USA offer favorable opportunities for achieving higher pay outcomes compared to the institutional factors affecting the level of CEO pay in other nations. I use institutional theory to identify factors that are likely to favor high pay outcomes within the USA and show how these enabling institutional factors may be less potent or absent in other institutional environments in other developed nations.

CEO pay in a global context

Agency theory models have been used extensively in studies that examine CEO pay and its antecedents (Gomez-Mejia *et al.*, 2003; Tosi *et al.*, 2000; Hambrick and Finkelstein, 1995; Zajac, 1990; Tosi and Gomez-Mejia, 1989). Agency theory reasons that principals, consisting of atomistic shareholders who are widely dispersed, and CEOs, who are agents hired to manage a firm for the benefit of shareholders, each have different risk preferences concerning how to deploy a firm's assets (Jensen and Meckling, 1976). Principals are risk neutral because their wealth is diversified between shareholdings in the focal firm and other investments. The CEO, who is an agent and professional manager, is risk averse due to the fact that the preponderance of agent wealth is derived from pay from the focal firm and future wealth is associated with sustaining incumbency in the job of CEO. CEOs are also aware of employment risk and the propensity for corporate boards to replace a CEO if firm performance does not meet strategic objectives (Wiseman and Gomez-Mejia, 1998). Moreover, agents/CEOs are more likely to deploy firm resources in lower risk projects that enhance CEO wealth such as growth through mergers and acquisitions, while principals/shareholders preferences would favor firm resources to be deployed in rent seeking projects that produce income and enhance the value of the firm's shares (Bebchuck and Fried, 2003; Wiseman and Gomez-Mejia, 1998). Thus principals' and agents' interests are likely to diverge unless principals either directly monitor agent behavior or use incentives to align agent interests to coincide with that of principals (Jensen and Meckling, 1976; Fama, 1980). The high cost of direct monitoring of agent behavior makes this choice less attractive, so principals are more likely to focus on designing efficient contracts that include incentives (i.e. CEO short-term and long-term compensation) that align CEO and shareholder interests.

The logic of agency theory is based on the assumption that principals are the shareholders and the corporate board of directors is responsive to the interests of the shareholders (Fama and Jensen, 1983). The agency model assumes that a homogeneous principal represents shareholder interests and this model is most closely related to the American corporate governance system which requires that corporate directors have the legal duty of loyalty and the duty of care to represent shareholders' interests when serving on the board in a public corporation (Monks and Minow, 2001).

The lion's share of the extant literature on CEO pay is based on data gathered from US firms (Tosi *et al.*, 2000), so the assumptions used in agency theory concerning the principal are consistent with the rules of US corporate governance (Aguilera and Jackson, 2003; Crossland and Hambrick, 2007). Another factor that contributes to the ubiquity of the use of US data in the CEO pay literature is that the US financial regulations have required that public firms disclose CEO pay in reports accessible to the public which lowered the barriers to perform CEO pay research in that country. More recently, following the USA, other countries (the United Kingdom, France and Germany for example) enacted financial regulations that require public firms to disclose CEO pay. Subsequently CEO pay studies have been published with non-US data, including the United Kingdom (Conyon and Murphy, 2000) and Germany (Sanders and Tuschke, 2007).

However, when comparing CEO pay between firms in the USA and other nations, agency theory models are limited due to its assumptions that the principal's interests are interchangeable with those of the shareholders. Corporate governance systems in many countries outside the USA such as in continental Europe and Asia have more heterogeneous interests represented on the board of directors providing input into the CEO pay decision. Germany, Japan and France are nations that have relational corporate governance systems where large institutional shareholders such as powerful banks, corporations and the state form stable and direct relationships with the management due to having large ownership stakes in a firm (Gospel and Pendleton, 2005; Dharwadkar *et al.*, 2000). For example in Germany, the external board of directors (called the supervisory board) is comprised of shareholders, debtholders and employee representatives, with no company executive including the CEO permitted to sit on the board (Crossland and Hambrick, 2007). In Germany there is also an internal management board in its dual board system, but the management board is not involved in oversight decisions such as the CEO pay decision. In large German firms with more than 2,000 employees half of the supervisory board members must be employees, representing labor and having different priorities than shareholders. When analyzing global CEO pay relationships a theoretical model should account for differences in national governance systems, shareholder-based or relational, that determine CEO pay. In the section that follows, I suggest that institutional theory provides a useful lens to examine CEO pay across different national corporate governance systems and also offers insights into the factors that account for the high pay earned by CEOs in US firms.

Institutional theory and CEO pay

Unlike agency theory, institutional theory can accommodate different interests of principals as actors representing different stakeholders that have important stakes in the focal firm and how it deploys its resources. While agency theory focuses exclusively on the profit seeking interests of the principals (i.e. the shareholders), it overlooks the fact that in many national jurisdictions outside the USA principals in a focal firm have other core interests besides rent seeking and these interests may be at odds with each other (Aguilera and Jackson, 2003). Compromise between opposing strategic objectives linked to CEO pay is likely to occur due to fundamental differences of opinion and priorities on a corporate board. For example, employee representatives on a German supervisory board are likely to give a high priority to protect employment opportunities of domestic employees and thus are likely to oppose a profitable opportunity to outsource labor to a low wage country in order to protect jobs in the local labor market. A compromise decision may need to be worked out that balances the priority of firm profits with a competing priority of maintaining job security for employees. In this illustration, the German board collectively agrees not to outsource labor, appeasing employee representatives on the board, and as a tradeoff obtains their acceptance of a more modest wage settlement for employees in order to sustain the objective of firm profitability. As this German example illustrates, lower employee wages are a result of a compromise in order to protect the jobs of employees. The compromise balances the objectives of the employee representatives on a German board (job security) with the objectives of shareholders and debtholders (profits). From this example it is not difficult to reason that on a German board the interplay of different stakeholder interests over the CEO pay decision may result in outcomes that are less than optimal for a CEO as I will show later in this chapter. Similar tradeoffs are likely to occur on boards of other countries with relational governance systems such as France and Japan.

Institutional theory reasons that organizations face environmental uncertainty in forming structural units such as corporate governance boards, which is relevant since boards are given the responsibility to determine CEO pay. Due to environmental uncertainty organizations seek that their structures and business practices are perceived to be legitimate by external parties as a way to reduce uncertainty and ensure survival (Zucker, 1987). Certain structural forms within a specified environment such as a state become standardized and are adopted by other organizations within it as a way to signal legitimacy to parties such as regulatory agencies or financial institutions (DiMaggio and Powell, 1983). Once a standard structural form is established, powerful forces emerge within an environment that press for change, so that organizations within an environment become similar to each other in structure (Kostova and Roth, 2002; Zucker, 1987). Thus institutional theory explains homogenization of structural forms and management practices within specific domains. For example, in the American textbook industry, Coser and colleagues (1982) describe how the industry evolved from a period of diverse structural forms to one consisting of only two dominant structural models; a large bureaucratic generalist and a small specialist. Similarly, civil-service reform was pioneered and achieved legitimacy by early adopting jurisdictions that developed innovative change in employment rules and that was later accepted by other governments seeking legitimacy for their employment practices (Zucker and Tolbert, 1981).

The concept of isomorphism is used by institutional theorists to capture the process of homogenization of organization structures and practices among firms that face the same environmental conditions (DiMaggio and Powell, 1983). In this chapter I focus on institutional isomorphism, which takes into account forces for change that organizations try to accommodate in order to achieve institutional legitimacy (Kostova and Roth, 2002; Aldrich, 1979; Carroll and Delacroix, 1982).

Three mechanisms have been identified through which isomorphic change occurs (DiMaggio and Powell, 1983; Meyer and Rowan, 1977). First, there is *coercive* isomorphism that comes from pressures from other organizations on which a focal organization is dependent to conform to the cultural expectations of the society (Mizruchi and Fein, 1999). Government regulatory agencies such as the US Securities and Exchange Commission (SEC) can apply a coercive isomorphism type of pressure on an organization that does not adhere to a regulation, such as the disclosure of its CEO pay.

Second, there is *mimetic* isomorphism which results from standard responses to uncertainty from a peer organization that is successful. The unprecedented pay practice of allocating a mega-stock option grant (2 million options) in 1984 to Michael Eisner, CEO of the Walt Disney Company, a highly successful media company, generated a mimetic isomorphism type of pressure on other organizations to offer large stock option grants to the CEO (Morgenson, 2006). In the parlance of management, mimetic pressures may be perceived as "best practices" innovated by leading firms that are imitated by other firms that seek symbolic ways to signal that they are well managed to outside constituencies.

Third, there is *normative* isomorphism which is associated with norms that develop in professions that receive similar training (such as accountants or physicians) as well as individuals in closely linked networks. Normative isomorphism can also be observed between nations that differ in the cultural values within a society (Crossland and Hambrick, 2007; Kostova and Roth, 2002). National cultures that have an emphasis on collectivistic values such as Japan may not be as tolerant to a large discrepancy between the pay of the CEO and other executives as would be tolerated within a national culture that emphasizes individualism, a cultural norm held by individuals in the USA.

Each of these three isomorphic change mechanisms is linked to factors that are favorable to high CEO pay in the USA due to the makeup of its institutional environment. However, these factors are expected to have weaker linkages to high CEO pay in other institutional environments in the United Kingdom, Germany, France and Japan, countries that are comparable to the USA in its level of economic development.

Coercive isomorphism and CEO pay

Coercive mechanisms that favorably influence high CEO pay in the USA consist of the corporate governance system and its practices or regulations affecting CEO pay practices and include the following: (1) the corporate governance system; (2) financial regulations that require the disclosure of CEO pay; (3) early adoption of regulations that legitimized the use of stock options for CEO pay; and (4) decentralized rules of incorporation that are favorable to the CEO's interests.

Corporate governance system

The characteristics of the US system of corporate governance that is conducive to high CEO pay include the prominence of shareholder interests on the board of directors and the presence of a powerful CEO who is likely to assume both roles as the CEO and chairman of the board (Pepper, 2006). As mentioned previously, in the USA directors on boards of public corporations have legally mandated duties of loyalty and care to exercise their role prudently in ways that uphold the interests of shareholders. Directors are held accountable to shareholders and shareholders can use the courts to punish directors who have failed in their duties at exercising loyalty or care. Boards of directors in the USA are composed mainly of outside directors that are expected to have no direct affiliations with management, such as occurs in continental European and Japanese boards which contain bankers and long-term suppliers or customers. The design of the US system of corporate governance depends on the market as a key mechanism to discipline management that is not performing effectively, through the process of a change of management control imposed by outside parties. However, it is not unusual for a market failure to occur when a CEO acts opportunistically. Moreover, a majority of stock in public US corporations is in the hands of millions of individual investors as well as large, institutional investors, and the latter are required by financial regulations to maintain highly diversified portfolios of stocks. Most of these private investors have a short-term investment horizon and will sell the stock of a poorly performing company rather than try to impose change on a CEO through exerting influence on the board of directors (Monks and Minow, 2001). A party who aims to replace a poorly performing management of a US corporation will offer a premium price for the stock in order to purchase a controlling number of shares. However, US CEOs seeking high pay can take advantage of the broad dispersion of shareholders by selecting outside directors that are beholden to the CEO's interests (Bebchuck and Fried, 2003) and use entrenchment mechanisms such as poison pills and golden parachutes to frustrate the attempts of outside takeovers in many instances (Tosi *et al.*, 2000; Davidson *et al.*, 1998; Schleifer and Vishney, 1989). Corporate governance in the United Kingdom, similar to the USA, also depends on the market to correct instances of inadequate CEO performance. Both the US and UK systems of corporate governance are shareholder-based systems.

Unlike the US and UK corporate governance system, the relational governance systems in continental Europe (including Germany and France) and Japan rely on a large concentration of shareholdings in the hands of banks (Germany, Japan), families (France) or other corporations (France, Japan) who can exert influence on the CEO and management by being represented on the board (Pepper, 2006; Weimer and Pape, 1999). It is reasonable to expect that when a greater diversity of interests can be voiced on boards within relational governance systems, this dynamic will present a less favorable context for high CEO pay than is likely to occur within shareholder-based systems such as in the USA. The CEO pay that emerges under a relational governance system should be the result of the interplay of diverse interests from parties with long-term interests in the focal firm (i.e. bankers, suppliers, customers, government) that is likely to be less sympathetic to high pay for the CEO than would be the case in the USA.

The US system of corporate governance offers CEOs a great deal of power to influence CEO pay compared to the rules of corporate governance in other countries (Bebchuck and Fried, 2003; Monks and Minow, 2001). One of the key factors sustaining powerful CEOs in the US system of corporate governance is the practice of CEO duality which assigns the CEO a dual role as chairman of the board. This practice is used in 80 percent of large, public firms in the USA and it dilutes the ability of the board of directors to exercise its responsibility as an oversight function (Monks and Minow, 2001). One way CEO duality can weaken a board's ability to exercise its oversight is by controlling the information given to directors on the board to make decisions. US CEOs can also translate their concentrated power as a dual CEO–chairman into ways to influence the selection of external board members who serve on the compensation committee which determines CEO pay. Moreover there is evidence that suggests that powerful CEOs exert influence on pay by selecting other highly paid CEOs to serve on the board of directors and these board members are likely to be sympathetic to high CEO pay at the focal firm (Westphal and Zajac, 1995).

Beyond the US system of corporate governance, a dual CEO–chairman structure does not exist in Germany because the supervisory board does not permit a CEO or other inside executives to serve on the governance board, let alone as chairman. In the United Kingdom there exist norms of good corporate governance which have been established under the highly respected Cadbury report of best corporate governance practices and one of its precepts recommends against the practice of CEO duality because of its potential to inhibit the board from performing its monitoring function, and consequently the practice of CEO duality is rare in the United Kingdom. In Japan the chairman of the board is usually a retired company CEO or retired government official. The Japanese CEO's power is also limited due to strong social norms that require consensus within the company (Monks and Minow, 2001). The company cultures that exhibit a traditional preference for teamwork within Japanese firms tend to reject high levels of pay dispersion between the CEO and other employees (Fackler and Barboza, 2006). In France, the CEO is powerful and has a dual role as chairman similar to its counterpart in the USA. However, the power of the French CEO can be offset by large and powerful shareholders (the five largest shareholders average 48 percent of stock ownership) who are represented by directors on the board (Weimer and Pape, 1999).

Regulations for CEO pay disclosure

In the USA the Securities and Exchange Commission (SEC) since 1992 requires public companies to disclose comprehensive information about the pay of the CEO and the four other most highly compensated executives each year in a company's annual proxy statement and its annual report. Disclosure includes full detail on salary, bonuses, stock options, stock awards, other long-term incentives and perquisites. The disclosure of CEO pay information puts pressure on a firm to be sensitive to the market for CEO pay and public perceptions of how the CEO is paid. Moreover, according to institutional theory, the pay regulation that requires the disclosure of CEO pay puts pressure on compensation committees on boards of directors to seek legitimacy in the way CEO pay is reported. Subsequently, compensation committees provided CEO pay with a strong emphasis on short- and long-term incentives that were linked to firm performance objectives. Reinforcing this trend was a 1993 tax rule that limited the amount of an executive salary, with the exception of performance contingent pay, that companies were permitted to deduct as a business expense to a ceiling of $1 million. The unintended result was to raise CEO salaries to the threshold of $1 million and offer additional compensation in the form of incentive pay. CEOs paid less than the threshold quickly saw their salary rise to this amount (Milkovich and Newman, 2008). As a consequence total CEO pay rose much faster than the pay of other employees in the USA. By 2005 CEOs in the S&P 500 stock index received on average 369 times the pay of the average worker, up from 42 in 1980 for the ratio of CEO pay to average worker pay (Sasseen, 2007). In a 2006 survey by *USA Today* of CEOs of the 50 largest US companies, median CEO pay was $17.7 million which includes $1.4 million in salary, $4.2 million in short-term incentives, and $9.6 million in stock and option awards (Farrell and Hansen, 2007). CEO short- and long-term pay incentives accounted for 78 percent of total CEO compensation in the 50 largest US firms in 2006. Further, more than half of the total compensation of CEOs in 2006 was accounted for by stock and options awards.

Regulations that require transparent reporting of CEO pay are present in the United Kingdom, France and Germany (Pepper, 2006). In the United Kingdom disclosure rules for CEO pay were enacted in 1995 and 1998 and follow similar requirements as in the USA (Conyon and Murphy, 2000). France and Germany enacted their executive pay disclosure regulations only since 2001, or later in the case of Germany. In Japan, disclosure of CEO pay is more opaque because regulations in that country only require the disclosure of the collective pay of its top executives (Fackler and Barboza, 2006). Thus, Nissan reported that the pay of its 10 top executives amounted to be on average the equivalent of $2 million in total compensation, which included its CEO Carlos Ghosn.

Early adoption of stock options

The USA was an early adopter of stock options as a key component of long-term compensation for CEOs and executives. Stock options were recognized under generally accepted accounting principles in 1972. Until 2005 stock options were not treated as an expense against company profits, while other forms of compensation did not have this unique status. This "no expense rule" contributed to the prevalence of stock options as the dominant form of long-term CEO compensation in the USA (Sanders, 2001, *The Economist*, 2007). A 2006 survey of CEO pay in the 50 largest US companies reported that long-term compensation consisting mainly of stock options accounted for the largest portion of CEO pay (Farrell and Hansen, 2007). As the use of stock options became the standard form for long-term CEO pay incentives, stock option pay gained legitimacy. Compensation committees on boards were likely to be influenced by the prevalence of other CEOs serving on the board who were recipients of stock option pay. While, after 2005 firms were required to expense stock options, they continue to be a key component of long-term compensation for CEOs. The main effect on a firm's compensation practices of the current accounting treatment of stock options appears to be a diminishing frequency of broad-based stock options to large groups of non-executive employees.

The diffusion of stock options for CEO pay in the United Kingdom and France closely followed the US practices, while Germany and Japan were late adopters of stock options (Pepper, 2006). Until 1998 companies were not permitted to grant stock options to CEOs and managers under German law. Germany enacted a law legalizing stock options in 1998 in response to some early adopters such as Daimler Benz and Deutsche Bank that found loopholes in the law in 1996 that enabled them to offer stock options to their executives (Sanders and Tuschke, 2007).

Stock options were banned in Japan until 1997 and by 1999, 160 listed companies offered stock options to executives (Bremmer, 1999). In Japan companies most likely to use stock options are those multinationals with a large presence in the USA such as Sony or Honda (Fackler and Barboza, 2006). The early adoption of enabling regulations for stock options in the USA and United Kingdom was likely to contribute to the wide diffusion and sense of legitimacy concerning the use of stock options as a major component of CEO pay in those countries, leading to a greater tolerance for the prodigious payouts to CEOs when the options are exercised. Later in this chapter it will be shown that with the exception of the USA, other nations contained institutional mechanisms that could limit the amount of stock options granted to a CEO. In the USA there are few institutional mechanisms that can deter compensation committees from allocating large stock option grants to CEOs.

Decentralized rules of incorporation favorable to a CEO's interests

Corporate law is decentralized in the USA which gives companies the opportunity to incorporate in a state such as Delaware, the state with the most management-friendly corporate laws and courts (Monks and Minow, 2001). More corporations are chartered in Delaware than any other state. Other states seeking to attract the corporate chartering business enter a "race to the bottom" to adopt management-friendly laws similar to those found in Delaware. As a consequence, shareholders in the USA by and large are not given the right to vote on CEO pay after it is approved by the board of directors. Shareholders in the USA who disapprove of CEO pay will need to challenge the board of directors in a proxy contest (where a dissident group of shareholders run a competing group of directors in an election) which can be very costly and as a consequence is a rare event (Monks and Minow, 2001). The management-friendly corporate rules in the USA can insulate CEO pay from the criticisms of disapproving shareholders that would prefer to limit the upper bound of CEO pay.

As a contrast, in the United Kingdom shareholders have won the right to vote on CEO compensation, and though their vote is non-binding, boards ignore the vote at their own peril (Fabrikant, 2006). Recently, in the United Kingdom angry shareholders voted against a $35 million severance payment promised to the CEO of GlaxoSmithKline in an employment contract. Ultimately the board decided to cut the size of the CEO's severance payment in half. Similarly in France shareholders have the right to vote on CEO pay components such as stock options and golden parachutes (Pepper, 2006). Empowering shareholders to vote on CEO pay can put institutional pressure on boards in the United Kingdom and France to limit the amount of CEO pay. For example, the newspapers in the United Kingdom regularly run front-page stories of "fat cats" such as CEOs that are perceived to be overpaid, and the stories include pictures of their homes, wives and vacation activities (Fabrikant, 2006). A CEO portrayed as a fat cat in the media may have a more difficult time convincing employees or unions to tighten their belts during a jolt in the business cycle. While shareholder voting on CEO pay does not occur in Germany or Japan, we will observe that other institutional pressures are present in those countries that can limit the upper bound of CEO pay.

Mimetic isomorphism and CEO pay

A mimetic isomorphism that has profoundly influenced high CEO pay in the USA is the pay practice of allocating mega-stock option grants that exceed one million stock options to CEOs (Chrystal, 1991). The mega-stock option grants were first given to the CEOs of the Walt Disney Company and Chrysler, Michael Eisner and Lee Iacocca. This precedent established a practice of long-term pay incentives that contain huge potential upside rewards and was imitated by other large corporations within the USA. Contributing to the diffusion of the practice of mega-stock option grants was the fact that both Eisner and Iacocca were early exemplars of celebrity CEOs during the 1980s which gave rise to high expectations for financial rewards to CEOs who are successful (Hayward *et al.*, 2004). Eisner and Iacocca were also given credit as change agents that succeeded in turning around the performance of their companies accompanied by sizeable increases in the stock value that produced substantial wealth for company shareholders (Chrystal, 1991). Adding to the celebrity status of these two CEOs was the fact that CEO Eisner was viewed weekly on the popular primetime Disney television series while CEO Iacocca wrote a best-selling autobiography. The strong market performance of the two companies under the stewardship of Eisner and Iacocca conferred legitimacy to the mega-stock option grants allocated to them and that enabled the diffusion of this reward practice to other firms that adopted it.

Lee Iacocca was recruited as an outsider to become the CEO of Chrysler in 1979 during a low point in its fortunes when it faced the prospect of bankruptcy. While taking a symbolic $1 in salary to indicate his willingness to postpone his compensation until Chrysler turned a profit, Iacocca was given what was then a record 400,000 stock options in compensation. Iacocca's performance subsequently was rewarded with additional large stock option grants in the 1980s so that in the six year period between 1981 and 1987 he received a total of $35 million in stock option gains (Chrystal, 1991).

Michael Eisner was also recruited as an outsider to become CEO of the Walt Disney Company in 1984 and granted two million stock options in his initial employment contract, which was unprecedented for that period. Other large stock option grants to Eisner followed due to the strong performance of Disney in the subsequent ten years, and by 1995 the value of his unexercised stock options was estimated to be $318 million (Byrne, 1996).

The practice of providing large stock option grants to CEOs spread rapidly to other large public US corporations following the grants to Iacocca and Eisner. Moreover, the value of the stock options given to the top 20 highest paid CEOs in the USA in 1995 ranged from $8 million for CEO Wayne Calloway of Pepsico to $44 million for CEO Sanford Weill of Travelers Group (Byrne, 1996). By 2006 the value of stock options of the 20 highest paid CEOs ranged from $11 million for CEO Sam Palmisano of IBM to $45 million for CEO Ray Irani of Occidental Petroleum (Farrell and Hansen, 2007).

While large stock option grants became standard pay practices for long-term compensation for US CEOs due to mimetic pressures on firms to adopt practices that confer legitimacy on pay decisions made by company boards of directors, outside the USA companies were slower to adopt these pay practices due to several of the institutional factors previously explained in this chapter. These factors include the facts that: (1) outside the US stock options were not legally recognized until the late 1990s in Germany and Japan; (2) regulations that require the disclosure of CEO pay were not present in Germany and France until 2001 or later and are still not present in Japan so that firms were less aware of the pay practices of their peer organizations; and (3) in the United Kingdom and France shareholders are empowered to vote on CEO pay allocations so that boards in those countries may decide to limit the size of option grants to avoid shareholder disapproval. Therefore in other countries the mimetic pressures to adopt large CEO stock option grants should be offset by coercive pressures to either use other forms of compensation such as cash, which is less available (due to the more profound tax implications that cash compensation has for the company), or to be more parsimonious with the number of stock options that are granted to the CEO. Consequently, the mimetic pressure to adopt the practice of allocating mega-stock option grants to CEOs in countries outside the USA is likely to be perceived as less compelling to boards than would be expected for US firms and thus it seems reasonable to expect that the number of options conferred to CEOs outside the USA should be more bounded.

Normative isomorphism and CEO pay

National cultural values influence people's perceptions, preferences and behaviors systematically in different societies and nations (Crossland and Hambrick, 2007; Hofstede, 1980). Normative isomorphism influences the CEO pay decision through the cultural values embedded in the members of the board of directors within a country. In particular, the individualism/collectivism value, one of five critical organizational work values identified in Geert Hofstede's (1980) research, is expected to influence the tolerance of board members within a given country with respect to unbounded CEO pay. In individualistic national cultures board members are expected to give a CEO more discretion to make decisions unilaterally and attribute more credit to a CEO for firm performance when the outcomes are successful (Crossland and Hambrick, 2007).

Following this logic, it stands to reason that there should be greater tolerance for high CEO pay in countries that have individualistic cultures. In Hofstede's seminal cross-cultural study of work values in 40 nations, the USA was ranked highest and the United Kingdom was ranked just below the USA in individualism. Some recent evidence that concurs with the Hofstede (1980) findings on individualism/collectivism comes from an analysis of gini coefficients of national income inequality performed by the United Nations (2006). A gini coefficient of 100 represents perfect economic inequality and a gini coefficient of 0 represents perfect economic equality. The United Nations study of national income inequality reported that in a peer group of developed nations (which included the USA, the United Kingdom, France, Germany and Japan) the USA (41) and the United Kingdom (36) were at the top of the range of income inequality compared to peer countries having similar levels of economic development. It can be inferred that individuals on boards in a nation with higher levels of income inequality are likely to be more tolerant of high CEO pay since income inequality is a more prominent feature of the nation's economic landscape.

The level of individualism of Japanese employees in the Hofstede (1980) study was ranked second lowest of 22 industrialized nations, which indicated that Japan is low on individualism and instead is a more collectivistic society. CEOs in Japan can be expected to consult more frequently with their peer group of executives and make more consensus-based decisions in Japan (Crossland and Hambrick, 2007). Further, the gini coefficient of Japan (25) was also lower than that of the other developed countries, which indicates less dispersion of incomes and greater income equality. It follows that individuals on boards in Japan can be expected to be less tolerant of high CEO pay since high pay dispersion is likely to produce social tension among executives with collectivistic values.

The levels of individualism in Germany and France in the Hofstede (1980) study were observed to be in the middle of the range between that of the extremes of the USA and the United Kingdom on the high end of the range, and Japan on the low end. This finding indicates that both individualistic and collectivistic work values are likely to be reflected in the cultures in those nations. Moreover, the same pattern was also repeated for the gini coefficients of Germany (28) and France (33) which were lower than the USA and the United Kingdom but higher than Japan. Boards in Germany and France can be expected to reflect cultural values that give CEOs some discretion to make decisions on an individualistic basis and therefore tolerate higher CEO pay than the Japanese but offer some resistance to paying a CEO at the levels that boards endorse within the USA and the United Kingdom due to the fact that German and French societies reflect more collectivist values than would be found within the Anglo-American peer nations.

Conclusion

This chapter applied the lens of institutional theory to offer an explanation why CEO pay in the USA significantly exceeds CEO pay in firms of comparable size in some other advanced developed countries – specifically, France, the United Kingdom, Germany and Japan. Institutional factors present in the USA favorable to high CEO pay were identified and each factor's presence, or its absence, was examined in the other countries. The institutional factors included: (1) the system of corporate governance; (2) regulations that require CEO pay disclosure; (3) regulations that facilitate the early adoption of stock options; (4) decentralized rules of incorporation; (5) mega-stock option grants diffused as a CEO pay practice; and (6) cultural norms that emphasize individualism. A cross country comparison of these six enabling institutional factors favorable to high CEO pay is summarized in Table 15.1.

Table 15.1 shows that all six enabling institutional factors are present within the USA, which offers a highly favorable institutional environment for boards of directors to provide high pay allocations to CEOs with a minimum amount of interference from the shareholders or the government. The institutional environment in the United Kingdom contains five out of the six favorable factors, with the exception being that rules of incorporation are centralized and contain rules that empower shareholders to vote on CEO pay once it is determined by the board which may inhibit the board's unbounded generosity to remunerate the CEO. In the USA by way of contrast a corporation under decentralized rules of incorporation can incorporate in a state with rules that are more favorable to the interests of management and a CEO with respect to pay. The conditions for high CEO pay in the United Kingdom were therefore classified as somewhat favorable, but less favorable than within the USA.

The table also shows that in Germany and France the institutional environment contains the presence of only one favorable factor for high CEO pay in the case of Germany and two favorable factors in the case of France. Both countries have relational governance systems that reflect the presence of a greater heterogeneity of interests on the board of directors representing not only shareholders but can also include labor, bankers, corporations with stakes in the focal firm and government, serving on the board. The complexity of interests represented by the directors on these relational boards are more likely to make a decision to cap CEO pay before it reaches comparable levels observed in the USA. Neither Germany nor France have a culture that reflects a strong emphasis on individualism, or decentralized rules of incorporation, or have embraced the broad diffusion of the practice of mega-stock option grants to CEOs. Consequently Table 15.1 classifies Germany and France as somewhat unfavorable institutional environments for high CEO pay compared to the USA.

Table 15.1 Cross country comparison of institutional factors favorable to high CEO pay

Institutional factor	United States	United Kingdom	Germany	France	Japan
Shareholder-based corporate governance system	Yes	Yes	No	No	No
CEO pay disclosure regulations	Yes	Yes	Yes	Yes	No
Regulations for early adoption of stock options	Yes	Yes	No	Yes	No
Decentralized rules of incorporation	Yes	No	No	No	No
Broad diffusion of mega-grants of stock options	Yes	Yes	No	No	No
Cultural values with emphasis on individualism	Yes	Yes	No	No	No
Degree of institutional favorability for high CEO pay	Highly favorable	Somewhat favorable	Somewhat unfavorable	Somewhat unfavorable	Highly unfavorable

Finally, Table 15.1 shows that in Japan the institutional environment contains none of the factors favorable for high CEO pay that would be present in the USA. Japan contains a society that emphasizes collectivism rather than individualism, a relational governance system and regulations that are late to adopt innovations in CEO pay related to stock options or pay disclosure, factors that have the potential for providing fertile conditions for high pay to a CEO. Therefore the institutional environment in Japan was classified as highly unfavorable for a CEO to obtain high pay compared to the USA.

In conclusion the findings suggested by Table 15.1 should be viewed as dynamic and not static, and are expected to change in the future as institutional environments in countries yield to pressures from global competition that influence CEO pay decisions. It is expected that the gap in CEO pay between the USA and other countries such as the United Kingdom, Germany, France and Japan will diminish as the market for talented CEOs more frequently breaches national boundaries and with it local pay expectations should be more attuned to global market patterns.

References

Aguilera, R.V. and Jackson, G. 2003. The cross-national diversity of corporate governance: Dimensions and determinants. *Academy of Management Review*, 28: 447–65.

Aldrich, H. 1979. *Organizations and environments*. Englewood Cliffs, NJ: Prentice-Hall.

Bebchuck, L.A. and Fried, J.M. 2003. Executive compensation as an agency problem. *Journal of Economic Perspectives*, 17(3): 71–92.

Bordet, M. 2003. The pay of top executives. *Le Point*, November 28: 86–7.

Bremmer, B. 1999. The stock-option comes to Japan. *Business Week Online*, April 19: 1–2.

Byrne, J. 1996. How high can CEO pay go? *Business Week*, April 22: 100–6.

Carroll, G.R. and Delacroix, J. 1982. Organizational mortality in the newspaper industries of Argentina and Ireland: An ecological approach. *Administrative Science Quarterly*, 27: 169–98.

Chrystal, G. 1991. *In search of excess: The overcompensation of American executives*. New York: W. W. Norton Company.

Conyon, M.J. and Murphy, K.J. 2000. The prince and the pauper? CEO pay in the United States and the United Kingdom. *The Economic Journal*, 110(447): F640–F671.

Coser, L., Kadushin, C. and Powell, W.W. 1982. *Books: The culture and commerce of book publishing*. New York: Basic Books.

Crossland, C. and Hambrick, D.C. 2007. How national systems differ in their constraints on corporate executives: A study of CEO effects in three countries. *Strategic Management Journal*, 28(8): 767–89.

Davidson, W.M., Pilger, T. and Szakmary, A. 1998. Golden parachutes, board and committee composition, and shareholder wealth. *The Financial Review*, 33: 128–52.

Dharwadkar, R., George, G. and Brandes, P. 2000. Privatization in emerging economies: An agency theory perspective. *Academy of Management Review*, 25: 650–69.

DiMaggio, P.J. and Powell, W.W. 1983. The iron cage revisited: Institutional isomorphism and collective rationality in organizational fields. *American Sociological Review*, 48(2): 147–60.

The Economist. 2007. In the money: A special report on executive pay. January 20: 3–10.

Fabrikant, G. 2006. US-style pay deals for chiefs become all the rage in Europe. *The New York Times*, June 16: A1, C4.

Fackler, M. and Barboza, D. 2006. In Asia, executives earn much less. *The New York Times*, June 16: C4.

Fama, E.F. 1980. Agency problems and the theory of the firm. *Journal of Political Economics*, 88: 288–307.

Fama, E.F. and Jensen, M.L. 1983. Separation of ownership and control. *Journal of Law and Economics*, 26: 301–25.

Farrell, G. and Hansen, B. 2007. CEO compensation: A peek at the perks of the corner office. *USA Today*, April 16: 1B–3B.

Gomez-Mejia, L.R., Makri, M. and Lazara, M. 2003. Determinants of executive compensation in public family-owned firms. *Academy of Management Journal*, 46: 226–38.

Gospel, H. and Pendleton, A. 2005. *Corporate governance and labor management: An international comparison.* New York: Oxford University Press.

Hambrick, D.C. and Finkelstein, S. 1995. The effects of ownership structure on conditions at the top: The case of CEO pay raises. *Strategic Management Journal*, 44: 96–117.

Hayward, M.A., Rindova, V.P. and Pollock, T.G. 2004. Believing one's own press: The causes and consequences of CEO celebrity. *Strategic Management Journal*, 25: 637–53.

Hofstede, G. 1980. *Culture's consequences: International differences in work-related values.* Thousand Oaks, CA: Sage.

Jensen, M.L. and Meckling, W.H. 1976. Theory of the firm: Managerial behavior, agency costs, and ownership structure. *Journal of Financial Economics*, 3: 305–60.

Kostova, T. and Roth, K. 2002. Adoption of an organizational practice by subsidiaries of multinational corporations: Institutional and relational effects. *Academy of Management Journal*, 44: 215–33.

Meyer, A. and Rowan, B. 1977. Institutionalized organizations: Formal structure as myth and ceremony. *American Journal of Sociology*, 83: 340–63.

Milkovich, G.T. and Newman, J. M. 2008. *Compensation* (9th edition). Burr Ridge, IL: McGraw-Hill.

Mizruchi, M.S. and Fein, L.C. 1999. The social construction of organizational knowledge: A study of the uses of coercive, mimetic, and normative isomorphism. *Administrative Science Quarterly*, 44: 653–83.

Monks, R.A. and Minow, N. 2001. *Corporate governance* (2nd edition). Malden, MA: Blackwell.

Morgenson, G. 2006. Corporate America's pay pal. *The New York Times*, October 15: Section 3: 1, 7.

Murphy, K.J. 1999. Executive compensation. In O. Ashenfelter and D. Card (eds), *Handbook of labor economics*: 2485–563. Amsterdam: North Holland.

Pepper, S. 2006. *Senior executive reward: Key models and practices.* Aldershot, UK: Gower Publishing.

Sanders, W.M. 2001. Behavioral responses of CEOs to stock ownership and stock option pay. *Academy of Management Journal*, 44: 477–92.

Sanders, W.M. and Tuschke, A. 2007. The adoption of institutionally contested organizational practices: The emergence of stock option pay in Germany. *Academy of Management Journal*, 50: 33–56.

Sasseen, J. 2007. A better look at the boss's pay. *Business Week*, February 26: 44–5.

Schleifer, A. and Vishney, R. 1989. Management entrenchment: The case of manager-specific investments. *Journal of Financial Economics*, 25: 123–39.

Tosi, H. and Gomez-Mejia, L.R. 1989. The decoupling of CEO pay and performance: An agency theory perspective. *Administrative Science Quarterly*, 34: 169–89.

Tosi, H., Werner, S., Katz, J.P. and Gomez-Mejia, L.R. 2000. How much does performance matter? A meta-analysis of CEO pay studies. *Journal of Management*, 26: 301–39.

United Nations. 2006. *Human Development Report 2006*, 335.

Weimer, J. and Pape, J.C. 1999. A taxonomy of systems of corporate governance. *Corporate Governance Theory Papers*, 7(2): 152–66.

Westphal, J.D. and Zajac, E.J. 1995. Who shall govern? CEO/Board power, demographic similarity, and new director selection. *Administrative Science Quarterly*, 40: 60–83.

Wiseman, R. and Gomez-Mejia, L.R. 1998. A behavioral agency model of managerial risk taking. *Academy of Management Review*, 23: 133–53.

Zajac, E.J. 1990. CEO selection, succession, compensation and firm performance: A theoretical integration and empirical analysis. *Strategic Management Journal*, 11: 217–30.

Zucker, L.G. 1987. Institutional theories of organization. *Annual Review of Sociology*, 13: 443–64.

Zucker, L.G. and Tolbert, P.S. 1981. *Institutional sources of change in the formal structure of organizations: The diffusion of civil service reform, 1880–1955.* Paper presented at American Sociological Association annual meeting, Toronto, Canada.

16 Beyond financial performance

Is there something missing in executive compensation schemes?

Pascual Berrone and Luis R. Gomez-Mejia

Exorbitant levels of executive pay have been the subject of intense public debate and have attracted the interest of researchers and the business press alike. Boards and executives have been criticized as the level of executive compensation has risen dramatically when compared to the pay of the average worker and to the actual growth of companies. Recently, this attention has been renewed due to the notorious corporate scandals in the USA such as those of Enron, Worldcom, Arthur Andersen, Tyco International and Adelphia. These business failures affected investors and pension holders – with estimated losses of US pension and 401(k) plans in the neighborhood of $7 trillion (Siebert, 2002) – but also had important social costs: thousands of workers have lost their jobs and they and their families are suffering the consequences. This situation has led scholars to call into question the efficacy of executive pay and brings to the forefront the issue of business ethics and corporate social responsibility in the context of managerial compensation.

Despite the wealth of research on executive compensation, the link between corporate social performance (CSP) and executive pay remains limited at best. These spectacular scandals and failures, however, may be evidence of a worldwide crisis in current corporate governance practices and therefore a revision of these practices is largely needed.

In this chapter, we analyze the stakeholder view of the firm as an alternative to the neoclassical model of the firm. Under this alternative approach, we argue that firms, in order to achieve sustainable development, should design executive compensation schemes including criteria that account for the interest of other constituencies as an addition to financial objectives.

The chapter is structured as follows. First, we argue that the excessive emphasis of incentives on financial measures could have negative consequences to the firm. We later analyze the basic underpinnings of stakeholder theory, and after revisiting some empirical studies, we present some of our ideas regarding the link between executive pay and corporate social responsibility. We conclude the chapter with a discussion of its main ideas, limitations and challenges for future research.

The traditional approach to the corporate objective and executive compensation

The relationship between financial performance and managerial pay has pervaded the field of executive compensation since its inception. A very plausible justification for this is that the majority of executive compensation research has relied on the neoclassical tradition in economics. Specifically, agency theory (Fama, 1980; Jensen and Meckling, 1976) has been the dominant framework used to analyze executive pay issues. In the basic agency setting, it is assumed that principals (shareholders), whose primary (and unique) objective is the maximization of the firm's value, delegate tasks to an effort–risk averse, rational and self-centered agent (manager). Principals design compensation contracts to ameliorate a moral hazard problem (i.e. manager opportunism).

Assumptions of agency theory fit neatly to the actual structure of Anglo-American firms characterized by widely dispersed ownership and the resulting separation of ownership and control (Berle and Means, 1932). Because investors rely on their top management teams to take the strategic decisions of the firms, they need mechanisms intended to dissuade managers from pursuing self-serving actions at the expense of shareholders. A common prescription suggested by agency theory is to establish incentive programs for managers which result in pecuniary payments that are closely linked to the achievement of financial objectives. In this way, a common fate between managers and shareholders is created as their interests are expected to be aligned.

The above rationale has translated into compensation practices, such as stock option awards, which have been largely adopted by firms. In the USA, over 90 percent of firms included in the Fortune 500 list have adopted stock options for their senior managers and these represent more than half of their compensation packages (Hymowitz, 2003). Outside the USA, these ratios are lower but exhibit a growing trend as companies are increasingly benchmarking governance practices following the US business model.

Under this neoclassical economic view, the sole corporate purpose is to maximize the value for shareholders. But the social role of the firm is, accidentally or intentionally, ignored. In the best case, it is tangentially addressed and always under the rubric of maximizing shareholders' value. The Nobel prize winning Milton Friedman (1970) provides the best example of this statement. He is categorical about the social function of firms: "there is one and only one social responsibility of business – to use its resources and engage in activities designed to increase its profits" (Friedman, 1970).

Given the value maximization objective, any financing or investment decision that is not expected to improve the value of the shareholders' stake in the business is not acceptable. In order to assure managers achieve the value maximization goal, compensation packages include performance criteria that focus on accounting and market based measures of performance. Indeed, Murphy (2000) provided evidence for the dominance of financial performance criteria in executive compensation plans. But these plans very rarely contain other criteria that would account for the interests of varied stakeholders, not just the firm's shareholders, such as environmental performance, employee relations, diversity and other social issues for which the link to financial performance is not straightforward. For example, Berrone and Gomez-Mejia (2006), who analyzed over 450 companies from polluting industries over seven years, found that only 5 percent of these companies had an explicit environmental pay policy for their executives.

However, recent studies have cast doubts on the efficacy of linking executive pay exclusively to firm performance as this practice may lead to unintended consequences since option holders and holders of underlying equity securities may have different interests (Deyá-Tortella *et al.*, 2005). Some authors have gone even further in explicitly blaming the overwhelming focus on financial performance of incentive systems for the recent scandals of corporate malfeasance including those at Enron, Worldcom and Arthur Andersen in the US, and Parmalat, Elf and ABB in Europe. For instance, Kochan (2002: 139) argued that the real root cause of corporate malfeasance is "*the overemphasis . . . corporations have been forced to give in recent years to maximizing shareholder value without regard for the effects of their actions on other stakeholders*" (emphasis in the original). Even scholars like Sundaram and Inkpen (2004: 358), who feverishly defended shareholder value maximization as the preferred objective for corporations, recognized that "the excessive use (and inadequate policing) of such compensation schemes helped fuel the corporate crisis of 2001 and 2002, and must be reined in." Recent evidence seems to support this idea. O'Connor and colleagues (2006) showed that large Chief Executive Officer (CEO) stock option grants were associated with greater incidence of fraudulent financial reporting when (1) the CEO also served as the chair of the board of directors and directors did not hold stock options and (2) the CEO was not the chair of the board but directors had stock options.

In the light of the above, key questions emerge in this discussion. If maximizing no more than shareholder value can lead to undesirable consequences, shouldn't this model be revisited? Shouldn't we focus beyond the value maximization objective? Shouldn't we examine whether or not incentive systems should include additional criteria? This is the purpose of this chapter.

An alternative approach to the corporate objective and executive compensation

The traditional neoclassical perspective and its shareholder maximization viewpoint were first challenged by Dodd (1932), who viewed the firm as an entity separate from its shareholders. As such, it has citizenship responsibilities and should act on behalf of all constituencies even if it means a decrease in shareholder value. Dodd's article was a response to an earlier article by Berle (1931) who argued that firms should use their power solely to maximize shareholders' benefits. This intellectual discussion is known as the Berle–Dodd debate, which was finally conceded to Dodd by Berle in 1954 (Weiner, 1964). More recently, Freeman's book (1984), *Strategic Management: A Stakeholder Approach*, set the basis for what today is known as the stakeholder theory. Freeman's main thesis is that the manager is responsible for coordinating the constellation of competitive and cooperative interests of various constituencies or stakeholders of the firm. A stakeholder is broadly defined as "any group or individual who can affect or is affected by the achievement of the organization's objectives" (1984: 46). As a consequence, stakeholders include not only financial claimants, but also employees, customers, communities, governmental officials and the environment.

A clear distinction between the traditionalist economic viewpoint and stakeholder theory is that the latter rejects the idea of a single-minded firm. In the words of Freeman and McVea (2001: 194):

> The stakeholder framework does not rely on a single overriding management objective for all decisions. As such it provides no rival to the traditional aim of "maximizing shareholder wealth." To the contrary, a stakeholder approach rejects the very idea of maximizing a single-objective function as a useful way of thinking about management strategy. Rather, stakeholder management is a neverending task of balancing and integrating multiple relationships and multiple objectives.

Thus, the firm has multiple goals in addition to the singular end of maximizing shareholder's value and stakeholder theory prescribes that they should be included as an integral part of its strategy.

The stakeholder approach of the firm is tied closely to the concept of social responsibility and entails the notion of corporate social performance (CSP). Firms that attend the needs of consumers, employees, NGOs, government and other groups of society are considered to perform in a socially responsible fashion, which reflects a broader orientation of the firm. CSP then evaluates how well the company performs in its efforts to develop practices to deal with and create relationships with its numerous stakeholders. Most normative approaches of stakeholder theory (Donalson and Dunfee, 1994; Evan and Freeman, 1983; Philips, 1997; Wicks *et al.*, 1994), with strong emphasis on ethical and moral standards, argue that the interests of all legitimate stakeholders have intrinsic value and that no particular interest should dominate those of the others. This implies that CSP is an end to itself regardless of the consequences to the firm's value. More instrumental (and perhaps realistic) approaches (Berman *et al.*, 1999; Donalson and Preston, 1995; Jones, 1995; Jones and Wicks, 1999), however, do not reject profitability but recognize that firms must manage and serve stakeholders' interests other than shareholders' in order to generate profits. Under the instrumental view, CSP is seen as a source of competitive advantage because when the firm meets the needs of a wide variety of stakeholders it enhances its corporate reputation, improves trusting and cooperative relationships, provides access to superior resources, lowers liability exposure, and enhances social legitimacy, which ultimately is expected to contribute to the bottom line (Hillman and Keim, 2001; Waddock and Graves, 1997). In this view, the risks of misfit between stakeholders' expectations and firms' actions can be deadly for the firm since they would involve prejudices such as unfair contracts, greater firm risk, loss of legitimacy, poorer performance and higher likelihood of failure. Thus, the firm's success and survival is a consequence of its capacity to establish and maintain a relationship with its network of stakeholders (Clarkson, 1995; Post *et al.*, 2002).

A significant amount of research has been devoted to understanding whether or not CSP serves as a means to the end of corporate financial performance (CFP), with inconclusive results. However, even among most skeptical authors, it is mostly conceded that CSP would have a positive, though indirect, affect on CFP, particularly in the long term. Although the CSP–CFP relationship is still open for debate, a recent review and meta-analysis seems to support this positive relationship (Margolis and Walsh, 2003; Orlizky *et al.*, 2003). If CSP is a broader measure of the firm's overall performance and it is expected to enhance the long term value of the firm, shouldn't it be considered as a criterion in the executive pay schemes? Let's see what the evidence tells us.

Empirical studies on the relationship between CSP and executive pay

Notwithstanding hundreds of articles written over more than eight decades of executive compensation research (e.g. Taussig and Baker, 1925), very little is known about the relations between CSP and managerial pay. This is because the field traditionally has concerned itself overwhelmingly with financial performance (Barkema and Gomez-Mejia, 1998; Gomez-Mejia and Wiseman, 1997).

Only recently have scholars started to analyze this relationship. The first authors to analyze this issue were Stanwick and Stanwick (2001), who studied the relationship between environmental reputation – a dimension of CSP measured with the Fortune environmental reputation index – and CEOs' salaries for 188 US companies in 1991. The authors argued that because there is a mismatch between stakeholders who benefit from environmental reputation (the community at large), and shareholders who evaluate CEOs based on financial performance and establish the CEOs' compensation, a negative relationship between environmental reputation and CEO salary was hypothesized. Results confirmed their expectations. The authors concluded that "CEOs are encouraged not to have a high environmental reputation" (180).

Similarly, Coombs and Gilley (2005) tested the effects of different dimensions of CSP on CEOs' salaries, bonus, stock options and total compensation. The authors used stakeholder-agency theory (Hill and Jones, 1992) to argue that CEOs ought to be compensated for effective management of both shareholders' and non-shareholders' needs. The authors tested their prediction using the Kinder, Lydenberg, Domini and Company, also known as KLD, index, which contains data on five dimensions of CSP: community performance, diversity performance, employee performance, environment performance and product performance. Their longitudinal analysis covered 406 firms over seven years and revealed that most of the dimensions of CSP had a negative impact on CEOs' salaries and no influence on bonus, long term and total pay. However, the authors found that CEOs who simultaneously maximized environmental and financial performances were rewarded with greater salaries, whereas CEOs who maximized diversity and financial performances obtained higher bonuses. Yet, the authors concluded that in general boards of directors negatively value proactive social initiatives and consequently CEOs "pay the price" for socially correct behaviors.

Also using KLD data, McGuire and colleagues (2003) examined the relationship between CEO incentives and CSP but, contrasting the work of Coombs and Gilley (2005), the authors used compensation measures as antecedents of CSP. An additional difference is that McGuire and colleagues used two measures of CSP: social strength and social weakness. The scholars found that different forms of incentives (measured as salary, bonus and long term incentives) did not have a significant relationship in those firms that adopted a social proactive stance (i.e. strong social performance) but high levels of salary and long term incentives were related to poor social performance.

Like McGuire and colleagues' study, Deckop and colleagues (2006) – who used a combined measure derived from KLD data – also found that short term CEO focus (measured as the ratio of annual bonuses and total pay) had a negative impact on CSP. However, the authors also found that long term CEO focus actually improved CSP. The latter finding is consistent with those by Berrone and Gomez-Mejia (2006) who found that long term pay had a positive impact on subsequent environmental performance, suggesting that long term pay provides incentives to managers to engage in socially responsible strategies. Furthermore, Berrone and Gomez-Mejia analyzed whether or not CEOs in polluting industries receive higher total pay for good environmental performance. The authors combined institutional and agency theories and argued that, within polluting industries, firms are expected to tie the CEO's compensation to environmental performance since this would provide social legitimacy to the firm. At the same time, this would shield top executives from the uncertainty environmental strategies involve given that the cause–effect relationships of these strategies are highly ambiguous. Using data on 469 firms from US polluting industries over seven years, the authors found that environmental performance was indeed a determinant of CEO total pay, even after controlling for accounting and market based measures of performance and other traditional determinants of executive compensation.

Also using environmental performance as a measure of CSP and based on a congruence model of organizational design, Russo and Harrison (2005) studied the monetary incentives for environmental performance for plant and environmental quality managers. The authors found electronic plants performed environmentally better if there was an explicit tie between environmental performance and pay, but only for facility managers, not for environmental quality managers. They speculated that environmental quality managers may see such a tie as redundant, given that their main task is to minimize toxic emissions. For facility managers, however, this tie represents a new incentive to shift attention to environmental issues.

Unfortunately, the evidence provided by the foregoing studies is far from being conclusive. These studies are exemplary efforts in providing rich and textured insights to understanding the links between CSP and executive compensation but they are just a small drop in the ocean of executive compensation research. Much more research is still needed to fully comprehend the relationships between incentives and social goals beyond financial performance. In the next section, we attempt to provide some guidelines in this direction.

Research conclusions and instrumental implications

After reviewing a large number of studies, Gomez-Mejia and Balkin (1992) noted that maximizing a sole set of criteria is one of the biggest dangers in poorly designed incentive programs, as those affected are tempted to engage in criterion manipulation. This is in line with the argument proposed by several authors: Relying exclusively on financial performance measures as the single criteria to which to link executive pay might well be the cause of undesired corporate behaviors such as fraudulent financial reporting, corruption, tax evasion, exploitation of underage workers and other forms of opportunism, malfeasance and white-collar crime.

In addition, pay schemes that only reward financial performance may deter managers from engaging in corporate social initiatives since the link between social actions and financial performance is not straightforward and could actually hinder more immediate results (Berrone and Gomez-Mejia, 2006). As a consequence, relying exclusively on financial performance measures can lead managers to avoid social strategies and allocate resources to more conservative investments. Stakeholder theory suggests, however, that overemphasis on financial performance and ignoring stakeholders' expectations can seriously damage the normal functioning of firms. For example, when a company acquires a particular economically useful input that is harmful to the environment, it risks the support of customers, regulators, local citizens, public interest groups or other firm stakeholders for the firm's products or services. Thus it appears that executive compensation schemes that merely contain financial performance measures are likely to dissuade managers from engaging in corporate socially responsible actions and can generate undesirable consequences for stakeholders, including shareholders.

Related to the above point is another: that other criteria in addition to financial performance should be included when designing the compensation package that accounts for the interests of other stakeholders affected by the firm's actions. This implies the adoption of a stakeholder approach, which focuses on the firm's long term survival by balancing interests of multiple stakeholders. As a consequence, criteria that capture these interests should be included in executive compensation schemes.

From a normative perspective, including CSP as a criterion in executive compensation may be seen as the "right thing to do." From the instrumental perspective, it would stimulate the development of capabilities and the creation of intangible assets that will positively affect financial performance. Even if corporate social initiatives do not boost financial performance directly, they are certainly intended to satisfy stakeholders' requirements. And satisfied stakeholders can directly or indirectly enhance the firm performance. Berrone and colleagues (in press) argue theoretically and show empirically that firms with satisfied stakeholders have better long term financial measures than those whose stakeholders are not fulfilled.

Yet, managers may be reluctant to adopt social strategies because of the inherent ambiguity that these strategies involve. Thus, only if social efforts are considered in the incentive scheme, socially responsible investments are likely to be enhanced (Berrone and Gomez-Mejia, 2006). In turn, better stakeholder management is expected to translate into superior firm performance (Hillman and Keim, 2001; Waddock and Graves, 1997). Therefore we believe that executive compensation schemes that incorporate CSP measures in combination with financial performance measures will generate sustainable value for all stakeholders, including shareholders.

Social criteria are hardly ever included in executive compensation contracts in an explicit fashion (Berrone and Gomez-Mejia, 2006). This fact is a source of uncertainty for managers since they do not know whether or not they would be compensated in the case of good CSP, which is a clear disincentive to engage in socially responsible activities. However, when criteria are explicit, they are expected to promote the desired behaviors. Indeed, Russo and Harrison (2005) show that environmental performance is enhanced when there is an explicit tie between environmental performance and plant managers' pay.

In addition, a problem with social criteria is that they may be hard to quantify (Deckop *et al.*, 2006; Russo and Harrison, 2005). Therefore, criteria that are measurable and available across time are needed to secure steady social actions. Otherwise, only isolated and sporadic social initiatives will be conducted. By including explicit and quantifiable CSP measures in the contract, (1) managerial uncertainty is reduced as firms assume a commitment to managers letting them know how their performance will be assessed, and (2) permanent orientation on stakeholder expectation is guaranteed. Thus, it appears that explicit and measurable social criteria in executive compensation contracts will induce effective and stable CSP, enhancing sustainable value for all stakeholders, including shareholders.

A subsidiary problem could emerge when including multiple CSP measures in the compensation contracts. Just like with any financial performance measures, executives may be tempted to maximize easier to attain CSP measures and manipulate indicators at the expense of other measures. This may be particularly severe for CSP measures given that "decisions in the area of CSP are likely to reflect both high information asymmetry and low programmability" (Deckop et al., 2006: 331). In order to mitigate this problem, vigilant bodies, information systems and cognizant assistance should be in place to curb opportunism and manipulation. Thus, we believe that proper monitoring mechanisms will reduce the chances of manipulating CSP measures and deter managers from impression management practices, avoiding undesirable consequences for stakeholders, including shareholders.

Related to the above proposition is the role of the board of directors. Traditional corporate governance literature has long stressed boards of directors and their composition as one of the primary mechanisms to monitor managerial actions (Fama and Jensen, 1983; Jensen and Meckling, 1976). It is generally assumed that board members represent shareholders' interests against the potentially self-serving behavior of the management team (Finkelstein and Hambrick, 1996; Jensen, 1993). We argue that the presence of stakeholders (non-shareholders) in corporate boards is a direct means through which firms can (1) assess the value of socially responsible initiatives; (2) monitor managerial social actions; and (3) safeguard different stakeholder interests. Because of these, the inclusion of CSP criteria in executive compensation will not only be more likely but also more efficient given the supervision function of board members. Therefore, we believe that stakeholder (non-shareholder) representation on boards of directors and in their committees will increase the use of CSP measures in executive compensation and its efficacy in promoting sustainable value for all stakeholders, including shareholders.

Firms differ in terms of size, resources, strategy and markets. But they also differ in terms of the environment they face. Each company operates within a particular context comprised of distinct stakeholders, who establish idiosyncratic rules, belief systems and practices deemed to be appropriate. Given that CSP is a multidimensional construct (Carroll, 1979), it is reasonable to assume that different dimensions of CSP will have different weight and importance based on the context in which the firm operates. This idea is captured in the work by Berrone and Gomez-Mejia (2006), who analyzed environmental performance as a determinant of CEO total pay *within* polluting industries. Unfortunately, other previous studies have ignored contextual and institutional factors that may influence the relationship between CSP and executive pay, but it would explain the mixed results.

Previous studies in executive compensation have emphasized the importance of contingencies and factors such as decision, strategic and environmental contexts in successful design of pay schemes (Barkema and Gomez-Mejia, 1998; Gomez-Mejia and Wiseman, 1997). Following this line of thought, we argue that the firm that successfully grasps key characteristics and demands of its stakeholders and designs its compensation packages accordingly will better fit to the requirement of its environments and consequently obtain a better overall performance. Thus, we suggest that the importance of different dimensions of corporate social responsibility is contingent on contextual and institutional factors and that firms that design their executive compensation packages accounting for these contingencies will outperform firms that do not consider them.

An important environmental factor is the country in which the firm operates. Each country has its political, legal, economic, social, cultural and institutional contexts that define values and norms deemed praiseworthy. Cross-cultural management research has long studied the importance of national culture and its different dimensions. For instance, Hofstede (1983, 1997) examined the individualism–collectivism dimension of societies. In individualistic societies, ties between individuals are very loose, people are supposed to look after their own self-interests and are expected to rely primarily upon themselves. Conversely, in collectivist countries, social ties or bonds between individuals are very tight, group harmony is valued and people are concerned for the well being of the group to which they belong. Presumably, CSP – which entails a broad orientation and concern for a wide range of interest groups – will be more esteemed in collectivist societies than in individualistic cultures. Given that these national differences are likely to influence the way social issues are valued and the importance they have in corporate governance and organizational decision making, we predict that collectivist societies will include CSP criteria in executive compensation schemes to a greater extent and with a larger impact on firms' sustainable value than individualistic societies.

However, many firms operate in multi-country settings. This allows managers to opportunistically conduct social initiatives in those countries where these initiatives are deemed important while performing poorly in those countries where social issues are neglected. A case in point is the environmental performance of firms. A company with low environmental impact in one specific country does not necessarily mean that the overall environmental performance of the firm is superior. Companies can relocate their dirty operations in regions with lax environmental standards (also known as pollution havens) to avoid stricter ones (Christmann, 2004).

However, according to stakeholder theory, a stakeholder is anyone who is affected by the organization's actions, regardless country of origin (Freeman, 1984). As a consequence, systematic advantages of locating activities abroad to face weaker standards are dubious. Indeed, Dowell and colleagues (2000) argued that different interest groups and nongovernmental organizations expose dirty firms by stimulating consumer awareness and pressuring local governments to discipline poor environmental performers, even if the pollution is in overseas locations. This suggests that while some fines and penalties could be eluded by locating polluting activities in countries with lax environmental regulations, legitimacy losses are unavoidable. Similarly, Kostova and Zaheer (1999) showed that the legitimacy of subsidiaries abroad influences the legitimacy of the whole organization. These studies suggest that transnational corporations operating poorly in countries with weak social regulations face serious harm to their reputation and legitimacy, with their resultant drawbacks. Conversely, companies that adopt global social standards are likely to enhance their social legitimacy and their corporate image, so executive pay plans that consider CSP as a criterion should include comprehensive measures. Therefore, we believe that firms that include global CSP criteria in executive compensation schemes will generate greater sustainable value for all stakeholders, including shareholders, than those that do not include global CSP criteria.

In our review of studies linking CSP and executive compensation, we found plausible arguments to justify both direction of causality and positive and negative relationships. Indeed, an unresolved issue in executive pay research is whether compensation design is a consequence of the firm's strategy or whether it actually drives firm strategy (Gomez-Mejia, 1994). An incentive system, however, is expected to play two main functions. On the one hand, it should reward past performance to recompense an executive for good management, and as a consequence CSP can be seen as an antecedent. At the same time, incentive schemes can be used to stimulate certain strategies such as social actions. Thus, CSP can be seen as an outcome. Therefore, the relationship seems to be a continuous sequence where proper combination of short and long term incentive structured around CSP can be expected to both reward and promote social and financial goals. Hence, it appears that the way executive compensation is structured affects and is affected by corporate socially responsible actions.

Conclusion

Understanding the relations between CSP and executive compensation is relevant for compensation designers, shareholders, managers and particularly for advocates of corporate governance reform. In this chapter, we argued that corporate functions go beyond financial performance maximization and executive compensation should be designed accordingly. In contrast to the neoclassical theory, we presented the arguments of the stakeholder theory which entertains the firm as a network of relationships with multiple constituencies, not only shareholders. As such, executive effectiveness should be assessed, rewarded and stimulated from the global perspective of multiple constituencies.

Our position is by no means that firms should ignore financial concerns or that shareholders are less important than other stakeholders. We are, however, somewhat skeptical of the argument that the sole social function of the firm is to maximize profit. In any case, we believe that if social goals are included in addition to financial objectives, enhanced outcomes can be obtained for multiple stakeholders worldwide and the firm as a whole. As recently conceded by one of the most renowned agency theorists, Michael Jensen,

> We can learn from stakeholder theorists how to lead managers and participants in an organization to think more generally and creatively about how the organization's policies treat . . . not just the stockholders and financial markets, but employees, customers, suppliers, and the community in which the organization exists . . . *[W]e cannot maximize the long-term market value of an organization if we ignore or mistreat any important constituency.*

> (2001: 16, emphasis in the original)

Viewed in the long term, stakeholder and shareholder interests are not necessarily mutually exclusive. In other words, the two approaches do not conflict unless posed in the extreme. Firms do not succeed financially by neglecting the expectations of employees, customers, suppliers, creditors and local communities; nor are they able to satisfy stakeholder needs by failing to meet shareholders' expectations.

Regardless what view of the corporate objective is taken, effective governance should ensure that managers are accountable for pursuing it. We proposed the inclusion of social goals in compensation schemes as a means of urging managers to expand their strategic scopes and engage in activities believed to provide benefits to firms and stakeholders. However, our conclusions represent major challenges to compensation designers given the complexity that multiple objectives entail. To start, multiple goals can create confusion about what type of decisions managers should take. There is also the risk of criteria manipulation and preference for easier to attain goals. Conditional compensation schemes and alternative monitoring systems may be required to successfully implement a compensation system that accounts for the interests of multiple stakeholders. Another challenge is how to measure CSP. While financial measures are well developed, social performance measures are still an open field to be explored. This is an important issue to avoid the "folly of rewarding A while expecting B" (Kerr, 1975: 769).

Unfortunately, available studies do not provide definitive evidence as to whether firms reward or punish socially responsible strategies and what combination of incentives promotes corporate social behaviors. Neither have they suggested the proper combination between short and long term forms of pay to stimulate adequately social strategies. This indicates the need for more research to fully understand the causal relationships between corporate governance and corporate social performance. To succeed in this endeavor, future research must move beyond financial performance and broaden its view to consider different dimensions of organizational effectiveness.

References

Barkema, H.G. and Gomez-Mejia, L.R. 1998. Managerial compensation and firm performance: A general research framework. *Academy of Management Journal*, 41(2): 135–45.

Berle, A.A. 1931. Corporate powers as powers in trust. *Harvard Law Review*, 44(7): 1049–74.

Berle, A.A. and Means, G.C. 1932. *The modern corporation and private property*. New York: Macmillan.

Berman, S.L., Wicks, A.C., Kotha, S. and Jones, T.M. 1999. Does stakeholder orientation matter? The relationship between stakeholder management models and firm financial performance. *Academy of Management Journal*, 42(5): 488–506.

Berrone, P. and Gomez-Mejia, L.R. 2006. *Do firms compensate their CEOs for good environmental performance?* Paper presented at the Academy of Management, Atlanta.

Berrone, P., Surroca, J. and Tribo, J. in press. Corporate ethical identity as a determinant of firm performance: A test of the mediating role of stakeholder satisfaction. *Journal of Business Ethics*.

Carroll, A.B. 1979. A three-dimensional conceptual model of corporate performance. *Academy of Management Review*, 4(4): 497–505.

Christmann, P. 2004. Multinational companies and the natural environment: Determinants of global environmental policy standardization. *Academy of Management Journal*, 47(5): 747–60.

Clarkson, M.B.E. 1995. A stakeholder framework for analyzing and evaluating corporate social performance. *Academy of Management Review*, 20(1): 92–117.

Coombs, J.E. and Gilley, K.M. 2005. Stakeholder management as a predictor of CEO compensation: Main effects and interactions with financial performance. *Strategic Management Journal*, 26: 827–40.

Deckop, J.R., Merriman, K.K. and Gupta, S. 2006. The effects of CEO pay structure on corporate social performance. *Journal of Management*, 32(3): 329–42.

Deyá-Tortella, B., Gomez-Mejia, L.R., De Castro, J. and Wiseman, R.M. 2005. Incentive alignment or perverse incentives? A behavioral view of stock options. *Management Research*, 3(2): 109–20.

Dodd, M.E. 1932. For whom are corporate managers trustees. *Harvard Law Review*, 45(7): 1145–63.

Donalson, T. and Dunfee, T.W. 1994. Toward a unified conception of business ethics: Integrative social contracts theory. *Academy of Management Review*, 19(2): 252–84.

Donalson, T. and Preston, L.E. 1995. The stakeholder theory of the corporation: Concepts, evidence, and implications. *Academy of Management Review*, 20(1): 65–91.

Dowell, G., Hart, S.L. and Yeung, B. 2000. Do corporate global environmental standards create or destroy market value? *Management Science*, 46(8): 1059–74.

Evan, W. and Freeman, E.R. 1983. A stakeholder theory of the modern corporation: Kantian capitalism. In T. Beauchamp and N. Bowie (eds), *Ethical theory in business*: 75–93. Englewood Cliffs, NJ: Prentice-Hall.

Fama, E.F. 1980. Agency problems and the theory of the firm. *Journal of Political Economy*, 88: 288–98.

Fama, E.F. and Jensen, M.C. 1983. Separation of ownership and control. *Journal of Law and Economics*, 26: 301–25.

Finkelstein, S. and Hambrick, D.C. 1996. Board of directors and corporate performance. In their *Strategic leadership: Top executives and their effect on organizations*: 209–60. St Paul, MN: West Publishing Co.

Freeman, E.R. 1984. *Strategic management: A stakeholder approach*. Englewood Cliffs, NJ: Prentice Hall.

Freeman, E.R. and McVea, J. 2001. A stakeholder approach to strategic management. In M. Hitt, E.R. Freeman and J. Harrison (eds), *Handbook of strategic management*: 189–207. Oxford, UK: Blackwell Publishing.

Friedman, M. 1970. The social responsibility of business is to increase its profits. *New York Times Magazine*, 13: 32–33.

Gomez-Mejia, L.R. 1994. Executive compensation: A reassessment and future research agenda. In G.R. Ferris (ed.), *Research in personnel and human resources management*, vol. 12: 161–222. Stanford, CT: JAI Press.

Gomez-Mejia, L.R. and Balkin, D.B. 1992. *Compensation, organizational strategy, and firm performance*. Cincinnati, OH: South-Western Publishing Company.

Gomez-Mejia, L.R. and Wiseman, R.M. 1997. Reframing executive compensation: An assessment and outlook. *Journal of Management*, 23: 291–374.

Hill, C. and Jones, T.M. 1992. Stakeholder-agency theory. *Journal of Management Studies*, 29(2): 131–54.

Hillman, A.J. and Keim, G.D. 2001. Shareholder value, stakeholder management, and social issues: What's the bottom line? *Strategic Management Journal*, 22: 125–39.

Hofstede, G. 1983. The cultural relativity of organizational practices and theories. *Journal of International Business Studies*, 14(2): 75–89.

—— 1997. *Cultures and organizations: Software of the mind*. New York: McGraw Hill.

Hymowitz, C. 2003. How to fix a broken system: A rush of new plans promise to make corporate boards more accountable. Will they work? *Wall Street Journal*: R1–R12. New York.

Jensen, M.C. 1993. The modern industrial revolution, exit, and the failure of internal control mechanism. *Journal of Finance*, 98: 225–64.

—— 2001. Value maximization, stakeholder theory, and the corporate objective function. *Journal of Applied Corporate Finance*, 14(3): 8–21.

Jensen, M.C. and Meckling, W. 1976. Theory of the firm: Managerial behavior, agency costs, and ownership structure. *Journal of Financial Economics*, 3: 305–60.

Jones, T.M. 1995. Instrumental stakeholder theory: A synthesis of ethics and economics. *Academy of Management Review*, 20(2): 404–37.

Jones, T.M. and Wicks, A.C. 1999. Convergent stakeholder theory. *Academy of Management Review*, 24(2): 206–21.

Kerr, J.L. 1975. On the folly of rewarding A while hoping for B. *Academy of Management Journal*, 18: 769–83.

Kochan, T.A. 2002. Addressing the crisis in confidence in corporations: Root causes, victims, and strategies for reform. *Academy of Management Executive*, 16(3): 139–41.

Kostova, T. and Zaheer, S. 1999. Organizational legitimacy under conditions of complexity: The case of the multinational enterprise. *Academy of Management Review*, 24(1): 64–81.

McGuire, J., Dow, S. and Argheyd, K. 2003. CEO incentives and corporate social performance. *Journal of Business Ethics*, 45(4): 341–59.

Margolis, J.D. and Walsh, J.P. 2003. Misery loves companies: Rethinking social initiatives by business. *Administrative Science Quarterly*, 48(2): 268–304.

Murphy, K.J. 2000. Performance standards in incentive contracts. *Journal of Accounting and Economics*, 30(3): 245–78.

O'Connor, J.P., Priem, R.L., Coombs, J.E. and Gilley, K.M. 2006. Do CEO stock options prevent or promote fraudulent financial reporting? *Academy of Management Journal*, 49(3): 483–500.

Orlizky, M., Schmidt, F.L. and Rynes, S.L. 2003. Corporate social and financial performance: A meta-analysis. *Organization Studies*, 24(3): 403–41.

Philips, R.A. 1997. Stakeholder theory and the principle of fairness. *Business Ethics Quarterly*, 7: 51–66.

Post, J.E., Preston, L.E. and Sachs, S. 2002. Managing the extended enterprise: The new stakeholder view. *California Management Review*, 45(1): 6–28.

Russo, M.V. and Harrison, N.S. 2005. Organizational design and environmental performance: Clues from the electronics industry. *Academy of Management Journal*, 48(4): 582–93.

Siebert, N. 2002. To encourage recovery, encourage investors. *The New York Times*: A19. New York.

Stanwick, P.A. and Stanwick, S.D. 2001. CEO compensation: Does it pay to be green? *Business Strategy and the Environment*, 10(3): 176–82.

Sundaram, A.K. and Inkpen, A.C. 2004. The corporate objective revisited. *Organization Science*, 15(3): 350–63.

Taussig, F.W. and Baker, W.S. 1925. American corporations and their executives: A statistical inquiry. *Quarterly Journal of Economics*, 3: 1–51.

Waddock, S.A. and Graves, S.B. 1997. The corporate social performance–financial performance link. *Strategic Management Journal*, 18(4): 303–19.

Weiner, J.L. 1964. The Berle–Dodd dialogue on the concept of the corporation. *Columbia Law Review*, 64: 1458–83.

Wicks, A.C., Gilbert, D.R., Jr. and Freeman, E.R. 1994. A feminist reinterpretation of the stakeholder concept. *Business Ethics Quarterly*, 4: 475–98.

Index